HOLY WAR
FOR ∗ THE
PROMISED LAND

Israel's Struggle to Survive
in the Muslim Middle East

DAVID DOLAN
Jerusalem-based journalist reporting for CBS

THOMAS NELSON PUBLISHERS
NASHVILLE

Copyright © 1991 by David Dolan

Published in Nashville, Tennessee, by Thomas Nelson, Inc.,
and distributed in Canada by Lawson Falle, Ltd.,
Cambridge, Ontario.

Scripture quotations are from the NEW KING JAMES
VERSION of the Bible. Copyright © 1979, 1980, 1982,
Thomas Nelson, Inc., Publishers.

Library of Congress Cataloging-in-Publication Data

Dolan, David (David P.)
    Holy war for the promised land: Israel's struggle to
survive in the Muslim Middle East / David Dolan.
        p.   cm.
    Includes bibliographical references.
    ISBN 0-8407-3325-9 (pb.)
    1. Jewish-Arab relations.   2. Israel—History.   3. Dolan,
David (David P.)—Journeys—Israel.   4. Radio
journalists—United States—Biography.   I. Title.
    DS119.7.D64   1991
    956—dc20   91-7630
                                                        CIP

Printed in the United States of America
3 4 5 6 7 - 96 95 94 93 92 91

CONTENTS

ACKNOWLEDGMENTS

I wish to thank the many Jewish and Arab friends who have shared their lives and experiences with me, and so helped me to better understand the raging conflict over the Holy Land.

I am also indebted to author Lance Lambert for first alerting me to the large role Islam plays in the Arab/Israeli conflict and for offering the use of his extensive library, and to Thomas Nelson Senior Editor Bill Watkins for showing early and continuing enthusiasm for this work.

Special thanks to those in many parts of the world who prayed for me when I became ill while writing the manuscript.

I would like especially to express my gratitude to my friends and family in America, and especially my parents, who believed me when I said the turbulent Middle East was where I needed to be.

ABOUT THE AUTHOR

David Dolan has lived in Israel since 1980, and he has personally experienced the country's strife from its Arab neighbors and terrorists. He has also come to learn first-hand about the Palestinian struggle for a homeland.

Since 1982 Dolan has broadcast news from the Middle East, including from south Lebanon and Jerusalem, and since 1988 has covered the area for CBS radio. He is also a regular lecturer at Jerusalem's Institute of Holy Land Studies.

Due to his media work and personal Christian faith, he has researched the roots of the Arab-Israeli conflict for over a decade. Consequently, he has come to be recognized as an expert in this field, having been interviewed in *Christianity Today,* on Prime Time America, CBN, and CBS News, and having articles published in such magazines as *Moody Monthly* and the *Christian Observer,* and in the *Jerusalem Post* newspaper. He also writes a monthly news and analysis report called *Israel News Digest.* This report goes to thousands worldwide, and it is translated into five languages: French, German, Norwegian, Portugese, and Spanish. Several U.S. Congressmen and Senators receive this report, as well as members of the British House of Commons.

If you would like to subscribe to this report, please write:

CFI
P.O. Box 1813
Jerusalem, 91015
Israel

INTRODUCTION

The Arab/Israeli struggle is unique among world conflicts. On one side are Israeli Jews—descendants of an ancient people who, according to the Bible, are chosen by God to be his own. The other protagonists, the Arabs, are mostly members of the fastest-growing and most controversial religion on earth: Islam. Closely watching from the sidelines are millions of Christians whose faith stems from history's most famous Jew, Jesus of Nazareth. The world's leading powers are involved in the conflict, as is the United Nations, which oversaw the creation of modern Israel.

The problems are so complex and deep-rooted, one cannot understand the nature of the struggle without an overview of its causes and history. I will begin by taking a look at the persecution the Jews endured from the time of their exile from Jerusalem in A.D. 135 through the twentieth century. Then I will delve into a short review of Arab history—basically the story of Islam.

Most of the books I have read on the Arab/Israeli dispute either play down or ignore the religious struggle at the center of the conflict. Possibly because of my own spiritual convictions, I have spent much time examining the religious beliefs of both Arabs and Jews. It is impossible to comprehend the roots and continuing intensity of the Jewish/Arab struggle without fully appreciating the enormous role ancient beliefs and prejudices play in it. I believe that *Holy War for the Promised Land* will especially make the reader aware of the significant role Islam has played in fueling the conflict.

Most chapters, and in many cases even single sentences, have themselves been the subject of entire books. While it is good to closely examine every aspect of the dispute over the Holy Land, I believe it is easy to get caught up in side issues and, therefore, not see the forest for the trees. We will attempt to step back and look at the broad picture, and especially at the religious canvas on which the conflict has been painted.

Throughout this book, I have woven many of my personal experiences in Israel. Some explain why I came to this controversial land in 1980. The rest, I live out daily as a radio broadcaster working in southern Lebanon. The final two chapters are my own personal assessment of the conflict and of the chances for a peaceful resolution.

I do not claim to be a professional historian or theologian; I am simply a journalist who has lived and worked for the past decade with the people at the center of the conflict. While doing so, I have come to understand their religious beliefs, political positions, and personal attitudes.

I have tried to write in such a way that those unfamiliar with the history of this struggle can comprehend what has happened and is happening in the Middle East. Yet I believe *Holy War* will also be of interest to those better acquainted with the topic, especially to anyone desiring a clearer picture of the fundamental religious elements behind the dispute.

Now, on to the ancient Temple Mount and to the odyssey that brought me to the tiny land of promise.

CHAPTER 1

MY ROAD
TO ISRAEL

"Saddam will avenge us!" shouted someone in the angry crowd, which rapidly dispersed as the shooting continued. Blood flowed thick and fast. Tempers flared on both sides.

"You will *not* take over our sacred mosques!" screamed a woman who held a dying young man close to her bosom.

"Stop shooting, stop shooting! *Allahu Akbar!*" cried a male voice from mosque loudspeakers as people ran for cover in two nearby Muslim shrines. Several minutes later Israeli security forces did stop firing at Palestinian rioters on Jerusalem's Temple Mount, but only after killing at least seventeen and injuring scores more, one of whom died several weeks later.

Tension had begun building well before dawn at the site where King Solomon and Zerubbabel had erected the first and second temples to the God of Israel. From 3 A.M. onward, hundreds of Muslims had started to gather on "the Noble Sanctuary," located in the southeastern corner of Jerusalem's ancient, walled "Old City." By 9 A.M. several thousand Palestinian Muslims, most of them men, had assembled on the Mount. They were ready for holy war.

Devout Muslims came to defend the Temple Mount

from a group of about thirty-five Jews who wanted to march to the site. It wasn't the first time that the small Jewish "Temple Mount Faithful" group had tried to hold ceremonies on the Mount during the Jewish Feast of Tabernacles. But this year was different. The Faithful— considered eccentric, if not extremist by a majority of Israelis—had declared their intention to bring with them a three-ton cornerstone of the *third Jewish Temple*.

Muslim leaders were officially informed the week before that Israel's Supreme Court had banned the group from holding the "cornerstone dedication" ceremony on the Mount. The Israeli justices agreed with police that the proposed ceremony would likely trigger wide-scale disturbances at Islam's third holiest site. The high court's ban had been published in all east Jerusalem Arabic newspapers. Still, thousands of Muslims showed up on October 8, 1990, in answer to calls by Islamic and Palestinian leaders to "defend 'Haram al-Sharif' from Jewish plots to destroy our sacred mosques."

The warm, sunny Monday morning was a special day for religious Jews. It was the fifth day of the Feast of Tabernacles, when Jewish men of priestly descent come to the Western Wall of the Temple Mount to say a levitical benediction over the assembled worshipers. About twenty-five thousand Jews had gathered for the blessing in the large Western Wall plaza, located just below Judaism's most sacred site, where the sons of Levi once ministered in the ancient Jewish temples.

As the priestly ceremony ended, the Temple Mount Faithful came marching into the plaza, singing religious and nationalistic songs and waving Israeli flags. Forbidden to march to the Mount itself, the Faithful quickly made their way out of the Old City's Dung Gate, heading toward the Kidron Valley, where King David had built his capital city. Near the bottom of the valley, just south of the Temple Mount, the Faithful stopped at the pool of Shiloah to reenact an ancient Jewish water purification ceremony.

Just as the marchers were leaving the Old City, Temple Mount loudspeakers started to broadcast sermons from inside al-Aksa Mosque, situated at the southern end of the Mount. The assembled Muslims packed into the sacred Islamic shrine were urged to wage *jihad,* or "holy war," to defend Haram al-Sharif from the Jews planning to march to the sacred site. Palestinian men congregating outside al-Aksa and the nearby Dome of the Rock (also known as the Mosque of Omar) began to gather building blocks, stones, and metal bars from various Temple Mount construction sites. Holy war was about to begin.

Suddenly, all hell broke loose in the City of Peace. "Come, all Muslims, and defend us! The Jews are invading!" cried a Muslim official from a loudspeaker on a mosque in Silwan Village, where the pool of Shiloah is located.

Muslims on the southern edge of the Temple Mount heard the cry and sounded the alarm. "The Jews are coming!" Several hundred primed and ready Palestinians then rushed to the western edge of the Mount, with rocks and other weapons in hand. An enraged crowd of several thousand Muslims quickly began to move in the same direction. As they did so, a tear gas canister was hurled into the crowd by an Israeli policeman, who apparently tossed the canister at random after it accidentally went off while being thrown to him by a fellow officer.

Taught that a Muslim who dies defending Haram al-Sharif goes immediately to the highest state of paradise, the jihad-frenzied Arabs then attacked a row of forty-four Israeli policemen standing near the edge of the Mount above the Western Wall.

The vastly outnumbered security forces, some wounded from the barrage of stones and other objects, shot tear gas canisters and rubber bullets at the Palestinians. But the crowd kept surging forward, seemingly impervious to injury or death. Within minutes, the overwhelmed Israeli policemen were forced to flee the Temple Mount through two nearby gates.

Angry Muslims took advantage of the police retreat to move up to the edge of the Mount. Two policemen standing on a ledge above the Western Wall called to Jews near the wall to quickly evacuate the area. Soon afterward many of the Palestinian rioters began to hurl rocks and stones onto the Western Wall plaza below. A majority of the thousands of assembled Jewish worshipers had already left the plaza, but hundreds were still in the vicinity of the wall. Jerusalem police said that about a dozen Jewish worshipers were injured in the barrage. Some of the wounded were hit by stones, while others fell down and were bruised during the rush to get away from the wall. None were hurt seriously.

The pavement in front of the ancient Temple Mount Wall was soon carpeted with rocks and stones. Lying amid the debris were a number of Jewish prayer books, knocked off their stands by the deluge of missiles.

As Israeli marksmen began shooting from a police lookout on the Mount, Muslim rioters attacked a nearby police outpost. Two Arab guards stationed inside the outpost called over a two-way radio for help. Minutes later the two were allowed to flee the outpost as the rioters entered the building. Beefed up security forces preparing to reenter the Mount heard the appeal for help over hand-held radios.

Soon afterward, the Israeli force broke through, met by a hail of stones and other objects. Their main goal was to get to the police outpost as fast as possible to free the two guards whom they assumed were being held captive. Unaware that the Muslim rioters had freed the two police guards, and suspecting that they had stolen guns and other weapons from the sacked outpost, the entering security forces quickly opened fire. In many cases, they seemed to be shooting to kill.[1]

Many Palestinians in Jerusalem and elsewhere stayed up late on the night of the tragedy, waiting for Iraqi chemical-tipped missiles to wipe out Tel Aviv, Israel's largest Jewish city. But their hoped-for avenger and savior, Saddam Hussein, did not come through, at least not right away. . . .

The Palestinians, echoed by Saddam and other Arab leaders, called the Israeli shootings a calculated massacre. The Israelis, suspecting that the attack on Jewish worshipers at the Western Wall was planned in advance by the PLO, in collusion with Saddam, said their security forces had acted in justified self-defense. The United Nations, supported by the United States, condemned Israel, calling for a special U.N. investigative commission to go to Jerusalem. The Israeli government demurred, saying all of Jerusalem, including the Old City, was sovereign Israeli territory, and therefore, the Israelis would handle the matter themselves.

Several weeks later, a special Israeli government-appointed committee blamed the Palestinians for starting the riot, and for no justifiable reason. But the committee also charged police officials with negligence in being unprepared for major rioting on the day of the clash, and said without elaboration that there had been "unsupervised use of live ammunition" by police trying to quell the rioting. The Palestinian uprising leadership, having already issued leaflets ordering revenge knifings and other attacks on Israeli soldiers and civilians, called the report a whitewash.

The riot and shootings took place just one mile north of my Jerusalem apartment. I was home on the morning of the violent clash, leisurely sipping coffee and reading the *Jerusalem Post* newspaper. Since I was not on duty that day for CBS Radio, I didn't react too quickly when the barely audible sounds of distant shooting and police sirens began to filter into my living room. Such sounds are, sad to say, not all that uncommon these days in the City of Peace. But after the noise continued for more than ten minutes, I thought I'd better find out what was going on.

FROM IDAHO TO ISRAEL

It was on an earlier October morning during another Jewish holiday that I first noticed the rumbling sounds of the distant Arab/Israeli conflict. The autumn sun shone brightly as I settled into my stuffed pillowchair, newspaper and coffee in hand. Local news dominated the headlines on that warm Saturday morning—another fatal road accident, city council intrigues, ongoing preparations for the Expo '74 World Fair in nearby Spokane, Washington. There were also the usual daily reports on the deepening Watergate crisis. After a quick glance at these stories, I turned to something a bit more interesting: Charlie Brown and his Peanuts gang.

After taking a serious look at the comics and sports pages, I switched on the radio to catch the latest news. "War has broken out in the Middle East," said a very somber voice. "Egyptian and Syrian forces launched a full-scale military attack against Israel several hours ago. Israeli troops and army reserve forces are being quickly mobilized to counter an Egyptian assault in the Sinai Desert, and a Syrian offensive on the Golan Heights. The surprise attack came as most Israelis were observing the holiest day of the Jewish year—Yom Kippur, the Day of Atonement."

When the newscast was finished, I turned off the radio and quietly mulled over this unexpected and obviously serious development. But instead of coherent thoughts, I found myself overwhelmed with emotion. Tears welled up in my eyes from somewhere deep inside of me. Waves of sorrow were rippling through me as the tears began to pour down my cheeks. Why was I reacting like this? Just out of high school and eighteen years old, I was only marginally interested in the Arab/Israeli conflict, even though my friends considered me a bit of a news-hound. I didn't know any Jews or Arabs who might lose loved ones in this latest chapter of the decades-old dispute. True, I had become somewhat sensitized to the horrors of war by watching television reports from Vietnam, as had many Americans, yet I realized that this alone couldn't explain the depth of my sorrow. It was as if some other being—maybe even God himself—were crying deep within me.

The Arab oil embargo following the 1973 Yom Kippur War was just beginning to produce major disruptions in America's life-style when my childhood faith in Jesus was renewed in January 1974. Increasing international attention was focused on the Middle East as drivers in the United States and parts of Europe suddenly found themselves waiting in long lines to fill up their gas tanks. Against this background, I soon found myself devouring various Christian prophecy books that pointed to the Arab/Israeli dispute as the centerpiece of God's prophetic "end-time plan" for the world. These books usually portrayed Israel in a very positive light. However, I was soon exposed to other, less charitable views of the Jews and Israel.

"It's all part of the Jewish conspiracy to take over the world," said my friend Doug, referring to the crisis that followed the Arab decision to cut off oil supplies to the United States because of its support for Israel.

"How could that be," I responded, "since the embargo is designed to hurt Israel?"

"Oh, the Jews are very clever," Doug assured me. "This is just part of their international deception. They're lulling the world to sleep while preparing for their final moves. We white Americans and Europeans must do everything we can to stop them!"

Doug was echoing the teachings of a group he had just joined, the Church of Jesus Christ Christian, Aryan Nation. Several years earlier, the group's leader had moved from California to Hayden Lake, Idaho, just a few miles north of my hometown, Coeur d'Alene. Many of the neo-Nazi white supremacists who followed him to Idaho were busy recruiting local people to their movement. Doug, of Germanic background, turned out to be easy prey, to everyone's great surprise.

Despite my new-found intense interest in the Arab/Israeli dispute, I didn't think I had ever met any Jews, or Arabs for that matter (although I later discovered that the father of a childhood classmate was Jewish when his Hayden Lake restaurant was painted with swastikas and set on fire by Aryan Nation followers). But now I was meeting Nazis, or their 1970s American equivalent, in my own hometown!

I was increasingly shocked, as were most of my fellow Idahoans, to discover the things that were going on in the Aryan Nation compound just outside of Hayden Lake. Hitler's Nazi flag was prominently displayed. Armed men in Nazi uniforms marched in "training exercises" around the compound. Wooden crosses were burned in the worst tradition of America's white supremacist underground movement, the Ku Klux Klan.

I easily resisted Doug's repeated invitations to attend a "Sunday service" in the fenced compound, but several mutual friends did go.

"Their leader said only white people in white robes

would make it into heaven," chuckled one of them. "He also insisted that we white Christians must overthrow what he called ZOG, the Zionist Occupation Government, which he said has long controlled Washington, D.C."

Several years later I experienced Aryan Nation persuasion firsthand. I was working at a Coeur d'Alene radio station after completing a year-long broadcasting course in Spokane. The radio station's news director was preparing a story about an armed attack on the home and car of a local attorney who had represented several Aryan Nation members and others in a lawsuit against a Spokane dental clinic. Doug told me the claimants had been "ripped off" by the previous owner of the clinic, Jewish dentist Dr. David Cowan. It seemed that the new owners of Cowan's denture clinic would not honor his lifetime guarantee on every set of false teeth he had sold. The attorney had apparently been attacked by disgruntled claimants unhappy with his out-of-court compromise settlement, which they complained did not give them sufficient compensation.

The radio station's news director showed up late one evening while I was on the air. "I interviewed that guy the neo-Nazis tried to kill," he told me. "I'll get the story to you for your next newscast."

"Good for you!" I replied. "I'll be waiting for it."

Soon after our brief conversation, the telephone rang. I could see the news director pick up the phone in a nearby editing room. I was pretty sure I knew who was calling. The day before, the owner of Coeur d'Alene's only newspaper, who also owned the radio station, had received a telephone threat: The publisher's family would be much better off if he stopped printing the attorney's allegations that Aryan Nation members were responsible for the attacks against him.

I listened in on the call over a nearby studio monitor. "We understand you did an interview with that man whose house and car were firebombed and shot at," said the unidentified caller. "We will be very glad if you do not run it. Your children and wife will be glad too."

After pausing for a few minutes, the news director walked into the on-air studio and announced that the story would not be available that evening.

"They threatened you," I said, not revealing that I had monitored the conversation. He frowned, but didn't answer. "We mustn't let these people intimidate us," I insisted with rising emotion. "This is how Hitler got started!"

"Then *you* run the interview," he shot back, "but it won't have my voice on it!"

I went ahead and played part of the interview on my 11 P.M. final newscast. Immediately two phone lines lit up. I decided not to answer. Soon afterward, in the spring of 1978, I left Coeur d'Alene for what I hoped would be saner pastures in California.

"Down with the oppressive Shah! Down with the satanic puppet!" shouted the Iranian students over loudspeakers as they drove around the University of California campus in Berkeley. It was there, where the 1960s "free speech movement" began, that I first met Arabs and Jews. I didn't, however, meet any dissident Iranian students, although I and everyone else was awakened many mornings by their anti-Shah slogans broadcast over an automobile loudspeaker. Within a year their wishes would come true, as the Shah of Iran was overthrown in early 1979 by a Shiite Muslim leader named Khomeini.

My next-door neighbor didn't think the Iranian Muslim fundamentalists were going to succeed in ousting the pro-Western Shah. Aaron was a Jewish law student at the university. He was interested to hear that I had come to California to work with a Christian anti-cult group called the Spiritual Counterfeits Project. "Sounds far out to me," said Aaron. "There are certainly enough religious kooks around the Bay area to investigate!"

Aaron was quite right, as I soon discovered. The folks at Spiritual Counterfeits had conducted an investigation of an unusual San Francisco "church" headed by the Reverend Jim Jones. Four months after I arrived in Berkeley in May 1978, Jones and hundreds of his followers committed suicide in Jonestown, the cult center he set up in Guyana, South America. Some of the survivors of Jones' cult threatened to harm members of those groups, such as the one I was now with, who had conducted investigations of it. Shortly after the horrific mass suicide occurred, the mayor of San Francisco and a city councilman were assassinated.

The cult-induced deaths of so many poor, mostly black San Franciscans in Guyana, followed by the killing of the two most prominent politicians in the city, left most Bay-area residents in a state of shock. Such things were a bit too much for an Idaho boy, even one who had already experienced neo-Nazi close encounters of a weird kind. My thoughts turned increasingly toward the relative sanity of northern Idaho. In December, I returned to the snowy Pacific Northwest. Several months later, I began working as a radio announcer at a station owned by the Moody Broadcasting Network in Spokane.

My sensation-filled time in the San Francisco area taught me that California, while a nice place to live in many ways, is definitely *not* the Promised Land. But it was there that I had my first deep longings to visit the *real* Promised Land, Israel.

During my third month in "Berzerkeley" (as the city is affectionately called by many), I had been invited to attend a Tuesday night Bible study at the Jews for Jesus headquarters in San Francisco. Almost every week after that, I would pile my car full of Christian friends and

cross the Bay Bridge into beautiful, troubled San Francisco. Although we were mostly Gentiles, the "Berkeley
crew" always received a warm welcome at the study.

I especially remember one meeting just before Yom
Kippur. Tears filled my eyes as I listened to the beautiful
songs sung by the musical group Liberated Wailing Wall.
As the Bible study leader spoke of Yom Kippur, I recalled
the first time I ever heard of the holy day—sitting in
my pillowchair listening to news about a new war in
the Middle East. *Maybe I'll live in Israel one day,* I mused.
But I dismissed the idea as highly unlikely.

Yet Israel was indeed in my future. Two years later,
in November 1980, I was on my way to live in the Promised
Land, but only for a year, I assured my not-too-thrilled
parents. I still couldn't believe I was really going, even
as I boarded an Israel-bound airliner with a group of
twenty young American Christians. We were on our way
to live and work for a year on an Israeli "kibbutz"—the
world renowned collective agricultural settlements that
played such a vital role in the formation of the state of
Israel earlier this century.

Many passengers applauded as our plane touched
down at Ben Gurion Airport near Tel Aviv. We were in
the Holy Land! After a harrowing taxi ride that should
have taken twenty minutes but only lasted ten, we arrived
at Baptist Village, a Southern Baptist Christian center
near Tel Aviv. There we were joined by another ten
young people from Britain, Denmark, Africa, and Australia. The next day we began a six-week orientation program to prepare for our year-long stay in Israel. We
had come under the sponsorship of Project Kibbutz, a
U.S.-based ministry that placed teams of young Christian
workers on Israeli kibbutz settlements.

Despite a severe case of jet lag, I enjoyed the "P.K."

orientation program. Well, maybe I wasn't exactly thrilled about the mandatory 5 A.M. daily jog around the village, but the continuing excitement I felt at being in the Promised Land made any other feelings, including exhaustion, irrelevant. My main goal besides staying awake was to visit the "City of the Great King," Jerusalem, just thirty miles away. We were scheduled to have a three-day tour of Israel's capital city at the end of the program. There was no way I was going to wait that long.

Niels Christiansen from Denmark had the bunk bed just above mine. While the rest of us flew to Israel from various parts of the globe, Niels pedaled his bicycle from Jerusalem, where he had worked as a volunteer with a Danish group helping the elderly for a year. Every day during the first few weeks of the program he would gleefully describe the city to me, knowing my eagerness to get there.

"Oh, Lord," I prayed, "you must have some way to get me to Jerusalem soon. I can't stand being so close to your city, yet having to wait another month to see it." The Lord heard my cry.

"I need someone to go up to Jerusalem to help me pick up the rest of my belongings," said Niels with a glint in his eye. "You wouldn't be interested, would you?" Several days later we were on a crowded Israeli bus, weaving our way up the tree-lined hills to Jerusalem.

My first experience in this holy city was nothing less than delightful. After arriving at the almost empty central bus station in western Jerusalem, Niels suggested we go and visit friends of his in a nearby apartment building. We walked in just as his Israeli friends were about to light the Friday evening Sabbath candles.

It was a special Sabbath, coming in the middle of the week-long Jewish festival of Hanukkah. The holiday marks God's deliverance of Jerusalem in 165 B.C. from Syrian-Greek control, and the miraculous restoration of the ancient Jewish Temple, which had been defiled by Greek pagan practices. We were handed Jewish skullcaps, or *yarmulkes,* to put on our heads before the woman of the house lit the candles. *"Baruch Ata Adonai Eloheinu, Melech ha Olam,"* she proclaimed, which is Hebrew for "Bless You, O Lord Our God, King of the Universe." After the prayers were finished, we retired to the kitchen to eat jelly doughnuts, the traditional Hanukkah treat.

"This is not the way the city usually looks," Niels assured me as we walked along almost empty streets heading for Jerusalem's ancient walled Old City. "This place really shuts down on Friday nights and Saturdays. The Sabbath is the Sabbath in Jerusalem!" To me, the quiet only added to the awesomeness I already felt at being in the city where Jesus died and rose again—the city where, according to the Bible, he will return one day in glory.

My excitement grew as we spotted in the distance the high stone wall surrounding the Old City, beautifully lit up by pink and white floodlights. Soon we were walking through the Damascus Gate, the main northern entrance to the Old City. All was quiet as we made our way along deserted narrow lanes. Finally we reached the Western Wall plaza. Here thousands of religious Jews gather daily to pray for the coming of the Messiah and the rebuilding of the Temple. Their heartfelt, sometimes tearful prayers over the years have led many Western visitors to dub it "the Wailing Wall." I was bubbling with excitement and anticipation as we entered the plaza. "We're approaching the heart of Jerusalem—and of the whole world," proclaimed Niels.

I was certain I had died and gone to heaven! Five large, gas-powered candles positioned close to the Western Wall shed a beautiful, otherworldly, reddish-orange light all over the empty plaza. The flickering firelight danced on the venerated ancient Wall and on all the surrounding buildings. The burning candles were part of the eight Hanukkah lights lit by Jews around the world each year, one day at a time. The candles commemorate a miracle said to have occurred in the ancient Temple, which once towered just above where we were standing. When the Jews drove the Syrian-Greeks out of the Temple, records the Jewish Talmud, only enough oil remained to fuel the seven-pointed Temple lamp for one day. But miraculously, the oil lasted eight full days. As Niels and I marveled at the sight before us, we spotted one lone Jew praying silently next to the Wall. He didn't seem to notice us as we quietly approached the Wall and began praying to the God of Israel through his anointed Messiah.

Although I was on cloud nine for several days, I didn't fully appreciate until a month later just how special my first visit to Jerusalem actually had been. When I saw the city a second time, it was as most visitors see it: full of the hustle and bustle, the crowds and the noise, of any city on earth. Our Project Kibbutz tour bus hobbled through streets packed with cars and noisy, smelly city buses. Shoppers carrying packages lined the route, darting to and fro between the slow-moving vehicles. Even the Western Wall plaza was not the same. Hundreds of tourists, many in odd-looking blue hats provided by their tour guides, mingled with Jewish worshipers. Arab vendors busily sold breadrolls nearby. This was the Jerusalem that I became quite familiar with over the next decade. But the memory of my first visit will never leave me.

Nor will the memory of my first tour of the Yad vaShem Holocaust Memorial, located near Mount Herzl in southwest Jerusalem. I, like my companions, was familiar with the Nazi holocaust of World War II that wiped out one-third of world Jewry. I was aware that well over a million Jewish children were among the dead. I knew millions of Jews had perished in gas ovens; had been shot near open pits; had been dissected like frogs; had been burned alive, raped, pillaged. Still, I was not fully prepared for what I would see on that cold day in December.

The others in my group went through the horrifying hallways—lined with pictures, documents, maps, and actual remains of history's worst mass slaughter—more quickly than I did. Maybe I took longer to absorb what I was reading and seeing because I knew firsthand that Nazi ideology is not just a thing of the past. Maybe it was because of my experiences with the Church of Jesus Christ Christian, Aryan Nation that I alone was moved to tears by a large photograph prominently displayed at the end of the first hallway.

The picture, the only one without an accompanying text, showed a large outdoor crucifix located in the yard of a German monastery. Just outside the yard, in the direction the head of the crucified, bloodstained Christ was facing, was posted a large sign in German: *Juden Sind Heir Nicht Erwunscht,* "Jews are not welcome here."

How could such a wholesale slaughter have happened anywhere on earth in the twentieth century? I asked myself as I neared the exit door. And, even more puzzling, how could it have taken place in Germany, one of the most advanced "Christian" nations in the world? Despite the fact that I knew the others were waiting for me outside, I had to take a few minutes at the end to find a dark corner—and weep.

CHAPTER 2

RACHEL
WEEPS

"You have two choices," said Art Carlson, the founder and leader of Project Kibbutz. We were at the end of our six-week orientation program, which included full lectures on Israel's history and the Middle East, plus Hebrew language lessons. "You can either go to a kibbutz in the south near the town of Ashkelon, or to one along the Israeli border with Lebanon. But I have to warn you," he continued gravely, "the northern kibbutz is sometimes shelled by PLO forces located just over the border in south Lebanon."

Naturally, as a radio broadcaster, I wanted to spend my year near the action, so I chose the northern kibbutz called Hagoshrim (the "bridge builders"). My Danish friend Niels also anticipated an adventure in the north, as did a dozen other orientation participants. It was undoubtedly for the best that none of us realized just how much action we were about to experience!

I arrived at Hagoshrim on Christmas Day 1980, along with my two team leaders, who were both from Great Britain. The three of us were sent up before the rest of the team to make sure that everything was in order. It was a bright, warm Christmas Day, marred only by what sounded like a distant thunder storm. But there were no clouds on the horizon.

"I bet you're wondering what that noise is," said Eliyahu, a delightful Turkish-born Jew who was in charge of overseas volunteer workers at Hagoshrim. "That's the PLO's traditional Christmas gift to the Christians of south Lebanon!" My puzzled expression prompted a further explanation. "The PLO always shoots extra shells at the south Lebanese Christians on their religious holidays," Eliyahu told me. As I began to digest this, he said, "Let's just hope they don't send anything our way." I could have gone all day without hearing that comment!

"Are people being killed?" I asked.

"Maybe some, but not many. The Israeli Army provides bomb shelters for them."

What a sad way to spend Christmas Day, I thought, *and how different from what I'm used to!*

Not much time passed before we began living in underground bomb shelters ourselves. Tension rose sharply in mid-January after the nearby Israeli town of Kiryat Shmona was shelled. The PLO had used the town as a frequent target of attack ever since setting up a mini-state in south Lebanon in the mid-1970s. The Palestinian attack began a new round of tit-for-tat shelling from both sides of the border. It climaxed in several weeks of heavy bombardments in April. One of the main Israeli gun emplacements was just next to Hagoshrim, a fact we were constantly reminded of. The shooting calmed down for several months, but intensified again in late June. July was a real blast! We ate and slept in our sweltering shelter for several weeks straight while bombs crashed down around us.

The Jews of Hagoshrim, who had lived through similar bombing blitzes for decades, were certain that some of us would return home. Taking off was the normal, and quite understandable, reaction of most foreign volunteers during periods of heavy shelling. Yet, although we were tempted at times, and despite some parental encouragement to come home, none of us left the kibbutz. We wanted to show our Jewish hosts that we would not run away at the first sign of trouble.

Our determination to stay was noted and appreciated by Hagoshrim's five hundred or so Israeli residents. A few would drop by our bomb shelter to hear us sing songs of praise and worship to the Lord. "The Lord is my life and my salvation. Whom shall I fear, whom shall I fear?" We especially liked to sing "Hiding Place," written in late 1980 by Project Kibbutz member Michael Ledner. He taught the song to me, then together we taught it to several P.K. teams gathered for a spring seminar on the shores of the Dead Sea—the lowest place on earth. "You are my hiding place./ You always fill my heart/ with songs of deliverance./ Whenever I am afraid,/ I will trust in you,/ I will trust in you./ Let the weak say, 'I am strong/ in the strength of the Lord!' " Comforting words indeed while sitting in an underground bomb shelter, or at the lowest spot on earth.

A late-July cease-fire, engineered by U.S. special envoy Philip Habib, gave us a break from the shelling for the remainder of our stay on Hagoshrim. Finally, we were able to get to know the kibbutz members in a relaxed atmosphere. Many of them immigrated to Israel from Turkey, whose once-great Jewish community consisted mainly of descendants of Jews expelled from Spain in the late 1400s. Some had fled Europe during World War II. One woman had lost more than two hundred relatives in Hitler's gas ovens. A few had come before the war, foreseeing that Hitler meant it when he said that Europe must be rid of its Jews. Several had fled from Iraq and other Arab countries in the early years of the Jewish state. Only a handful were survivors of Hitler's death camps.

I was overwhelmed by the stories I heard—some heroic, some pitiful, most a mixture of the two. As I listened,

I realized that I knew so very little about the Jewish *diaspora,* or "dispersion," which had lasted for most of the past two thousand years.

"Diaspora is a Greek word," somebody on the kibbutz pointed out to me. "The word we use in Israel is *galut,* Hebrew for 'exile.' We weren't simply dispersed. We were cast out, exiled from our land."

I soon realized that knowledge about the many years of Jewish *galut* is essential if one is attempting to comprehend what lies behind the creation of the modern state of Israel and the Arab/Israeli conflict. I vaguely knew that the history of "Christian" persecution of the Jews didn't begin with Hitler's Germany. Still I was shocked to discover in subsequent research that it was only the tip—even if an excessively horrendous one—of a very ugly iceberg.

MARTYRS AND HEROES

As I begin writing this brief overview of Jewish history from the time of the Jewish dispersion from the Holy Land in the second century A.D., Israel is observing its annual Holocaust Martyrs and Heroes Remembrance Day. This morning I stood on my balcony at 10 A.M. as sirens wailed for two minutes across Jerusalem and the rest of the country. Cars and trucks came to a halt as Jews throughout the land stood in silence to commemorate the millions killed by Hitler's Nazi death machine. This special day also reminds many people of the centuries of persecution their ancestors endured in Christian Europe and Russia. Last evening, as the sad day began (all Jewish days begin at sunset), I was in the home of Messianic Jewish author Lance Lambert, whose father and other relatives perished in the Auschwitz death camp. I sat quietly as Lance and his sister Teresa lit a candle in their father's memory.

Lance's father was taken to Auschwitz from his home country of Italy, where a thriving Jewish community had lived for many centuries in relatively peaceful conditions. Yet despite the traditional warmth and moderation of the Italian people, the Mediterranean nation of Italy is generally not fondly remembered by Jews. The reason for this is quite simple. The heart of Italy is Rome, and for centuries the heartbeat of Rome has been the Vatican, the seat of the Roman Catholic church. It was the Vatican that gave an official Christian imprimatur to the persecution suffered by the Jewish people in the early days of Christianity and beyond, an imprimatur that was at least partially carried on by most of the Reformation churches.

The ancient church laid the foundation upon which the holocaust was built. In fact, a thousand years before Hitler took control of Germany, Jews were being slaughtered throughout "Christian" Europe. It must be noted that anyone holding religious views dissimilar to the Church of Rome's was liable to be ostracized, if not actually persecuted, be they Jew or Gentile. But no other sect or nationality suffered such deep and consistent hostility, hatred, and violence as the Jews.

"The vast majority of Christians, even well educated, are all but totally ignorant of what happened to Jews in history, and of the culpable involvement of the Church," writes Edward H. Flannery, a Roman Catholic priest, in the introduction to his excellent, if very sad, book *The Anguish of the Jews: Twenty-three Centuries of Antisemitism.*[1] The author's lament, which I can verify from my own experience, is followed by the observation that Christians are generally ignorant of the church's historical anti-Semitic record because most Christian history books omit or play down its intensity. Christian anti-Semitic teachings and actions were hardly even mentioned in the Catholic school I attended in the 1960s. Father Flannery then goes on to note that most Jews are *acutely* aware of this historical hatred and persecution, which so often ended in violent death. After more than a decade in Israel, I can confirm that statement as well.

Was the Church's record really that bad? some may ask. *And didn't the Jews deserve it just a little?* The answer to the first part of that question can be found in history, which we will look at briefly in the coming paragraphs. The answer to the second part is a matter of opinion. As someone who has lived with Israeli Jews since 1980, I can testify that they are as human as anyone else. It was, after all, the ancient Jewish prophets who pointed out the sinful and fallen state of the chosen people of God. Many Jews are wonderful people, and others not so nice. Whatever the case, true Christians have no excuse for hating or persecuting anyone, being followers of the Jew who taught us to love all people equally, whether we like them or not. Yet it was the Bible, and especially the New Testament, which was so often quoted to justify Christian attacks against the Jews.

A LEGACY OF HATRED

Within several centuries after Jesus' death and resurrection, many of the church fathers seemed to have forgotten that their Savior, his mother Mary, his earthly father Joseph, all of the apostles, all but possibly one of the New Testament writers, and most members of the early church, *were Jews.* They began preaching from churches—mostly named after these Jews—that God had forever cursed the physical brethren of Jesus who had totally rejected him as Messiah. They taught that the New Testament church is the new Israel, which has totally supplanted the old. The church accepted this interpretation as authoritative despite the contextual evidence throughout the New Testament that, although the Gentiles are now partakers of the covenant blessings of God, the term *Israel* still refers, with one possible exception, exclusively to the Jewish people.

These same church leaders apparently overlooked the fact that many thousands of Jews accepted their fellow Jew, Yeshua, as the Messiah *before* Gentiles even had a chance to hear the gospel. We know from the New Testament book of Acts that in the immediate years after the Lord's ascension, "the number of the disciples multiplied greatly in Jerusalem, and a great many of the priests were obedient to the faith" (6:7). Even before this, just after Jesus' crucifixion, many Jews were sympathetic to him, deeply regretting and mourning over his death. Luke records that following the crucifixion and the darkness which fell over the land, "and the whole crowd who came together to that sight, seeing what had been done, beat their breasts and returned" (Luke 23:48), which was a sign of great mourning. Yet in the writings of many of the early church fathers, the Jewish multitudes were pictured as totally evil, jeering the Lord as he was led to the slaughter.

Flannery points out that church fathers such as Origen, Justin, and Chrysostom seemed to have forgotten that any Jews had ever trusted Jesus as their Savior. Jewish Pharisees and priests were exclusively portrayed as conniving and totally hostile to the gospel. The fathers used selected statements made by the apostle Paul to attack these groups, ignoring Paul's own testimony that he was proud of his Jewish heritage, including his upbringing as a Pharisee. Nicodemus, a leading Pharisee in Paul's day, confessed to Jesus that many of his contemporaries were awestruck by this rabbi from Nazareth: "We know that You are a teacher come from God; for no one can do these signs that You do unless God is with him" (John 3:2). Many church fathers seemed to have assumed that none of the people spoken of by Nicodemus, and none of the multitudes who beat their breasts over the Lord's awful crucifixion, ended up following the one who proclaimed himself the long-awaited Messiah of Israel. Of course, even if none had believed, there was no Christian basis for vicious attacks against the Jewish people.

Paul's affection for his kinsmen and their religion, spelled out in his letter to the Romans, was not emulated by these early Roman church leaders. Instead there was enmity, hostility, and finally outright hatred of the Jews. Paul taught that God's rejection of that part of the Jewish nation which did not believe led to "riches for the Gentiles" who were then grafted in as "wild olive branches" onto the tree of Israel. (How can the church be grafted onto a tree it has completely replaced?) Many of Paul's successors seemingly wanted to destroy the Jewish roots of the tree, along with the rejected branches, apparently ignoring the fact that a tree without roots will soon die.

The Roman destruction of the Jewish nation of Judea in A.D. 135 was deserved, wrote Justin to an unidentified rabbi in his *Dialogue with Trypho,* "because you have murdered the Just One."[2] This theme would be echoed frequently down through history by Christians persecuting Jews. The fact that Jesus himself taught that he *had to die* in order to redeem mankind somehow escaped Gentile persecutors, along with the fact that it was *Roman* soldiers who actually killed him.

Origen concluded that the Jews "will never be restored to their former condition. For they have committed a crime of the most unhallowed kind, in conspiring against the Savior of the human race."[3] Apparently overlooked was Paul's teaching that Gentile Christians should not behave arrogantly toward the broken-off Jewish branches, for "God is able to graft them in again."

Father Flannery cites many other instances of growing hostility toward the Jews by early church fathers, which reached its height in the sermons and writings of John

Chrysostom (A.D. 344–407). According to Flannery, Chrysostom "stands without peer or parallel in the virulence of his attack."[4] He quotes from eight sermons by Chrysostom—the most popular preacher of the fourth century—in which this preacher called the Jews "lustful, rapacious, greedy, perfidious bandits, inveterate murderers, destroyers, men possessed by the devil" with the "manners of the pig and the lusty goat." Jews "worship the devil," and their religion is "a disease." They have fallen into such a state because of their "odious assassination of Christ." Therefore, God hates the Jews, who will always remain without the Temple or a sovereign nation. If all of this did not lead to obvious conclusions among his Christian audience, Chrysostom spelled it out even more explicitly for them, calling for a perpetual Christian "holy war" against the Jews: "He who can never love Christ enough will never have done with fighting against those who hate Him."[5]

Such statements as these would be of only marginal historical interest if it were not for the awful, tragic fact that many Christian leaders and laymen used them as a basis for persecuting, and even killing, their Jewish neighbors. It does not matter that Jewish hostility against Christians might have, at times, preceded Christian persecution of Jews, as Justin argued in his *Dialogue With Trypho*. It was, after all, Christians, and not nonbelieving Jews who were supposed to be the bearers of the full revelation of the Messiah. It was Christians who had the high moral and ethical standards of the Jew Jesus to emulate.

There were, of course, individual Christians down through the years who followed the Messiah's teachings and example of love, compassion and forgiveness in dealing with their Jewish neighbors. But, as in Nazi Germany, such people were always relatively few. And most of them were forced to go against official church teachings and laws in order to fulfill Christ's command to "love your neighbor as yourself."

ENFORCED DISCRIMINATION

It wasn't long before anti-Jewish sentiments emanating from various pulpits around the Roman empire were turned into anti-Jewish church legislation. Around A.D. 306, church leaders meeting in Elvira, Spain, issued a decree forbidding close relations of any kind between Christians and Jews. In particular they banned Jewish/ Christian marriages, which was understandable in light of Paul's admonition in his second letter to the Corinthians that Christians should not be "unequally yoked" with nonbelievers (6:14).

The Nicaean Council of 325 took another step to insure that Christians would have "nothing in common with this odious people," ruling that the calendar date for Easter should be unlinked to the Jewish Passover Festival. The Council of Antioch in 341 explicitly prohibited Christians from celebrating Passover with their Jewish neighbors (a command I've broken many times!). The long-running Council of Laodicea (434–481) told Christians they could not keep the Jewish Sabbath, or receive gifts or unleavened bread from Jews observing the Passover.

The Roman Emperor Constantine converted to Christianity in 312 and later declared his new faith to be the official state religion. His subsequent moves regarding the Jewish people were not exactly sterling displays of the Golden Rule. Constantine ordered all Jews to leave Rome in 325, signaling hard times ahead for the ancient chosen people of God. British Old Testament scholar H. L. Ellis wrote that Constantine's legalization of Christianity was a turning point for the Jews: "When the church became recognized by Constantine, legal discrimination against Jews increased and they were gradually deprived of all rights."[6]

At least Constantine and his successors frowned on the growing Christian practice of burning down Jewish synagogues (a practice fanned, no doubt, by Chrysostom's sermons in Antioch). There was still some appreciation for the fact that the Jews had been the first to bring knowledge of the one true God of Israel to Rome and its provinces, but it was insufficient to hold back the tidal wave of anti-Semitism that was about to crash on the Mediterranean shores and flood the entire Empire.

Conversions to Judaism, which had been a legally protected religion, were outlawed for all Roman citizens, while formulas were drawn up for Jews converting to Christianity, which included renunciations of the "detestable practices" of Judaism. Jewish converts were to break off all ties to any family member or friend still practicing the "nefarious religion." The official slide into anti-Semitism was halted only briefly during the reign of Julian (361–363), who did not claim to be a Christian, but resumed again with his successors, who were professing Christians.

Emperor Theodosius banned all Jews from holding any form of public office in A.D. 438. This law, along with other restrictions enacted around this time, constituted the legal basis on which all later European anti-Semitic legislation was formulated.

With the legal door now closing on Jewish life, persecution began in earnest. The ancient Jewish community in Alexandria became the first victims of wide-scale attack early in the fifth century. Zealous, misguided preachers encouraged the sacking of synagogues all over the Empire. Many thousands of Jews perished in these attacks.

The official Roman Catholic church attitude toward the Jews—which was more benign than the practice of many of its members—was solidified by Pope Gregory, who ruled from 590 to 604. Physical violence was condemned, but other forms of persecution were tolerated and even encouraged. God did not intend for Christians to kill Jews, said Gregory. Instead, the Jews were meant to exist alongside Christians as an "active witness" that sin was always punished by God. The Jews, in their degradation, provided such a testimony. While their conversion was to be worked for, force should not be used. The Jews could keep their synagogues, but no new ones should be built.

Popes down through the centuries were generally able to enforce these policies in the immediate vicinity of Rome, even as the Empire fell apart. But elsewhere, many bishops and secular rulers, believing that the Jews were eternally cursed by God, carried the official church position to its logical conclusion. Forced conversions under penalty of death were ordered in many places (not a few Jews died rather than undergo baptism). The burning and looting of synagogues continued in many places. Jewish children were forcibly taken from their parents and raised as Christians. Jews were forbidden to work in many professions. They were, however, encouraged to be moneylenders since the church forbade Christians to be involved with usury. (Thus, the anti-Semitic charge, heard to this day, that Jews control all the money, was to a certain degree true, but only because of the church's own laws!)

JUDENRIND

The first mass expulsion of Jews from their homes was ordered by King Dagobert of Gaul in 626. This was rapidly emulated in nearby Burgundy and in the kingdom of Lombardy in northern Italy. These expulsions came as King Sisebut of Spain was outlawing the practice of

Judaism in his country. Still, the great Spanish Jewish community continued to flourish for many centuries, despite growing persecution, and some Jews even attained to positions of power and influence.

However, Jewish fortunes declined sharply in the ninth century as Christians and Muslims fought over the Iberian Peninsula. Jews were expelled from the kingdom of Granada in 1066. Many were put to death by Muslim conquerors in southern Spain. Muslim victories in Spain only added to the growing cry in Europe for a holy war against the Islamic "infidels" who had conquered the Holy Land four centuries earlier.

The first "Crusade" to retake Zion from Islam was launched by Pope Urban II in 1095. For the next several hundred years, Jews would be viciously slaughtered throughout Europe and the Middle East by European soldiers and civilians who believed they were doing the will of God. Hatred of the Jews exploded into mass violence everywhere. Jews were burned alive in their synagogues; raped; driven from many towns; accused of killing Christian children in order to use their blood in Passover rites; accused of poisoning water wells. Jews were forced to wear distinctive hats or yellow patches for identification. Their property was seized and plundered, their crops destroyed, their animals stolen or killed. All of this happened, and much more, in the name of the Jewish Messiah.

When the Crusaders "captured Jerusalem for Christ" in 1099, they gathered the small Jewish remnant of David's ancient capital city into one of Jerusalem's synagogues and set it on fire, killing everyone inside. In 1189 during the third Crusade, the Jewish quarter of London was set aflame, leaving many people dead. Jewish centers were then destroyed all over England, as they had been earlier in France and Germany. Anti-Jewish rioting against "the Christ killers" was usually at its worst around

Easter. Jews came to dread this Christian holiday more than any other—even though it was a holiday meant to proclaim the Messiah of Israel's victory over sin and death.

As the Crusades came to an unglorious end with Jerusalem back in Muslim hands, a wave of expulsions began in Europe. Jews were ordered out of England and Wales in 1290, from Paris and other parts of France in 1306, from the Rhineland in 1348, from Hungary in 1349, from southern France in 1394, from Spain in 1492, and from Portugal in 1497. The expulsions came in the wake of the forth Lateran Council of 1215, which strengthened earlier Roman Catholic legislation aimed at restricting the Jews. Among other things, the Council ordered Jews to begin wearing a yellow or crimson badge in order to prevent unwitting sexual intercourse between Christians and Jews, an offense punishable by death in most places.

In the midst of these expulsions, Europe experienced its most deadly plague ever—the Black Death. The scourge, which wiped out a third of the continent's population (including, of course, Jews) between 1347 and 1350, was blamed by the masses on the Jews. They had become the usual scapegoat for anything that went wrong.[7]

The populace believed that the Jews had poisoned Europe's water supplies with a concoction of sacred hosts, human hearts, and various insects and animals. Untold thousands of Jews were massacred in southern France, Spain, Switzerland, Germany, Austria, Poland, and Belgium because of this ridiculous charge. More than two hundred Jewish communities were entirely wiped out. To his credit, Pope Clement VI tried to stop the carnage, but he could not.

The expulsion of the Jews from Spain and Portugal followed what was probably the saddest feature of Roman

Catholic church history: the Inquisition. Pope Sixtus IV issued a Papal Bull in 1478 to set up the "Holy Tribunal" in Spain. Its purpose was to seek out and expose all heretics living in the land. The Roman Catholic Inquisitors ordered tens of thousands of people burned alive at the stake, most of them either Jews who had been pressured to convert to Christianity or their descendants. Many confessed, often under torture, that they had clung to Judaism despite their conversions.

The practice of forcing Jews to live in walled ghettos was already widespread when it was officially legislated by Pope Paul IV in 1555 as part of his fight against the dreaded Protestant Reformation. The idea was to keep Jews, thought to be sympathetic to Martin Luther's reforms, away from their Christian neighbors. The ghettos, usually overcrowded, were ordered sealed off at night and on Christian religious holidays. In Rome, Vienna, Prague, Frankfurt, and other European cities, Jews were forced to live like rats in a hole for no other reason than that they were Jews.

The Reformation was in fact welcomed by many Jews as a possible breath of fresh air in an otherwise stifling Europe. Martin Luther had proclaimed that Christians must be guided in their dealings with the Jews, "not by papal law, but by the law of Christian love." Yet a mere twenty years later, Luther—upset that "Christian love" had not won mass conversions—declared the Jews "disgusting vermin" who should be deported from Germany. His pamphlet "On The Jews and Their Lies" (1543) called for seven steps to be taken against the Jews, including the burning of their synagogues, the razing of their houses, the banning of their holy books, and the seizure of their assets.

Although conditions gradually improved for European Jews after the Enlightenment took hold in the late seventeenth century, persecution and discrimination still continued in many places, especially in eastern Europe and Russia. And Luther's suggestions were definitely not forgotten. They were put into effect four hundred years later (along with many other measures that would have horrified even Luther) by a German fuhrer whose ultimate aim was to make Europe, and ultimately the entire earth, *judenrind*—without Jews.

CHAPTER 3

BUSTING
OUT OF
ARABIA

The windows in my room shook fiercely as artillery and tank shells rained down onto the nearby Golan Heights. *This time,* I thought to myself as I quickly became fully awake, *I'm not in Idaho listening to radio reports about a Syrian surprise attack against Israel. . . . I'm in the valley right below the battle!*

It was the middle of the night, in September 1981. I was all alone in the Hagoshrim medical clinic, recovering from a bad case of hepatitis. The kibbutz resident doctor said I probably caught the disease by drinking untreated water from the Jordan River. "They'll have to carry me down to the bomb shelter," I reasoned out loud while listening to the heavy tank- and shell-fire on the heights above. But several hours passed and nobody came to rescue me. My imagination rapidly slipped into overdrive. Pictures of Syrian soldiers carting me off from the clinic flashed through my mind. As my sense of panic grew, I prayed fervently that God would send someone from my Project Kibbutz team to retrieve me before the Syrians began bombing Hagoshrim.

By morning, the noise of battle had died down. "Would you please tell me what's going on?" I demanded of my teammate Pat as he prepared to pass me breakfast through an open window near my bed.

"Oh, you mean the stuff during the night. Did it bother you?" he asked with a rather obvious sparkle in his eye. Before I could protest, Pat went on to explain that the sounds of war had come from an all-night Israeli Army exercise. "We were all a bit excited. Sorry I didn't come to clue you in on what was happening. Eliyahu came and told us what it was. Boy, was he mad, and so were the other kibbutzniks!"

"Why is that?" I asked, more than a little relieved to find out we were not at war.

"Well, it seems the army didn't inform them about the exercise in advance," answered Pat. "The kids were all sent down into the shelters, and the men were grabbing their uniforms and guns to go off and fight the Syrians before word came that it was only an exercise!"

Although the "battle" on that September night in 1981 proved to be one-sided, Israel and Syria would indeed clash in war before another summer passed.

One month later, I had recovered enough to begin the long journey back to North America. Yet somehow I didn't feel right as Niels and another teammate carried my bags to Hagoshrim's bus stop. Maybe I felt guilty because we only had a couple of months left of our year-long commitment to the kibbutz. Here I was, the one who had encouraged everyone else to stay during the heavy shelling earlier in the year, flying home because of a little illness! But Niels and the others, seeing my poor health, urged me to go and rest for a few months.

"I'm certain that I'll end up on another kibbutz after this one," he assured me, "a quieter one, I hope! So you can come back and finish your year with me in 1982!" Tears filled my eyes as I waved good-bye to my friends. With a heavy heart, I took one long last look at the Golan Heights, Mount Hermon, and the brown hills of Lebanon. The bus headed south toward Jerusalem.

By the time I spotted the Dome of the Rock Muslim shrine on the ancient Temple Mount four hours later, I was certain that, like Jonah, I was heading in the wrong direction. Still, I proceeded with my plan. My next stop was the Garden Tomb near the Old City—the place revered by many Protestants as the possible site where Jesus was buried and rose from the dead.

Good friends from Hayden Lake, Idaho—Claude and Jerry Carey—were serving as volunteer administrators at the Garden Tomb. The Careys met me with their usual warm hugs. However, my surrogate parents for the year were not pleased to hear that I was suddenly thinking of staying in Israel.

"You need to go home to your parents' place and really recover," said Jerry as Claude nodded in agreement. As longtime missionaries, they knew something about hepatitis.

"But I feel like I'm running from God," I responded.

"Well, why don't you go out to the garden and pray about it for a while, and then come in and we'll have a good meal," said Claude, seemingly certain that God would show me the way back . . . to Idaho!

As I sat down to pray in a quiet corner of the garden, one thing especially weighed heavily on my mind. I strongly believed that the Lord had shown me, while sick in bed, that I would be serving him in Lebanon the following year. I had even shared this belief with some of my Project Kibbutz teammates. Yet here I was journeying back to America, with little prospect that I would return halfway around the world to the Middle East in 1982. "Please, Lord," I prayed, "show me what you want me to do!"

His answer came quite quickly. I felt the Holy Spirit gently prompting me to walk over to another part of the beautiful, well-kept garden. There, I came upon a gathering of about fifty people just beginning a communion service. As I joined in singing the familiar Christian hymns, I noticed the light blue windbreakers worn by everyone in the group. "The Voice of Hope" was printed in large letters across the back of the jackets. The name belonged to a Christian radio station that I had often listened to at Kibbutz Hagoshrim. The Voice of Hope broadcasts from south Lebanon.

After the service ended, I announced to the Careys that God had clearly shown me that I was to return to the kibbutz. I didn't quite have the nerve to add that the Lord also confirmed that he was about to open a door of service for me in war-torn southern Lebanon.

In early 1982 there were really only two possible ways of entering the Land of the Cedars from Israel. You had to be an Israeli or United Nations soldier beginning a tour of duty in or near the south Lebanese security zone, a border enclave set up by Israel in the late 1970s to stop terrorists from infiltrating into northern Israel. Or you had to be an employee or guest of the American-owned Voice of Hope radio station.

I certainly wasn't about to join the Israeli army in order to get into Lebanon. But I was not overly eager to work at the Voice of Hope either. I knew that the station was a frequent target of PLO shelling from Beaufort Castle, a nearby Crusader fortress used as a forward military base by Yasser Arafat's fighters. On top of that obvious drawback, I had already decided to leave the field of broadcasting before I ever left the United States. I did not respond enthusiastically when station manager Chuck Pollack suggested during the summer of 1981 that I consider working with his crew in south Lebanon after completing my year at Hagoshrim.

"If you have any life insurance, don't count on anyone collecting on it for anything that happens here," said Chuck as we crossed the border into Lebanon, adding that "your insurer will say that anyone crazy enough to come here deserves to die."

I had met the Voice of Hope director again at a wedding soon after I returned from my "Jonah journey" to Jerusalem. He renewed his offer to me to come work with him. Chuck said he was beefing up his staff, especially the news department, in anticipation of a large-scale Israeli army operation sometime in 1982.

After touring the station, and after much thought and prayer, I finally decided to join the Voice of Hope's English language staff. My first day on the air was in mid-April. Less than two months later, thousands of Israeli soldiers poured across the border to push the PLO out of southern Lebanon—at least that's what everyone thought at the time.

The first Israeli citizens I met after arriving at Ben Gurion Airport in 1980 were Arabs. They were Christian Arabs from Nazareth who worked at Baptist Village. But from the time I moved to Hagoshrim, I was, naturally enough, surrounded by Hebrew-speaking Jews. It was quite a change to suddenly find myself at a Christian radio station in the Arab country of Lebanon, even if I was not far from the Israel/Lebanon border and only a few miles north of the kibbutz.

Several English-speaking Voice of Hope staff members, including myself, took turns broadcasting in the mornings. Several Lebanese Christians rotated as hosts of the afternoon Arabic show. I quickly became friends with my Lebanese co-workers, who all spoke passable English, and began picking up a few phrases in Arabic. I often practiced my newly acquired "pigeon Arabic" over a cup of thick, black Turkish coffee with several of the Christian and Muslim guards who protected the station from armed attack.

One of the conditions for working at the Voice of Hope was that I purchase my own vehicle—essential since we Westerners were not allowed to live in Lebanon and had to cross the border daily from our homes in northern Israel. A friend told me about a good, used Volkswagen station wagon that an Arab Christian pastor needed to sell in Haifa. Although the car was already ten years old, it seemed like just the right vehicle for the potholed roads of Lebanon.

After signing a purchase agreement with Samir, we discussed the Mideast situation. It wasn't long before I discovered that Samir had a very different perception of the fighting in Lebanon than did my Jewish or Lebanese Christian friends. I also learned that Samir termed himself a "Palestinian Israeli," not an "Israeli Arab" as Israeli Jews called him. Our discussions about the Arab/Israeli conflict continued whenever I took the car in for a checkup (Samir was also a good mechanic).

My growing contacts with Arabs from both Israel and Lebanon showed me just how little I knew of Arab history, even as my time on Kibbutz Hagoshrim had pointed out the large gaps in my knowledge of Jewish history. As I studied Arab history in depth, I quickly realized that it is largely a story springing from one man—a desert-dweller named Muhammad.

WHAT'S IN A NAME?

It is difficult to know exactly what we are talking about when we say "Arab history," because it is difficult to precisely define who an "Arab" is.

Historians say the original Arabs were a semi-nomadic, Semitic-speaking tribal people who dwelled in the northern section of the Arabian Peninsula, southeast of the Holy Land. The Bible records that the peoples who roamed the northern Arabian Desert area were largely the descendants of Abraham's firstborn son, Ishmael, and Isaac's son Esau, also known as Edom. God promised Abraham that he would make Ishmael a great nation, although he made clear that he would establish his covenant with Isaac (Gen. 17:20–21). The God of Israel also foretold that there would be enmity between the descendants of Isaac's twin sons, Jacob and Esau (Gen. 25:23). Esau's children began to fulfill that prophecy when they refused passage to the children of Israel who were on their way from Egypt to the Promised Land.

The Bible first uses the term *Arabians* in 2 Chronicles 17:11, where we are told the Arabs gave tribute, along with the Philistines and others, to the highly honored Jewish King Jehoshaphat, who ruled in the ninth century B.C. Later on we find the Arabs joining the Philistines in an attack against Jehoshaphat's son Jehoram (2 Chron. 21:16). With God's help, the youthful King Uzziah defeated the Arabians and the Philistines in the eighth century B.C. (2 Chron. 26:7). By the time of Christ, all of the desert peoples who lived east and southeast of the Promised Land were known as Arabs.

Arab/Jewish enmity was evident when the Jews returned to the homeland from the Babylonian Exile in the sixth and fifth centuries B.C. Arabs were apparently among the peoples who settled in the land during the exile, since they are listed as among those who were angry that returning Jews were rebuilding the destroyed walls of Jerusalem (Neh. 4:7). Earlier Nehemiah had told his opponents, including "Geshem the Arab," that God was behind the rebuilding project, adding that these Gentiles had "no heritage or right or memorial in Jerusalem" (2:20).

In modern terminology, an Arab is generally thought of as anyone whose native tongue is Arabic. This is basically how I have chosen to use the term in this book. However, the peoples who lived in the vast North African region from the Sinai Peninsula to the Atlantic Ocean only began to seriously mix with the warrior-tribesmen of Arabia in the seventh century A.D. Likewise, many of the inhabitants of Syria, Persia, Mesopotamia, Lebanon, and the Holy Land probably had very little Arabian blood in them before the Islamic conquests of that century.

Today most Arabic-speaking people have at least some

genuine Arab ancestry. However, this is probably less
true of those indigenous peoples who did not convert
to Islam in the centuries following the Arab conquest—
such as the Maronite Catholics of Lebanon, the Copts
of Egypt, and the Greek Orthodox and Syrian Orthodox
Catholics of the Middle East.

Except in Lebanon and Egypt, present-day Mideast
Christian communities are tiny minorities in the countries where they reside. This is true despite the fact
that Christianity became the dominant regional religion
by the fifth century. The Lebanese Christians, who belong
mainly to the Rome-affiliated Maronite church founded
in the fifth century by a Syrian monk, consider themselves
descendants of the Phoenicians who plied the ancient
seas from Lebanon's shores. In fact, they are probably
a mixture of various peoples, as is common in the region.
The Egyptian Copts, whose church was said to have
been founded by the Gospel writer Mark, say they are
the true descendants of the ancient Egyptians who once
ruled half the known world. This claim is also undoubtedly only partially true.

Mideast church historians believe that at least some
of the ancient ancestors of the indigenous Christians
of modern-day Israel, Jordan, Judea, and Samaria were
the original converts to the faith in the first century of
church expansion. In other words, many such Christians
actually have Jewish ancestry, since the early Church
was almost entirely Jewish. Their ancestors' Jewish memory faded as the church grew in strength and as rejection
of anything Jewish became a part of mainstream Christian
theology.

The Arabic-speaking Arabian tribesmen who conquered the Middle East, the horn and north of Africa,
and the Persian Empire for Allah turned the world upside
down in just a few short decades. The Arab/Islamic expansion into these areas was swift and complete. Some Christians and Jews fled the rapidly advancing Muslim warri-

ors, while many others were killed. Others converted—often at the point of a sword.

The common thread, then, that ties the histories of the Arabs of northern Africa and the Middle East together is a religion—Islam. But Islam is much more than a religion. It is an all-encompassing code of life which does not separate Caesar from God. The Islamic conception of the absolute unity of religion and government is very much a part of the Mideast drama unfolding in our days.

ALLAH'S ANOINTED

Arab history was most uninteresting until around A.D. 570. In August of that year (the date established by Muslim tradition), a baby boy named Muhammad was born in the Arabian trading town of Mecca. A member of the Quraish tribe which had seized Mecca more than a century earlier, the somewhat mystical, moody orphan had been brought up by one of his uncles following the death of his parents and beloved grandfather, who was one of the leading men of Mecca.

As an adult, Muhammad would often go out to meditate in the hills surrounding Mecca. It was there, during the month of Ramadan in A.D. 610, that the "Angel Jibril" (Gabriel) appeared to the thoughtful mystic. The "angel" instructed Muhammad to declare to the world what he would reveal to him.

Three years later, the forty-three-year-old Arabian stood in Mecca and proclaimed the revelations given to him. He spoke out against the pantheistic idol worship then prevalent in Mecca, and in favor of the one God associated with Gabriel: the God of Abraham, whom he called Allah. But it soon became apparent to Arabia's Christians and Jews—the first targets for conversion by Muhammad and his followers—that Islam's founder was definitely not speaking about the God they worshiped.

When he was twenty-five, Muhammad led a trade caravan to Syria on behalf of a local wealthy widow, Khadija, who later became his first wife (he had about fifteen all together). Scholars believe he may have absorbed much of his knowledge of Christianity while visiting the Byzantine-controlled city of Damascus. However, Muhammad apparently did not correctly comprehend several theological fine points. For one thing, the prominent position that the Eastern Orthodox church allotted to Mary led him to erroneously assume that she was the third person of the Christian Trinity (an assumption still held by the average Muslim today).

The Christianity with which Muhammad came into contact was largely corrupt and riddled with internal, often violent, disputes over theological and political questions. It is, therefore, perfectly understandable that an outsider would have difficulty determining exactly what the church's doctrinal positions really were.

Many Christian experts on Islam maintain that Muhammad's often-confused accounts of the life and mission of Jesus—recorded in the Muslim holy book, the Koran—may have been influenced by contacts with the heretical Christian Nestorian sect, which believed that separate divine and human natures and persons were manifested in Jesus Christ. Whether Muhammad's ideas about Jesus came from himself, from Nestorian members, from the "Angel Jibril," or some combination of the three, seems impossible to say for sure. However, one thing is quite clear: The Islamic Jesus is not the divine being portrayed in the New Testament or worshiped throughout church history.

According to the Koran, Jesus is not the Son of God, but "the son of Mary," since God could not have a son. Those who declare that Jesus is God are "unbelievers" who will be "forbidden entrance into Paradise, and shall be cast into the fire of hell," for "the Messiah, the son of Mary, was no more than an apostle" (Sura 5:73–75).[1]

The Galilean was a great prophet, but not the Savior of the world. He did not die on the cross, but only appeared to do so. He was actually taken up alive to heaven before an embodied spirit resembling him appeared to undergo crucifixion. Since Jesus did not die, he was not raised from the dead. His unshed blood did not atone for the sins of mankind. He will come again to earth just before the Day of Judgment, proclaim that Muhammad was God's final and most sublime prophet, and lead all of mankind into Islam. Then "the son of Mary" will die like any other mortal man and be raised to life along with everyone else on the last day.

The Koran's version of the birth of Jesus is very different from the Gospel accounts. In Sura Mary (*Sura* means "revelation"), the Holy Spirit is sent to Mary in the form of a full-grown man who tells the frightened Jewish maiden that he has "come to give you a holy son" (15–20). The koranic account then reveals that Jesus came into the world while Mary rested under a palm tree somewhere in "the east." Suddenly a voice comes "from below" her, apparently the newborn baby Jesus, who tells Mary to shake the tree and eat of its fruit (24–27). Later the infant surprises Mary's relatives by speaking from his cradle, saying, "I am the servant of Allah," and describing his mission on earth. The Koran then reveals that "this is the whole truth, which they [apparently the Christians and Jews] are unwilling to accept," adding that "Allah forbid that He Himself should beget a son!" (29–36).[2]

Islam has as many distortions in its portrayal of the Hebrew Bible, upon which Judaism is founded, as it does of the New Testament. For instance, the Koran says that Abraham had two sons, not eight as recorded in Genesis. The patriarch is said to have raised his family in Mecca, not in Hebron as the Bible says. Allah's covenant blessings were passed down through Ishmael, not through

Isaac. The Islamic holy book states that Moses was adopted by Pharoah's wife, not his daughter as recorded in Exodus 2:5–10. Haman, the evil Persian court official who opposed the Jews in the fifth century B.C., is said to have been a minister in Pharoah's court. The Bible records that Aaron molded the golden calf in the wilderness; the Koran says it was a Samaritan, despite the fact that the Samaritans did not appear in the Holy Land until the time of the Babylonian Exile.

The Koran, which calls itself a holy book sent by God from heaven to Muhammad (3:1–2), contains many denunciations of the Jews and their religion, especially in chapters 2 through 5. After the sins of the children of Israel in the wilderness are recounted, Allah castigates the Muslims for thinking that the Jews, who "knowingly perverted" his word, would trust the Muslims (2:75). Allah has forever cursed the Jews for their unbelief, and especially for deliberately rejecting his final revelation, the Koran, which they know to be a holy book (2:88–90). The Jews are evildoers who "love this life more than the pagans do," and are enemies of Allah, and of his angels, his messengers Gabriel and Michael (2:95–99). Jews worship their rabbis (9:31) who cast off the Islamic holy book, are influenced by devils, and teach spells and witchcraft to their followers (2:101–102).

The Jews have deliberately "perverted the words of the Scriptures" and, therefore, "Allah has cursed them" except for a few who have faith (5:13, 4:46). Although "a portion of the Scriptures was given" to the Jews, they are enemies of the Muslims, and want to see them "led astray" (4:44). Any Jew who does not repent and turn to Allah—along with all other unbelievers—will roast in hell, constantly receiving new skins to be burned in order to receive a thorough taste of Allah's "scourge" (4:55).

Muhammad was probably familiar with the basic tenets

of Judaism since many Jewish tribes lived in Arabia, especially around the town of Medina, which was where he fled after being rejected as a prophet in Mecca. Scholars say his negative attitude toward the Jews, partially founded on denunciations of them in the Bible, probably congealed after local Jewish tribes resisted conversion to his fast-growing faith in the early years of Islamic expansion.

Islam's founder is also thought to have learned something about Judaism and Christianity from visiting preachers who occasionally stopped off at Mecca's main tourist attraction—the Kaaba Shrine—to try and convert the crowds gathered at the cultic site. The Arabian Peninsula's most popular pagan shrine housed a black stone said to have fallen out of the sky in ancient times. Before Muhammad's reformist religion took hold, the Kaaba Stone was the centerpiece of Arabian polytheistic idol worship. Muhammad ordered the idols destroyed and declared the site to be an Islamic shrine. Muslim tradition later held that either Allah or Gabriel had given the black Kaaba Stone to Adam when he was cast out of the Garden of Eden. For more than twelve centuries, Muhammad's followers all over the world have turned to face the stone shrine while reciting their daily prayers.

Another tradition connected to the Kaaba Shrine illustrates how Islam reinterprets certain parts of the Hebrew Bible, along with New Testament accounts about Jesus. Muslims believe that God ordered Abraham, the first Muslim, to sacrifice his son Ishmael—not Isaac as the book of Genesis records. God then tells the obedient Abraham not to go through with the killing. The square shrine is said to mark the spot where God spared Ishmael's life. The thwarted sacrifice of Ishmael is celebrated each year on the tenth day of the twelfth month in the Islamic calendar. This is the end of the month-long *haj* pilgrimage to Mecca.

A NEW FAITH

Muhammad's new religion spread rapidly throughout the Arabian peninsula, due largely to the Koran's call for *jihad,* or "great striving," against all unbelievers, especially Christians and Jews. The Islamic holy book urges all Muslims to "make war" on the unbelievers "until idolatry is no more and Allah's religion reigns supreme" (Sura 8:39).[3] The reward for dying in a jihad struggle is instantaneous entrance into paradise, which the Koran makes clear is a place of great sensual pleasure. Modern Muslim apologists maintain that jihad does not necessarily mean actual fighting. Jihad is also waged by nonviolent struggle through education, propaganda, and economic boycott. But it is abundantly clear from the Koran (and from the *Hadith,* the codified Islamic oral tradition of Muhammad's actions and sayings) that the *primary* meaning of *jihad* is actual fighting—"holy war." That is why Islam has long been known as the religion of the sword.

The doctrine of jihad was avidly obeyed by newly converted Arabian warriors. Islam's founder certainly took it very seriously. Muhammad's many battles and victories are recorded in the Hadith. "Muhammad was much more than a prophet. He was a soldier—he took part personally in some of the early battles," wrote G. H. Jansen in his book *Militant Islam.* "He was wounded in the face and was known to have killed at least one of his adversaries."[4] Popular Muslim accounts say Muhammad personally killed many of his opponents, including some of Medina's most prominent Jews.

The early Muslim military campaigns were mainly designed to acquire booty, most historians agree. But before long the spirit of religious holy war was propelling Arab armies across the known world. Within a few years of Muhammad's death in 632, Muslim warriors were driving into the Holy Land and Syria. The corrupt Byzantine Empire could not withstand the rapid onslaught. Jerusalem was captured by Muhammad's successor, Omar, in 638. Egypt and Cyprus fell several years later. Some people, tired of corrupt Byzantine rule and frequent violent Christian feuds, welcomed the Arabs.

By 650 the fired-up Arabians, who saw their lightning victories as proof that Allah was with them, had driven deep into the territory of the other regional superpower, Persia, converting people everywhere they went. Within one hundred years, Muslim armies had conquered much of Spain, all of North Africa, the entire eastern Mediterranean region up to the Caucasus Mountains, the Persian Empire, the northwest portion of the Indian subcontinent, and were fighting their way into central Asia.

Conversion to Islam was a very simple matter, as it is today. One had only to recite three times the *Shahada,* the Islamic Affirmation of Faith: "There is no God but Allah, and Muhammad is the Prophet of Allah." This simple method of entering Allah's kingdom contrasted sharply with seventh-century Judaism and Christianity, which had elaborate conversion procedures. Muslim victors often forced whole communities of Christians and Jews to convert—or face execution.

The Affirmation of Faith is the first of Islam's Five Pillars of Faith to which every Muslim must adhere (some authorities add jihad as a sixth pillar). The others are: paying of the *zakat,* an obligatory alms tax; saying prayers five times a day while facing the Kaaba Shrine in Mecca; keeping the daytime fast during the Muslim holy month of Ramadan; and making the *haj,* or "pilgrimage," to Mecca at least once in a lifetime.

These pillars are observed by both Sunni and Shiite Muslims, the two main branches of Islam (there are more than one hundred fifty Muslim sects altogether.) The minority Shiites, most numerous in Iran, Iraq, and Lebanon, are followers of Muhammad's cousin and son-in-law, Ali. Disappointed that he had not been named the leader of Islam immediately after Muhammad's death, Ali's followers engaged in a violent struggle with the Sunnis. The more powerful Sunnis came out on top, keeping control of the holy sites in Mecca and Medina. Shiite and Sunni Muslims still battle each other today, as evidenced by the long and bloody Gulf War during the 1980s between Shiite Iran and Sunni-controlled Iraq, and intermittent skirmishes in Lebanon.

Naturally, neither Christians nor Jews were too happy with either form of the Arabian warrior's religion, and especially with Islam's rapid advance in obedience to the Koran's many jihad calls, such as these in Sura 4:74 and 76:

> Let those who would exchange the life of this world for the hereafter, fight for the cause of Allah; whether they die or conquer, We shall richly reward them. . . . The true believers fight for the cause of Allah, but the infidels fight for idols. Fight then against the friends of Satan.

HOLY PERSECUTION

The "infidels" were alarmed by Muhammad's insistence that the Koran was the final revelation of God sent to correct the many distortions and untruths that had been allegedly introduced into the Old and New Testaments over the centuries. (Muslims maintain that prophecies forecasting Muhammad's advent were deliberately eliminated from both Testaments.) Adherents of the two "corrupted" faiths would either submit to conquering Muslim armies and convert to Islam or burn in hell as a consequence. The Christian nations responded to this new challenge with armed might wherever they could. That option was, of course, not open to the stateless Jews.

In Christianity, the Jews already had to endure what they considered to be a major digression from the revealed religion of the God of Israel. Now, fired-up followers of an Arabian upstart were conquering the world with an even more distorted version of Judaism's revealed truth (although in some ways Islam is closer to Judaism than Christianity, especially in its dietary laws and emphasis on religious legislation).

The Jews were especially worried that the advancing armies would repeat the Islamic founder's killings and expulsion of their co-religionists in Arabia. In 624 Muhammad ordered the Jewish Banu Qainuqa tribe of Medina to flee without their possessions after they refused, at least for the most part, to convert to his newly revealed "final revelation from God." A second Jewish tribe was expelled in 625, after allegedly aiding Muhammad's opponents from Mecca, who defeated the Muslims in a battle just outside Medina.

After the Meccans attacked Muhammad's forces again in 626, the "Angel Jibril" supposedly told Muhammad that God was ordering him to fight against a third Jewish tribe living near Medina, Banu Quraiza. The prophet ordered every Jewish man killed (more than nine hundred were slain, according to some historians), and the women and children sold into slavery. Jewish men in groups of five or six were made to kneel in front of newly dug trenches. Muslim swordsmen then came along and sliced off their heads, which then fell along with their bodies into the trenches. The slaughter lasted all day and into the night. Many Muslims believe that Muhammad personally took part in the killings.

Jewish historians insist that none of the Jews converted to Islam, despite an offer by Muhammad that their lives would be spared if they did so. After Muhammad's death, the remaining Jews of Arabia, except for some living in the Yemeni enclave in southern Arabia, were either killed, forced to convert, or expelled from the peninsula. All remaining Christians were also forced to vacate the Islamic holy land.

The widespread Islamic conquests eventually persuaded Muslim leaders of the need to moderate their minorities policy somewhat. Mass murders and forced conversions declined, and a rich Muslim culture developed in much of the Islamic world—one in which Jews and Christians were often allowed to participate, at least to a certain extent. However, some modern historians believe that it was not Arab conquerors who brought about Islam's glorious age. They say that the cultural leaders in many Muslim-dominated regions were actually local Christian, Jewish, and Persian converts to Islam and their descendants.

Those Christians and Jews who refused to give up their faith were officially subject to the *dhimmi* (non-Muslim) laws laid down by Muhammad's successor, Omar. Patterned on koranic teachings, the laws clearly defined all unbelievers as second class citizens with restricted rights. Breaking some of the laws could mean the death penalty. Jews and Christians had to pay special head and property taxes. They could hold no position of authority over, or marry, a Muslim. They had to wear distinctive clothing to mark them out (the yellow patch so popular in Europe was first introduced by a Muslim *caliph,* or ruler, in the ninth century). They could not perform religious practices in public. They were forbidden to build new houses of worship. And they could not ride a horse in public (a symbol of authority).

In practice, some of these restrictions were ignored, modified, or imposed on a limited basis. Yet, when it suited the whim of a particular Muslim ruler, as it often did as the great Islamic civilization declined, the restrictions would be fully imposed—often with deadly consequences for the dhimmi peoples. On the other hand, any Muslim attempting to convert to either Christianity or Judaism was certain to be killed, in accordance with Islamic law.

The Koran orders Muslims to "take neither Jews nor Christians for your friends. They are friends with one another. Whoever of you seeks their friendship shall become one of their number. Allah does not guide the wrongdoers" (Sura 5:51). Another reason to stay away from the dhimmi peoples is because they "spare no pains to corrupt you. They desire nothing but your ruin. Their hatred is clear from what they say, but more violent is the hatred which their breasts conceal" (3:118). However, some Muslims ignored this rule throughout history, as many do today in Israel. But such koranic teachings meant that many Jews, and to a lesser extent Christians, were forced at times to live in special marked-off areas—the precursor of the ghetto in Europe. These areas were at times attacked, looted, and burned, and their residents murdered.

Some historians argue that Christian leaders derived much of their anti-Jewish legislation from Islam's dhimmi laws, just as they basically picked up the concept of holy war from the Muslims. Others say that Muhammad borrowed the ideas from the Christians with which he came in contact. Whatever the case, it is quite clear that Jews under Muslim rule endured nothing like the frequent wholesale slaughters that occurred in medieval Europe. Yet Muslim oppression was often harsh, even if generally less intense than in lands farther north. Anti-Jewish attacks became quite frequent in the 1800s, especially in North Africa, as European colonial rule began to wane. Violent attacks increased even further in the early part of the twentieth century as thousands of European Jews settled in the Holy Land.

A significant portion of the Arab world has experienced economic revival in the last few decades, due mainly to the black gold known as oil. The great Islamic culture which sprang up in the seventh and eighth centuries, and then declined sharply due to corruption and increasing European colonial power, has shown new signs of life, mainly as a result of generously flowing petrodollars.

Saudi Arabia and other Gulf states have used their new-found wealth to rebuild their long-dormant societies. Islam itself has also experienced a resurgence throughout the region, helped along by generous gifts from Muslim Gulf treasuries. The history of the Jews in Muslim lands and the Arab world's renewed power and influence play a significant part in the ongoing Arab/Jewish struggle over the land of Zion.

CHAPTER 4

SUFFER
THE LITTLE
HOLY LAND

"I'm dead," I announced to myself, as the long barrel of the tank gun came ever closer to my front windshield. However, my self-proclaimed death notice turned out to be, to my great relief, slightly premature. At the last possible moment, the Israeli tank crew raised the long, steel gun barrel several feet above my Volkswagen roof. I said an extra prayer of thanksgiving as I slowly continued on my way to the Voice of Hope radio station.

It had already been an unusual morning drive to the station, located about a mile north of the Israeli border. Most days the journey from my home in Kiryat Shmona took only twenty minutes or so, occasionally longer if army vehicles were waiting in line before me at the border checkpoint. But previous regular routines, such as the length of my morning drive, had gone out the window several days earlier when Israeli troops began pouring across the border into Lebanon. My commute to the radio station would never be the same again.

It was providence that I spotted the tank barrel coming over the crest of the hill. I would have definitely been the loser in a battle with the Israeli-made *merkava* ("chariot"). I quickly pulled off the road to let the fifty-six-ton armored vehicle pass. But another tank was right behind it, and then another, and another! I carefully inched my Volkswagen up to the edge of the ridge to see how many more army tanks were in this convoy.

I couldn't believe my eyes! There before me, stretched out along the narrow valley road for as far as I could see, were hundreds of Israeli tanks, slowly making their way from the Golan Heights into southern Lebanon. After waiting several more minutes, I still couldn't see the end of the long convoy.

"I can't be late for work," I told myself, as I slowly made my way forward down the hill. The tank drivers courteously steered their armored chariots as far as possible onto their side of the narrow road. Still, I just barely squeezed by them. I chuckled when I considered what the crews must be thinking of my Israeli-licensed white Volkswagen taking on hundreds of battle tanks alone in southern Lebanon!

Except for the jarring experience of almost having one of the tank barrels smash into my car windshield, I made it to the station unscathed. However, I signed on the air a little late, explaining to my listeners that I had gotten caught in heavy traffic.

Even though I suddenly had to contend with military traffic jams on south Lebanese roads, there were definite benefits to having the Israelis around. For one thing, PLO shells no longer rained down from Beaufort Castle, situated on a strategic crest just above the road to the station. The medieval Crusader fortress was captured from the PLO on June 6, 1982, the day after Israeli forces started pouring into southern Lebanon. The battle for the ancient castle had been fierce, and, I thought, a bit ironic. Despite all the modern tanks and warplanes in the Israeli armory, and the artillery and mortar shells the PLO possessed, they fought hand to hand in the end, just as in the days when European Christian defenders lost the castle, and several others like it to the south, to Muslim warriors.

THE ROMAN DESOLATION OF ZION

Warfare has been an almost constant feature of life in the land which the Bible calls holy (Zech. 2:12) ever since the final destruction of the Jewish state of Judea by chariot-driving Romans in A.D. 135. When Roman warriors had vanquished the hundreds-of-thousands-strong Jewish army, which had risen up in revolt against hated Roman rule, the Emperor Hadrian decided enough was enough. He would wipe out Judea forever.

The Jews who remained alive after the slaughter were driven out of Jerusalem and surrounding areas. The city where David had set up his throne was renamed "Aelia Capitolina," and a temple to the pagan god Jupiter was built on the site of the Jewish Temple, destroyed by the Roman warrior Titus sixty-five years earlier. Judea was given the Latin name "Syria Palaestina"—anglicized as "Palestine"—to erase any Jewish connection to the land that the God of Israel calls his own. The Romans plainly intended to insult the Jews by the choice of a name derived from the Philistines, Israel's ancient enemies who dwelled on the coastal plain.

The Jews did not entirely disappear from the Holy Land, however, as many people wrongly assume. In fact, Hadrian's successors allowed a Jewish mini-state to exist for several centuries in the Galilee. The ruling Sanhedrin was reestablished, and Jewish religious studies flourished. However, Jewish emigration increased significantly after the Roman Empire officially adopted Christianity in the fourth century. Synagogues in the Galilee were burned by Christian ecclesiastics, now protected by the state.

After the Roman Empire was divided late in the fourth century, Eastern Byzantine rulers stepped up persecution of the Jews. The Emperor Justinian tried to force remaining Jews in the Lord's land to convert to Christianity.

Many Jews fled east to Mesopotamia, also known as Babylon, which rapidly became the center of Jewish life and learning.

Yet many Jews remained in the land, and others joined them during periods of less intense persecution. Official records listed forty-three Jewish communities in the sixth century: twelve along the coast, in the Negev Desert and east of the Jordan River; and thirty-one in the Galilee and Jordan Valley.[1] Local Jews even briefly regained a foothold in Jerusalem in A.D. 614 after helping the Persians to invade and conquer the Byzantines. But Constantinople was back in the saddle within a few years, and the Jews paid dearly for their "treason."

Despite renewed Byzantine persecution, many Jews survived to see Arab-Muslim warriors push out the Christian empire in A.D. 638. Islamic rulers, keenly aware of the importance of Jerusalem to Christians and Jews, were fairly tolerant of their dhimmi subjects, who continued to outnumber Muslims in the land until the Crusaders were defeated five centuries later. Jewish and Christian communities flourished in many places, including Jerusalem.

The Muslims, however, made it quite clear that their religion was superior to the two older faiths, and would rule Jerusalem until Allah's judgment day. The ancient Jewish Temple Mount would naturally be the best place to make such a statement. Although there is no evidence that Muhammad ever visited Jerusalem, Muslim clerics declared that the Islamic prophet rode at night to the city on his faithful horse, al-Burak. After tying up his horse to the Western Wall, Muhammad is said to have bodily ascended from the mount on a short visit to heaven. The area was proclaimed a sacred Islamic site and work was begun on a magnificent shrine—the Dome of the Rock. In 691 the shrine was completed.

Among inscriptions from the Koran which line the

round dome are several ridiculing Christian belief in the deity of Jesus: "This is the whole truth about Jesus, the son of Mary, which they are unwilling to accept: Allah forbid that He Himself should beget a son!" (Sura 19:35–36); "Say: 'Praise be to Allah who has never begotten a son, who has no partner in His kingdom' " (Sura 17:111).[2]

NO REST FOR THE HOLY LAND

The Lord's land was ruled from 661 by Umayyad Arab Muslims based in Damascus. However, Umayyad rule was increasingly challenged by the basically non-Arab Abbasid dynasty of Baghdad. In 750, Abbasid armies overcame their Damascus-based adversaries and began to rule the Holy Land from the Mesopotamian capital. Just over a century later, General Ahmed Tulun, a Turkish governor of Egypt, went to war with the Umayyads. He overcame their armies in 878. After further bloody battles, Umayyad forces recaptured Jerusalem in 904.

The tenth century saw continuous struggle for control in the area. Egyptian Ikhshidi princes overthrew Umayyad rule in 934. Twenty-five years later the Fatimid Caliphs of Cairo defeated their Baghdad rivals and began to rule the land. In a preview of the coming Crusades, Byzantine leaders took advantage of the almost constant Muslim internal battles to invade in 970. They were finally defeated by Muslim forces in 976. Just prior to the first Crusade, Seljuk Turks conquered the land in 1070, holding it until 1080.

As the war-filled centuries progressed under one Muslim ruler after another, many local Christians and some Jews converted to Islam in order to escape oppression and better their social and economic standing. Despite such conversions of convenience, Islam was not the majority religion in the Holy Land until the large-scale slaughter of local Christians by victorious Muslim armies at the end of the Crusades (the Jews, as noted in Chapter 2, had already been largely eliminated by the "Christian" invaders).

Pope Urban's Crusader forces arrived to throw out the Muslim "infidels" in 1096. Many Jews, aware of the growing persecution of their brethren in Europe, helped the Muslims in attempts to repel the advancing armies. Battles raged in the area for many decades. Untold numbers of Muslims and Jews were slaughtered by the victorious Crusaders. The new European landlords defended themselves from a number of magnificent castles, such as Beaufort, which they constructed throughout the area. However the Muslims, under the Kurdish general Saladin, roundly defeated the Crusaders in a major battle near the Sea of Galilee in 1187. Islamic rule was reestablished in Jerusalem. The Pope's armies retreated to the coastal plain, where they suffered their final defeat and expulsion in 1291.

As Christian and Muslim armies slaughtered each other, Mongol forces from Asia swept into the area. They entered and sacked Jerusalem twice, in 1244 and 1260, and launched a full-scale invasion of the land in 1299. The Mongols were finally defeated by Muslim warriors in 1303.

Over the next several centuries, the by-now ravished Holy Land was ruled from either Damascus or Cairo. The various rulers, known as the *mamluks,* were mostly descendants of Turkish or Circassian slaves who had settled in one of those two great cities. Of course, they frequently fought each other, not allowing the decimated land to recover from its earlier, immense wounds.

The area was conquered yet again, in 1516, by the rapidly expanding Turkish-Muslim Ottoman Empire. As it had been in the past, Jerusalem was once again ruled from the ancient city of Constantinople, now under Muslim control and re-named Istanbul. Records show that there were about thirty Jewish communities living in the land of Abraham, Isaac, and Jacob, mostly around the northern towns of Safed and Tiberias, when the Turkish Muslims arrived. Some of these Jews had remained over the centuries—somehow surviving the frequent wars and massacres—others had slipped in over the years seeking refuge from persecution in Europe and elsewhere.

The Ottomans, whose renowned leader Suliman the Magnificent built the current walls of Jerusalem's Old City, treated their Christian subjects fairly well. They knew that persecution would bring the wrath of the great European powers, already quite concerned over the growth of the Turkish empire. At first the Jews were also treated with some respect. Suliman even allowed a leading member of the expelled Portuguese Jewish community, Joseph Nasi, to set up a semi-autonomous Jewish area around Tiberias. Persecuted Jews from the papal states joined others from the Muslim world in settling in and around the town, which was one of the four Jewish "holy cities" of the time. A local textile industry was set up, employing many Jews. Jacob's children also migrated into the other three holy cities: Jerusalem, Safed, and Hebron.

However, most of Suliman's successors were not so liberal-minded. Ottoman officials several times barred all Jewish immigration to the Holy Land. Jews were sometimes allowed to slip in after paying *baksheesh* (a Turkish word meaning "bribes") to appropriate officials. Such bribes sometimes helped Jewish "visitors" from abroad to stay in the land. Turkish Muslim authorities barred Jews, even local ones, from buying property anywhere in the land of their ancestors. In 1856 this policy was reversed at the request of Sir Moses Montefiore, a wealthy British Jew. However, the ban was reinstated later in the century as increasing numbers of Jews moved to their ancient homeland.

During the second century of Ottoman rule, a most interesting and unusual character marched onto the world stage. Shabbetai Zvi was born in Smyrna in 1626. In 1648 he announced to his Turkish friends that he was the long-awaited Jewish Messiah. The follower of the Jewish mystical Kaballah sect was quickly expelled from town. After wandering for more than a decade, Shabbetai ended up in Jerusalem where he proclaimed to all in 1665 that he was the messiah. His "John the Baptist" was a man named Nathan, from Gaza (then another center of Jewish settlement).

Nathan and others traveled far and wide with the good tidings of the "messiah's" advent. By 1666, hundreds of thousands, if not millions, of Jews from all over Europe and North Africa were preparing to depart for the Holy Land to be citizens of the Jewish state that Shabbetai promised to set up (after somehow neutralizing the Muslims). Many thousands had actually begun the journey to Zion when news came that the "messiah" had gone to Istanbul to lay his claim before Ottoman leaders. The Turks were not impressed, and ordered Shabbetai to convert to Islam or die. He chose the former, much to the dismay of his many hopeful Jewish followers around the world.

Persecution of the Jews, particularly by local Muslim officials, was frequent and sometimes fierce during the Ottoman years, especially after the anti-Jewish Mulrad III became sultan in the mid-1500s. (This, plus savage religious wars in Europe, may help explain why so many were eager to believe in Shabbetai.) Many of the estimated twenty thousand Jews in the holy Galilee town of Safed—home of the Kaballah movement—were massacred in 1660. Mob violence against the Jews of Hebron broke out in 1775. Safed, which had been restored by a liberal Turkish ruler after the 1660 massacre, was again sacked in 1799. At this time, a sadistic Albanian-born

Muslim nicknamed "the butcher" gained power in the region. He ordered the beheading of any subject who displeased him—especially dhimmi subjects.

Some historians believe that "the butcher's" mistreatment of French merchants in the port town of Acre prompted Napoleon to launch his invasion of the region at the end of the eighteenth century. The French Emperor tried to enlist Jewish support for his venture by promising to restore Jerusalem to Jewish control. But Napoleon's dreams of empire in the region were severely set back when his fleet of ships was destroyed by British forces during the battle for Egypt in 1798. The following year he launched a ground invasion of the Holy Land from the Mediterranean coast of Sinai. On March 6, French forces captured the coastal town of Jaffa. Napoleon then moved north to the port of Acre, near modern Haifa. However Turkish forces from Syria, with the aid of the British, withstood his siege of the town. Napoleon was forced to retreat to Egypt in June of 1799, his dreams of ruling the Promised Land shattered.

LET'S GO UP TO ZION

Ever-increasing numbers of Christians and Jews made their way to the Holy Land throughout the nineteenth century. In 1831 the land was conquered once again, this time by the Egyptian ruler Muhammad Ali. He had gained control of Egypt several decades earlier after French and British forces withdrew from the area. Although Ali had waged a number of wars against rival Muslim sects on behalf of the Ottomans, he turned against Istanbul after Turkish leaders refused to hand over Syria (which included the Holy Land) to him as a reward.

Ali's military occupation, spearheaded by his son Ibrahim, was met with little opposition from local citizens since, as Holy Land historian James Parkes put it: "Turkish rule had few admirers even among the Muslim peasants."[3] After Ibrahim captured Damascus and was heading for Turkey, Russia feared that a new vigorous ruler would occupy Istanbul. Russia sent forces to stop the Egyptian's northward advance. Things settled down for a few years until Ali's forces attempted a new northern thrust. The British then intervened against the Egyptians, bombarding Ali's positions in Acre and other coastal areas. Muhammad Ali's forces were finally pushed out of the Holy Land in 1840.

The Lord's frequently fought-over land, Parkes says, suffered constant internal warfare over the centuries between clans and villages, along with frequent invasions from without. But it also had to contend with a natural disaster during the nine years of Egyptian rule: A severe earthquake struck the Galilee region in 1837. Historians believe that half of Safed's ten thousand citizens perished in the quake, along with a third of Tiberias' twenty-five hundred residents. Many villages in the area were destroyed.

It was during the short period of Egyptian rule that British, American and other Western Christian missionary groups began to appear in Jerusalem and other parts of the Holy Land. This trend accelerated when the Ottomans regained control, with the Christian European powers wielding increasing influence over Istanbul. European consulates in Jerusalem took advantage of the situation to help the Church of England, the Lutherans, the Roman Catholics, and others set up churches, hospitals, and orphanages. The Eastern churches—Greek Orthodox, Greek Catholic, Armenian, Egyptian Coptic, and Syrian Coptic—watched uneasily as the powerful Roman Catholic Church established its first ever patriarchy in 1847.

Despite the growing influence of Christian Europe in the Lord's land, all of the churches from east and west were constantly reminded of their "protected" position under Islam. A sword-bearing Turkish guard, or *kawass,* accompanied church leaders wherever they went, and all church activities had to be cleared with Muslim Ottoman authorities.

Visitors to the Holy Land in the 1800s describe it as desolate, sparsely populated, and riven with lawlessness. Powerful local families known as *effendis* constantly fought each other. Roaming Bedouin tribesmen launched frequent attacks on the settled population, especially on villages which were sometimes overrun and destroyed. Turkish rulers generally ignored the effendi violence since they were dependent on the powerful clans to collect taxes and help raise armies for the constant Ottoman wars in central Europe. Like everyone else, they could do little to prevent the nomadic Bedouin pillaging, since the fast-moving Arabs were usually gone almost as soon as they arrived.

After so many centuries of almost constant warfare, it was no wonder that the Lord's land was such a miserable place. The American writer Mark Twain expressed great disappointment with the sad state of the land during a pilgrimage in 1867:

> Palestine sits in sackcloth and ashes . . . desolate and unlovely. . . . Nazareth is forlorn. . . . Jerico the accursed lies a moldering ruin. . . . Bethlehem and Bethany, in their poverty and their humiliation, have nothing about them now to remind one that they once knew the high honor of the Savior's presence.[4]

Describing the Jezreel Valley, the site of ancient battles and of the prophesied final battle of Armageddon, Twain wrote:

> There is not a solitary village throughout its whole extent—not for thirty miles in either direction. There are two or

three small clusters of Bedouin tents, but not a single permanent habitation.[5]

Despite the sad state of the land, things improved somewhat for the Jews as the century wore on. The European consulates, especially the British, often took up their grievances with Ottoman authorities. Still, such assistance was limited, and Jews continued to suffer frequent humiliations at the hands of local Muslims.

Throughout the years of Ottoman occupation, a steady stream of Jews trickled into the land of their forefathers. By the middle of the nineteenth century Jews were becoming the largest single group in Jerusalem—for the first time in more than 1,700 years. Their numbers had grown so much in the crowded Old City that a group moved out in 1878 in order to build a new Jewish town on the coastal plane of Sharon. They named their town Petach Tikva, Hebrew for "Gate of Hope." The Baptist Village, where I spent my first weeks in Israel, is just a few miles from what is today a large, modern city northeast of Tel Aviv.

During the four hundred years of Ottoman rule and before, local Muslim leaders knew of the centrality of Jerusalem, and the rest of the Holy Land, to Judaism. As the years wore on, they observed how the Jewish "People of the Book"—treated as second-class dhimmis in Christian as well as Muslim lands—were gaining increasing influence and stature in "enlightened" Europe. They knew that European Jews were bound to repeat Joseph Nasi's attempt to increase Jewish immigration and set up an autonomous area in Palestine. They realized that religious Jews in Europe and the Arab world expected that, one day, their God and his chosen Messiah would restore to them their Promised Land.

Muslim leaders in the 1600s had witnessed the fervent Jewish expectation of return passionately played out by hundreds of thousands of Jews desperately grasping on to Shabbetai Zvi's false messianic claim. They knew that many Jews had already come to live in the Holy Land over the centuries, despite the enormous obstacles put in their way by Muslim and Christian rulers. They knew that Jews around the world mentioned Jerusalem every day in their prayers as they faced in the direction of the Holy City. Muslim leaders must have sensed, to their dismay, that the time was fast approaching when Jews from the four corners of the globe would seriously attempt to fulfill their long-held yearning to return to the Promised Land—the land given by the God of Jacob to their forefathers, thousands of years ago.

CHAPTER 5

RETURN
TO
ZION

My apartment in Kiryat Shmona was not elegant, to say the least. However, the rent was extremely reasonable—seventy-five dollars a month for a two-bedroom flat. There was a simple explanation for the northern Israeli town's wonderfully low rental rates: Kiryat Shmona's sixteen thousand residents had received PLO shells so many times since the mid-1970s that well over half of them had moved to other, quieter parts of the country. Nonetheless, people were returning to Israel's northernmost town when I moved there in August 1982. The shelling had stopped in June.

My teammates and I often visited Kiryat Shmona during our year on nearby Kibbutz Hagoshrim. It was, quite honestly, a depressing experience. Few people ventured out into the town's business center for fear that a Russian-made Katuysha rocket would come crashing down on their heads. In fact, PLO gunners often waited until just after 4 P.M.—when stores reopened after the afternoon siesta—to shoot rockets toward the center of town. We often found ourselves the only customers at the few open ice cream stalls. All of us knew there was a risk of unexpectedly meeting our Maker during one of our afternoon outings, but then again, we reasoned, bombs had landed more than once on our kibbutz. An exploding rocket had even sent pieces of metal shrapnel into a wall just inches above the heads of several sleeping Hagoshrim children, one of them the son of the kibbutz gardener whom I worked for during most of 1981.

The road I traveled daily to the Voice of Hope radio station in south Lebanon took me right past the Tel Hai Museum located less than a mile north of Kiryat Shmona. The museum, clearly visible from the road, commemorates an earlier Arab/Jewish confrontation: an Arab attack on the Tel Hai ("Hill of Life") fortress in 1920 that killed eight Jews who defended the compound. Kiryat Shmona, the "town of the eight," is named after the victims.

Among the eight was Joseph Trumpeldor, a former Russian Army officer who had lost an arm in the Russo-Japanese war of 1905. Trumpeldor came to live in Turkish-controlled Palestine in 1912. He swiftly became one of the Jewish community's main military leaders. The words Trumpeldor is said to have cried as he and his comrades were fighting off the Arab attack—"It is good to die for your country"—became a symbol for a strong defense to the fledgling Jewish community in the Holy Land.

Trumpeldor settled in the Galilee area during the "second wave" of Jewish immigration, which occurred between 1904 and 1914. Like the first *aliyah* (the Hebrew word for "immigration," which literally means "going up" to Zion), most of the immigrants came from Russia. They were fleeing the Russian and east European "pogroms": the widespread, organized massacres of hundreds of thousands of Jews, which began in western Russia in 1881 and later spread to Poland, Romania, and other areas. The vicious attacks continued on and off for more than two decades. More than a million Jews left Russia and eastern Europe by the turn of the century because of the rioting, looting, and mass slaughter, which devastated the world's largest concentration of Jews. Most of the emigrants moved to the United States. However, more than fifty thousand managed to come to the ancient land of their forefathers, *Eretz Yisrael* (the "Land of Israel"), despite Ottoman immigration restrictions. Quite a few later left because of the tough conditions they found here.

Those conditions were spelled out for me and my Project Kibbutz teammates in 1981 during a lecture by historian Arieh Avneri, a member of Kibbutz Hagoshrim. He had just written a book in Hebrew on the pre-state conflict between the Arabs and Jews of Palestine, called *The Claim of Dispossession: Jewish Land Settlement and the Arabs.*[1] Avneri's book focuses on Jewish immigration and subsequent land purchases between the years 1878 and 1948. Some of the information presented later in this chapter comes from his well-documented book.

LA CHAIM!—"TO LIFE!"

As noted in Chapter 4, the Holy Land was not exactly at its prime when significant numbers of Jews began immigrating during the latter part of the nineteenth century. The area had been called Palestine in the West since the Roman destruction of Judea in A.D. 135, but was usually referred to as southern Syria in the Muslim world.

Reports from the British consulate in Jerusalem echo Mark Twain and others in describing a sparsely populated, underdeveloped land riven with violent Bedouin attacks and clan warfare. The land was divided into two Ottoman districts. The border ran just north of Jerusalem and Jaffa. The northern district, divided further into two subdistricts, was administered from Beirut. Jerusalem was the headquarters for the southern district. The area east of the Jordan River was administered from Damascus. The entire region was ruled by Muslim caliphs in Istanbul, nearly a thousand miles away. Although Turkish was the language of government, few people actually spoke it, save for a few well-known phrases and words.

The Western superpowers grew increasingly interested in the region as the century wore on, mainly because of the vital Suez Canal which the French and British were constructing in Egypt using local peasant laborers (many of whom died in the process). Other than this grand project, the Mideast economy had begun to stagnate, driving many people, especially better-educated Arab Christians, to seek their fortunes in America and elsewhere.

The few departing Jews were quickly replaced by others—especially religious Jews from Europe and North Africa—who took advantage of the growing European presence to slip into Jerusalem and other towns. Arab workers from Morocco, Algeria, and Egypt and other parts of the Ottoman Empire wandered into the Holy Land, which had no clearly defined borders other than the Mediterranean. They came in search of work as the economy improved during the second half of the century.

Protestant Christians came to live in the Lord's land in increasing numbers in the late 1800s. The first Protestant missionaries encountered fierce opposition from both the long-established Eastern churches and the Muslim Ottoman authorities.

An American church group, expecting the imminent return of the Lord, arrived in 1866. The American Protestants brought prefabricated houses with them which they set up near the port town of Jaffa. However, official and unofficial harassment and poor living conditions pushed most of the sojourners out of the Promised Land within a few years.

Just as the Americans departed, a group of twelve German Lutherans, taking advantage of improving German-Turkish relations, arrived to await the Lord's return. They set up a colony near Nazareth. But the scourge of malaria left all twelve dead within a year. Other determined Germans soon replaced them. The German colonists bought the abandoned American prefabs and erected them in two locations: one near Jaffa and the other just outside of Haifa. Additional settlements soon sprang up near Jerusalem (when I moved to the city in 1984, I lived in the "German Colony" neighborhood, located southwest of the Old City). Other locations attracted more Germans, and before long, about a thousand Germans were living in the land. Their advanced agricultural methods were slowly adopted by local farmers. The German colonies thrived until Hitler rose to power in the 1930s. British authorities ordered the whole community to leave after several leading members declared themselves Nazi sympathizers.

The long-established Greek Christian community continued to grow in size during the waning years of the Ottoman Empire. A Greek neighborhood was built just south of the German colony as Jerusalem expanded south early in the twentieth century. Most local Greeks were connected to the Greek Orthodox Church—the main Christian body in the land since the time of the Byzantine Empire.

Arab workers migrated to the Holy Land in increasing numbers in the late 1800s, seeking jobs. Ironically, growing Arab employment opportunities were largely due to the economic activity generated by immigrating Russian Jews! A Belgian company, contracted to build local railroad lines, imported many Arab workers from Egypt, Syria, and Lebanon. Not a few of them stayed in the country after the projects were completed. Turkish authorities brought in Circassian workers from the Black

Sea region. Hundreds of Maronite Catholics came to live in Jerusalem to escape bloody fighting going on (then, as now) in Lebanon. Armenian Christians, seeking to escape Ottoman oppression in Turkey, migrated to the area in increasing numbers.

A steady stream of Jews made their way to the Holy Land in the 1800s from Egypt and other North African countries. Many Syrian Jews fled to the Galilee and Jerusalem in 1840 following widespread anti-Jewish rioting in Damascus. Violence broke out in Damascus and surrounding areas after rumors spread that local Jews had murdered a priest in order to use his blood in unleavened Passover bread—the same "blood libel" pinned on the Jews down through the centuries in Europe. Yemeni Jews in the southern Arabian Peninsula continued to pine for Zion, and some found their way overland to the ancient homeland in the late 1800s.

In northern Europe, a rabbi in the Serbian town of Semlin was busy drawing up plans in the 1850s for a large-scale Jewish migration to Zion. Rabbi Yehuda Alkalay, a Sephardic Jew, (*sephardi* means Spanish in Hebrew, but the term in modern Israeli usage generally refers to Jews from Muslim and other oriental countries, whether or not their ancestors came from the Iberian Peninsula) published his plan in 1857. The rabbi's ideas caused considerable excitement among many of the millions of Jews in eastern Europe and Russia who were confined by law to live in "the pale"—specially marked off, crowded provinces in the Russian Ukraine and occupied Poland. Jews longing to live free of persecution "beyond the pale" eagerly studied Alkalay's plans for a return to the Promised Land.

Holy Land fever was also stirring during the nineteenth century in Great Britain, but not only among Jews. Various Christian leaders and writers were speaking out on the need for a Jewish homeland. In 1839 the Church of

Scotland sent out a two-man delegation to report on the condition of the Jews living in the land. Their report, detailing the discrimination and frequent persecution local Jews were forced to endure, was widely debated in Great Britain. The church then sent out a memorandum to Protestant monarchs throughout northern Europe, printed in full in the *London Times* newspaper, advocating support for a Jewish homeland in the Holy Land.

Christian associations were formed throughout Britain to help Jews return to the land. Of course, many Christian members had motives other than just helping persecuted Jews; they saw a Jewish return as a necessary, prophesied prelude to the second coming of Jesus. Meanwhile, several leading rabbis of undisputed orthodoxy began to teach that the messianic deliverance, so long hoped for and expected, would not occur before or concurrent with a Jewish return to the land, but would follow such a return.

As it became apparent that the pogroms were not just a passing phenomenon, but the worst sustained anti-Jewish violence since the Middle Ages, many east European and Russian Jews quickly searched for another home. The age-old Jewish migration was on again. Groups were formed called "Lovers of Zion" to promote Jewish emigration to the ancient homeland. Many packed their bags and fled, as their ancestors had done so many times in the past. But there was a difference this time: Thousands were on their way not to another Gentile nation, but to the Promised Land!

In the middle of the first aliyah wave, which brought around twenty-five thousand Jews to the land between 1880 and 1903, a young Jewish journalist from Vienna covered the trial of a French Jewish army officer in Paris. The officer, Alfred Dreyfus, was convicted of treason despite a lack of evidence against him. He was later acquitted in a retrial. The Jewish officer's trial unleashed a

wave of vicious anti-Semitism in what was then considered to be the most cultured city in Europe. The young
journalist, Theodor Herzl, had already begun to despair
of continuing anti-Jewish discrimination in "enlightened
Europe" before witnessing this latest outbreak of hatred.
Suddenly, as if inspired from above, he became a fiery
advocate for a Jewish state, seeing it as the only solution
for his perennially despised and persecuted people. But
Herzl was not content to sit around and wait for the
Messiah to set up such a state, as most Jews had been
since the Roman exile. Like the Lovers of Zion, Theodor
Herzl took action.

The Viennese-born Jew quickly penned a book which
would prove to be the main inspiration for what became
known as the "Zionist Movement." The book was titled
*The Jewish State: An Attempt at a Modern Solution to
the Jewish Question.* A year later, in 1897, Herzl convened
the First Zionist Congress in Basel, Switzerland. Delegates
voted to establish the World Zionist Organization, with
Theodor Herzl as its president, to work for the setting
up of a Jewish national home in Palestine. A Jewish flag
with the six-sided Star of David was adopted, along with
a national anthem entitled "Ha Tikva," ("The Hope")
which lifts up the "hope of two thousand years to be a
free people in our Land, the Land of Zion and Jerusalem."
Exactly fifty years later, the United Nations voted to set
up a Jewish state in the land that the God of Israel gave
to Abraham and his descendants almost four thousand
years ago.

COUSINS IN CONFLICT

There was one major problem facing the modern children of Abraham, Isaac, and Jacob. The Holy Land already
had people living in it who also traced their ancestry
to Abraham—through Ishmael, the patriarch's other son.

These Muslims, along with most Christians, were convinced that the Jews would never again be a sovereign people in the land of their ancient forefathers. It was inconceivable that the rejected Jews would once again wield authority over the biblical holy sites which had been in Muslim and Christian hands for close to two millennia. The Roman Catholic and Orthodox churches had long concluded that *they* were the new Israel of God, and the Jews but a perpetual witness to sin and folly. The Muslims were clearly triumphant over both older religions which had strayed from the true path of Allah. The idea that the wretched Jews would run the place once again was dismissed out of hand as a theological impossibility.

Still, alarm grew as the evidence on the ground outpaced religious certainties. The Jews *were* returning, and they were openly declaring that their goal was an independent state on the same ground where their ancient ancestral homeland stood. Meanwhile, the Turkish Empire was crumbling, and nobody knew exactly what would come in its place.

In 1858, some four decades before Herzl's Zionist Movement came into being, the selling of land to Jews was restricted by Turkish authorities. Local effendi families demanded a total ban in 1891. Still, as Arieh Avneri documents, many wealthy Arab families themselves sold land to Jews, mostly at inflated prices. Much land was also purchased from absentee owners living in Beirut, south Lebanon, Damascus, and elsewhere. Death threats were issued, and sometimes carried out, against anyone caught selling land to Jews. Immigrating Jews, backed by such European millionaires as the Rothschild family, were willing to pay almost any price to have a piece of the ancient homeland. Most of the property that Jewish settlers somehow managed to purchase lay in the sparsely populated coastal plain and the Galilee region.

Tension sprang up almost immediately between Jewish settlers and their Arab neighbors. Muslim Arabs in particular could not accept the fact that dhimmi Jews were establishing independent, successful farming communities near the heart of the Islamic world. Avneri writes that the two peoples had different views of property ownership: The Jews stuck to legally defined boundaries, while Arab farmers were more interested in landmarks and long-established grazing practices. Jewish farmers thought that each community should establish and use its own water resources, while Arab farmers and shepherds insisted that freshly dug Jewish wells be open to all.

Tension also resulted from initial Jewish reluctance to hire Arab workers. These factors led to a number of armed Arab attacks on Jewish settlements, especially in the area southeast of Jaffa and near the Sea of Galilee. Other assaults were simply the usual Bedouin raids every settled town or village was subject to at the time.

As Jewish nationalism manifested itself in the continuing waves of immigrants coming from Europe, Arab nationalism also began to stir in the region. Mideast Arabs had little love for their Turkish masters, even if they were fellow Muslims. They also resented British and French interference in the region. Still, most Arab leaders cooperated with the Allies against the Germans and Turks in World War I. They hoped to receive European support for the setting up of an independent state or states in the region once the weakening Ottoman Empire was finally dismantled.

While benefiting economically and medically from the European Jewish and Christian influx into the land, local Arabs realized early on that their chances of being included in a larger regional Arab state or states were threatened by Jewish hopes to establish a homeland. Very few expected at the time that the small area of

Palestine would become its own independent state. In 1914, as the first World War began to shake Europe, anti-Zionist societies were formed in Jerusalem, Jaffa, Haifa, Beirut, Cairo, and Istanbul to encourage Arab and Muslim resistance to the emerging Jewish national home.

The Great War was destined to change not only the face of Europe, but also that of the Middle East. Soon after Germany and Turkey were finally defeated by the Allied powers in 1918, politicians went to work redrawing national boundaries throughout eastern Europe. The Arabs waited patiently for the politicians to begin mapping out an independent state or states on the Arabian Peninsula and farther to the north.

In 1915, Arab Muslim leader Sharif Hussein of Mecca (the title *sharif* denotes ancestry from Muhammad) had been promised by the British High Commissioner in Cairo, Sir H. McMahon, that London would be "prepared to recognize and support the independence of the Arabs" following the defeat of the Turks. However, McMahon added that any independent Arab state or states could not include the Turkish district administered from Beirut—in other words, most of modern-day Lebanon and northern Israel. He also implied that the district of Jerusalem should be excluded from the proposed Arab-controlled areas.

Hussein replied that "the people of Beirut will never accept such isolation." He was, of course, referring to the Muslims of Beirut and surrounding areas, not the Christians who were eager to be isolated from their Muslim neighbors.

British insistence on the exclusion of the eastern Mediterranean coastal area made a lot of sense to the other victorious Allied powers. All were aware that Lebanese Christians had often suffered persecution during many centuries of regional Muslim domination. French Catholics were especially eager to see a French-protected area carved out for their Lebanese co-religionists. The British government was just as keen to see Christians and Jews in the Holy Land exempted from further Muslim domination. The United States generally backed these positions. It was obvious that the British and French had other reasons for wanting to protect Christian and Jewish interests in the region: Both, but especially the British, had far-flung empires to protect, and the strategic Middle East with its vital Suez Canal was of utmost importance to them. The two powers reasoned that having European-oriented enclaves in the area would add greatly to their empire-maintenance efforts.

The British had another, compelling reason for proposing that the southern coastal area be excluded from any Arab state. The government in London had sought, and received, Jewish assistance during the war. In return, and in line with general sympathy for the Jewish need for a homeland after so many centuries of wandering and persecution, British Foreign Minister A. J. Balfour, on behalf of the government, issued the following statement to Zionist leaders during the final months of World War I:

> His Majesty's Government view with favour the establishment in Palestine of a national home for the Jewish people, and will use their best endeavours to facilitate the achievement of this object, it being clearly understood that nothing shall be done which may prejudice the civil and religious rights of non-Jewish communities in Palestine or the rights and political status enjoyed by Jews in any other country.

Soon after the "Balfour Declaration" was issued on November 2, 1917, British General Sir Edmund Allenby drove the last Turkish soldiers out of Jerusalem, ending many centuries of Muslim control. The Holy Land was in British, Christian hands.

Although the wording of the Balfour Declaration was somewhat imprecise, historians such as Walter Laqueur say that the clear British intention at the time was to work for the setting up of a fully sovereign Jewish state in Palestine.[2] Laqueur records that there was some initial ambivalence and even acceptance of the declaration in the Arab world. However, the overwhelming reaction was one of rejection.

Arab leaders in Palestine said it would be impossible to set up a Jewish national home while at the same time guarding the civil and religious rights of non-Jews living in the land. Zionist leaders responded that the rights of local Arabs would indeed be respected in a Jewish state. They were optimistic, wrote Laqueur, that local Arabs would eventually accept the Jewish national home and live in peace with it.[3]

Jewish Zionist leaders considered "Palestine" to be the entire area that today comprises Israel, the territories captured by Israel in 1967, and Jordan. In fact, the whole area legally came under that name at the 1920 postwar San Remo conference, where the world powers voted to give Britain a mandate to oversee the setting up of a Jewish national home in Palestine. (See maps on pages 247 and 248.) The Zionists hoped they would be allowed to settle in all of what later became Israel, Judea and Samaria (later known as the West Bank), the Gaza Strip, and the east bank of the Jordan River up to the town of Amman. The mandate given to Britain stated that Jews could settle anywhere west of the river, but not necessarily east of it.

British authorities were eager to keep their pledges to the Arabs as well as the Jews. Therefore, Jewish settlement east of the Jordan River was banned in 1921, and the area—two-thirds of designated "Palestine" under the Mandate—was declared the Emirate of Trans-Jordan. Sharif Hussein's son Abdullah was installed upon the throne. The British continued to play a vital role in the new state until the mid-1940s, overseeing the setting up of various political institutions and an army.

Farther to the east, Britain created the Arab state of Iraq, with Abdullah's brother Faisal enthroned as king. Faisal Hussein, representing his father and brothers, had met in 1919 in Paris with the head of the Jewish Zionist Movement, Dr. Chaim Weizmann, a highly respected British scientist. At the meeting Faisal signed a joint, typed statement committing the Arabs to recognize "Jewish national aspirations" for a homeland in Palestine. But at the bottom of the paper he added in Arabic "provided the Arabs gain their independence." He seemed to be saying that a Jewish state would be permissible, but only if the Arabs, long controlled by Turkey and the European powers, were finally allowed to enjoy total sovereignty in the other areas where they lived.

While these momentous political decisions were being made, about ten thousand Jews came to live in the Holy Land. Most fled a new wave of anti-Jewish violence in Russia. The latest attacks, in which some seventy thousand Jews lost their lives, broke out as Russian Communists fought a bloody civil war with their noncommunist opponents for control of the country. By 1923 another twenty-five thousand Jews would join them in what later became known as the "third aliyah wave."

During this period the League of Nations—the precursor of the United Nations—endorsed the San Remo decision to give Great Britain a mandate to set up a Jewish national home in Palestine. The fifty-two nations voting in favor noted "the historic connection of the Jewish people with Palestine," and called for the establishment of a "Jewish Agency" to aid British authorities in accomplishing their Mandate.

The Arabs of Palestine were not too thrilled with the world body's decision, as they had not been with the April 1920 San Remo declaration of support for a Jewish state, although the League of Nations also approved mandates for Britain and France to oversee the setting up of independent Arab states in the rest of the region.

Soon after the San Remo Declaration, Muslim and Christian community leaders, led by the powerful Husseini clan, met in Jerusalem and issued a proclamation which totally rejected the British Mandate to set up a Jewish national home, adding that Palestine belonged exclusively to the Muslim and Christian worlds. They also poured scorn on Faisal Hussein's acceptance of Jewish nationalist aspirations in Palestine. Their Arab brethren would eventually live in sovereign Arab states, while they would have to reside with the Jews, who were compared with "poisonous snakes" in leaflets distributed in Jerusalem and Jaffa. No nation on earth had tolerated the Jews, said the leaflets, so why should the Arabs of Palestine have to?[4]

A month before the San Remo Conference, Joseph Trumpeldor and his seven colleagues were attacked and killed at Tel Hai. While the conference was underway, a Jewish settlement east of the Sea of Galilee was abandoned after Arabs murdered a settler. Arab bands attacked eight other settlements in the area during March and April. After debating how to respond to the violent assaults, the Jews decided to establish the Hagana defense force in June. It would later evolve into the main arm of the pre-state Jewish army.

In May 1921, widespread Arab violence broke out against the growing Jewish community. Armed Arab bands attacked Jews living in Haifa, Jaffa, Petach Tikva, and two other towns. The Jaffa riots were the bloodiest— forty-seven Jews lost their lives. Zionist leaders, still publicly speaking about their hopes of amicable Jewish/ Arab relations, were beginning to realize that local Arabs were determined to do everything in their power to prevent the establishment of a Jewish state. They feared that British authorities would cave in to the growing

Arab violence and go back on their pledge to set up a Jewish homeland.

Confronted by growing Arab opposition, British leaders began to redefine their Mandate in terms more acceptable to local Arabs. Colonial Secretary Winston Churchill issued a statement in 1922 saying that the British did not envision that "Palestine as a whole should be converted into a Jewish National Home, but that such a Home should be founded in Palestine." The statement did not placate local Arab leaders, who said the British were not adequately taking their fears or aspirations into consideration.

Many Jewish immigrants settled in kibbutz collective farms, which were established from 1909 onward in various parts of Palestine. The Hebrew word *kibbutz* means "ingathering." The founders of the kibbutz movement were mainly socialists who either ignored or had abandoned the faith of their fathers. Yet the name they chose for their communities had a definite, biblical, prophetic ring to it. Kibbutz settlements were established throughout the Jezreel Valley—the area Mark Twain had described as virtually without inhabitants a half century earlier. Stagnant swamps in the valley kept away most immigrants, as elsewhere in the northern part of the Holy Land. The tepid waters were breeding grounds for malaria-carrying mosquitoes. Many Jewish pioneers lost their lives in the process of clearing the swamps. But, as one of them told me when I briefly lived on a Jezreel Valley kibbutz in 1982, it was "better to die while doing something for your people than to be massacred in the Russian pogroms." A few of the settlers were immigrants from the United States. One of them, Golda Meir, later became Israel's first female prime minister.

The fourth aliyah wave (1924–1928) brought sixty-seven thousand Jews to the ancient Jewish homeland. This fourth wave of immigrants was comprised largely of urban Polish and Russian Jews who were more inclined to settle in the cities than on the farming cooperatives. Many went no further than Tel Aviv, a Jewish town established just north of Jaffa in 1909. The city rapidly became the main Jewish urban center.

Zionist leaders continued to voice hopes during the 1920s that Jews and Arabs could co-exist in peace in the Holy Land, despite the 1921 riots. A Zionist Congress held in Germany in 1922 proclaimed the desire of the Jewish people to "live with the Arab people in friendship and mutual respect, and together with them develop the homeland common to both into a flourishing community which would ensure to each of its peoples an undisturbed national development."[5]

There were regular political and social contacts between Jewish Zionist and Arab leaders in Jerusalem and elsewhere during the decade, and many Zionist leaders expressed optimism that the Arabs of Palestine would eventually see the growing Jewish presence in the land as a positive development leading to better living standards for all.

By 1929, about 150,000 Jews had settled in the land. Over half had immigrated since 1918. The Arabs numbered around 700,000. The overall population of Palestine had increased by only about 350,000 since 1880, despite the Jewish influx from eastern Europe and Russia.[6] Many more of the three million Jews who moved to the West during the period might have come to the Holy Land if Ottoman and British authorities had not enacted immigration restrictions at various times.

LIFT UP THE SWORD OF ISLAM!

The relatively small numbers of Jews that came were too much for most local Arabs, who were beginning to believe that the Jews just might succeed in setting up a sovereign state in Palestine. The generally better-educated and largely socialist or communist immigrants were seen as a major cultural threat to the conservative Islamic and Christian communities. Although Jews had succeeded in purchasing only about 4 percent of the land by 1929, and although there was plenty of room for growth, local Muslim Arab leaders whipped up passions and fears among their followers by warning of the dangers posed to Islam by the growing Jewish presence. The Jews, so long oppressed by both Muslims and Christians, were planning to take revenge on the Arabs, they maintained. Jewish fighters would attack and destroy the holy mosques of Omar and al-Aksa in Jerusalem, bringing humiliation to Islam. The fact that most of the immigrants were not at all religious did not impede the issuance of such warnings.

With such dire warnings sounded in many mosques throughout the land, Arab resistance to the growing Jewish presence took on an increasingly religious tone during the 1920s. It is no coincidence that the emerging leader of the Arab struggle against the Jews was the President of the Supreme Muslim Council in Jerusalem, the Grand Mufti Haj Amin Husseini. He would not echo the earlier, relatively moderate tone of Faisal Hussein or his father, the Sharif of Mecca. Husseini traveled to many Arab capitals raising money to repair Muslim holy sites in Jerusalem, warning in every place of the dangers of allowing the Jews to gain any sort of sovereignty in the Holy Land.

The Palestinian Muslim leader repeatedly preached that the sinister Jews were plotting to take over all local Islamic holy sites, and especially the two mosques located on what the Jews call *Har ha Biet,* the "Mount of the House" (of God). Husseini insisted that Jews should not be allowed to pray at the Western, or Wailing Wall of "Haram al-Sharif." He declared the wall an Islamic holy site, since the prophet Muhammad had supposedly tied up his horse, al-Burak, to the wall just after making his night journey to Jerusalem. Jews attempting to pray at the Western Wall, a traditional Jewish prayer site for centuries, increasingly found themselves the target of stonings and other physical attacks.

On August 23, 1929, at the Grand Mufti's instigation, hundreds of Muslim Arabs poured down from the Temple Mount and assaulted Jews praying at the wall. Then they burst out of the Old City to attack Jews living in nearby neighborhoods. Many Jews were killed or wounded. Some Arab Christians joined in the assaults, but most stayed on the sidelines. Arab attacks quickly spread to other parts of Mandatory Palestine. Fifty-nine Orthodox Jews, including many women and children, were brutally murdered in Hebron, south of Jerusalem.

Most of the dead, many of whom had been tortured and dismembered, were descendants of Jews who had lived in the town, where Abraham's tomb is located, for hundreds of years. Twenty Jews were killed in another of the four holy cities, Safed. Seven kibbutz settlements were attacked and burned. Armed Arab gangs also launched assaults in Haifa and Tel Aviv. British forces, refusing to allow the Jews to take up weapons and defend themselves, killed 110 Arabs before the rioting was stopped on August 26. A total of 133 Jews lost their lives during the three days of violence, and another 339 were wounded.

In 1930 the League of Nations sent a committee to Palestine to investigate the question of Jewish and Arab rights at the Western Wall. Islamic officials from various countries appeared before the committee, along with Amin Husseini. Jews must not be allowed to pray at the site, they urged, since the entire mount belongs to the Muslims. The matter was of utmost importance to the Islamic world, the committee members were told, since the Jews were openly praying for their ancient Temple to be rebuilt on its original foundations, where the sacred Dome of the Rock shrine is located. Jewish representatives pointed out their ancestors had built the Temple Mount, first occupied by Muslims in the seventh century A.D. It was only right that Jews should be allowed to pray at one of the remaining retaining walls of their ancient Temple Mount. The committee agreed that Jews should be allowed to pray at the wall, in light of the fact they had done so for centuries and Muslims have the entire mount to pray on, but ruled that Muslims held absolute ownership of it. However, the committee forbade the Jews to blow the traditional ram's horn, the *shofar,* near the Western Wall on Jewish holy days, a move that deeply offended religious Jews.

In order to further whip up Muslim opposition to the establishment of a Jewish state in the Holy Land, Husseini hosted a Pan-Islamic World Conference in Jerusalem in December 1931. Islamic delegates were told that they must rise up to defend the Muslim holy sites from Jewish plots to take them over. Sacred Islamic shrines such as Abraham's Tomb in Hebron (from where Jews had been banned from praying since the end of the Crusades) were under threat of being taken over by the "Zionist invaders," warned the Grand Mufti. Islamic leaders pledged their full support for Husseini's struggle, agreeing that everything must be done to keep a sovereign Jewish state from being formed in "sacred Palestine."

Despite growing Arab/Muslim opposition, the number of Jews immigrating to the designated Jewish homeland took a sharp upward swing in the 1930s. The main reason for the Jewish influx was the rise of the viciously anti-Semitic Nazi movement in Germany, Austria, and other portions of central Europe. There is little doubt that many, if not most of the 250,000 European Jews who came to live here during the decade (a quarter of them refugees from Germany) would have remained where they were if not for the rise of Adolf Hitler. Long-estab-

lished and successful Jews suddenly found themselves
under attack simply because they were Jews. Many ended
up at Haifa or Jaffa ports with little more than the shirts
on their backs. But at least they had their lives—something that could not be said after World War II for six
million of their fellow Jews. His Majesty's Royal Navy
forcibly prevented many Jewish refugees from landing
in Palestine between 1936 and 1939, as numbers began
to exceed official quotas. Others were intercepted and
interned in British prison camps set up along the coast.

European Jews fleeing Hitler's madness met with no
more Arab sympathy than had those Jews who barely
escaped with their lives from the pogroms in Russia
and eastern Europe. Indeed, Grand Mufti Husseini was
a strong supporter and personal friend of the German
fuhrer, and of Italian fascist leader Benito Mussolini, who
"adopted" the Palestinian leader and promised to aid
his struggle against the Jews.

Haj Amin Husseini's frequent sermons in support of
Hitler's anti-Jewish campaign were closely monitored
by British Mandate authorities. They ordered him arrested after the British governor of the Galilee district
was assassinated by the Mufti's men in 1937. However,
Husseini evaded British forces and escaped to Lebanon.
The Grand Mufti continued to encourage resistance to
the Jews as he traveled between various regional Arab
capitals.

When World War II broke out in Europe, he declared
a jihad against Britain. Husseini spent the war years in
Berlin, where he headed the Arab Office, a propaganda
and espionage arm of the Nazi war administration aimed
at strengthening Arab support for the Axis powers.

In the mid-1930s the head of the Jewish Zionist community in the Holy Land, David Ben Gurion, contacted various Palestinian Arab and Syrian leaders to present a
political proposal that he hoped would bridge the grow-

ing gap between Arabs and Jews. He proposed that the Arabs allow a majority Jewish state to be set up in Palestine, which would then join in a federation with nearby Arab states. Although local Arabs would be a minority in the Jewish state, they would form part of the overall Arab majority in the federated states. Every state in the federation would pledge nonbelligerency toward the others, with freedom of travel and commerce guaranteed. Thus, the rights and security of both Arabs and Jews would be protected. Ben Gurion's proposal was totally rejected by the Arab leaders he contacted, who again insisted that no Jewish sovereign state would be allowed to exist in the region.

Before Haj Amin Husseini fled to Lebanon, he helped organize an Arab general strike to protest stepped-up Jewish immigration from Europe and Zionist hopes to establish a sovereign Jewish state. Stores were closed for six months in 1936 following Arab attacks in April and May, which left twenty-one Jews dead. Jewish settlements and shops were attacked. Jewish crops were burned and tens of thousands of trees uprooted. Jewish buses were bombed, and individual Jews gunned down everywhere. In all, eighty Jews were killed and many more injured before the British succeeded in stopping the armed uprising in October.

British troops, who sustained thirty-three casualties, shot and killed more than one hundred Arab gunmen and rioters during the six-month revolt. Local Arab leaders met during the early part of the rebellion to demand that London stop all Jewish immigration to the Holy Land, forbid all Jewish land purchases, and set up an Arab majority government. But by the end of September, they realized that the British were not going to discuss Arab demands until all violence ceased.

In early 1937, after several months of relative calm, Britain sent a Royal Commission to Jerusalem to investigate the increasingly violent Arab/Jewish conflict. The commissioners ended up recommending that the mandate for a Jewish homeland in all of western Palestine be annulled. Instead, the land should be partitioned into separate Arab and Jewish states.

Although the Jews were deeply disappointed with the recommendation of a truncated Jewish state, most Zionist leaders were willing to accept it, saying it was better to have a tiny state than none at all, especially in light of the rise of the Nazi movement and the impending war in Europe.

As Jewish leaders debated the British partition plan, the Arab world moved swiftly to condemn it. Arab leaders meeting in French-ruled Syria in September 1937 declared that they would never permit the setting up of a Jewish state in any part of sacred Palestine. Shortly afterward, armed Arab bands began a new round of attacks against British soldiers and Jewish settlements. The attacks were much fiercer than the first round of disturbances in 1936. Arab leaders again declared a general commercial strike, which was often enforced by violent means. Rival Arab factions increasingly turned on each other, leading to many Arab deaths—a situation which would be repeated in another Palestinian Arab uprising fifty years later.

By the summer of 1938, Arab gunmen had taken control of most of the hilly regions in the Judea and Samaria district. The British reacted swiftly and forcefully, entering villages and towns in pursuit of armed bands. Homes of suspected or known Arab gunmen were destroyed, and widespread curfews were imposed. Security measures were tightened even further after Arab saboteurs blew up the British-owned Iraqi oil pipeline, which ran through the lower Galilee to the Mediterranean coast near Haifa.

Hundreds of Arabs and Jews were killed, along with

many British soldiers, before the violent revolt was halted in early 1939. Later that same year, German forces under the command of Adolf Hitler invaded Poland—then the country with the largest concentration of Jews in the world—beginning the worst war in mankind's long, bloody history. For the Jews, it would be a catastrophe of unimaginable proportions.

CHAPTER 6

JACOB COMES OUT ON TOP

I will probably never get used to it. In the middle of a conversation, while sitting next to somebody on a bus, or sometimes while standing in line at the bank or post office, you see it. Maybe it strikes me more forcefully than others because of my familiarity with the prophecy in the book of Revelation, which predicts that a world dictator will one day order everyone to have a mark placed on his or her hand or forehead. The jarring experience of having a good friend become a neo-Nazi in my own hometown heightens my sensitivity to the sight. Whatever the reasons, I am certain I will always recoil a bit when I see the numbers tattooed on the back of the hands of Jews who somehow survived the Nazi death camps of Europe.

I have never had the courage to ask any camp survivor what it was like to be in Auschwitz, Treblinka, or one of the other extermination camps which took the lives of millions of their fellow Jews. How can I ask them to relate the unspeakable things they saw, the things they experienced? I've read a few of the tortured accounts survivors have committed to paper. But to ask someone to speak about these things—it is just too much.

Very few survivors of Hitler's partially successful attempt to wipe out the Jewish people made it to the shores of pre-state Israel. It was not easy for Jews to get into the Promised Land in those days, despite the mandate given to Great Britain to oversee the setting up of a Jewish homeland. Mandate authorities had again placed severe restrictions on the numbers of Jews allowed to enter after the Arab revolts between 1936 and 1939. Those limitations continued during and after World War II, despite the obvious need for Jewish refugees fleeing Europe and north Africa to go somewhere, anywhere.

THE WHITE PAPER

As the second Arab revolt was finally put down in early 1939, the British convened a conference in London to hear Arab and Jewish proposals on how to resolve the deepening crisis in the Holy Land. The Jewish delegation, headed by Zionist leader Chaim Weizmann, pleaded for His Majesty's Government to honor the original mandate commitment to set up a national home for the Jews. Weizmann said it could either be part of a larger binational state in which the Jewish and Arab communities both ran their own affairs, or a small Jewish state in part of Palestine, as proposed in the earlier partition plan.

The Arab delegation, which included Palestinian representatives along with those of surrounding Arab states, refused to even sit in the same room with the Jews. They repeated earlier demands for a halt to all Jewish immigration and land sales and for the immediate setting up of an independent Arab state over every inch of Palestine. The Arabs made clear that one of the first acts of such a state would be to deport all Jews who were not already living in the land at the start of the "Zionist invasion" in 1881.

After the conference ended, the British issued a docu-

ment containing a proposed "final solution" of the Arab/
Jewish conflict. Known as the White Paper, the document
deeply shocked Zionist leaders. The Jews, facing annihilation in Europe, would pay the heaviest price for ending
the conflict, although they were the targets of armed
attacks from the Arabs.

The White Paper called for the establishment in Palestine of an independent Arab-dominated state within ten
years. Jews would only number about a third of the
overall population. Only 75,000 Jews would be allowed
into Palestine by March 1944, after which no more would
be let in without Arab consent (which the British, of
course, knew would not be forthcoming). Jewish land
purchases would be severely restricted, and Jews could
only settle in certain parts of the Arab-dominated state.
At a certain point, the British would withdraw, leaving
the minority Jews to fend for themselves against the
Arabs' openly declared threat to cremate them.

The White Paper solution was a disaster for the Jews,
who saw it as a sure recipe for total destruction at the
hands of their hateful Arab cousins. The proposed solution was also an embarrassment for many British members of Parliament, who said His Majesty's Government
was abandoning the Jews, along with the League of Nations' mandate to set up a Jewish homeland. One member, Herbert Morrison, who later served in Winston
Churchill's cabinet, called the British White Paper proposal a "cynical breach of pledges."[1]

Although the White Paper was very much in their favor,
Palestinian leaders rejected it, despite advice from Egypt
and Iraq that they accept it. The grand mufti insisted
that all colonial Jews who had invaded Palestine since
the 1880s had to leave the land, and no more should
be let in.

Jews in Tel Aviv and elsewhere took to the streets
to protest the British proposal. They charged, among

other things, that London was deliberately ignoring the Arab pledge to throw most Jews out of the proposed state. The White Paper solution, they maintained, would certainly lead to a bloody confrontation between Arabs trying to enforce the expulsion and Jews fighting to remain in their ancestral homeland. Outraged Jewish leaders said that Britain was selling them down the drain in order to buy Arab support during the coming war. Hitler had already invaded Czechoslovakia by this time, making war in Europe almost a certainty.

In fact, British officials quite openly admitted to Zionist leaders that securing such Arab support was indeed one of the main reasons for the White Paper solution. The Jews of Palestine felt abandoned, betrayed. Many refugees from prewar Europe, who had barely escaped Hitler's clutches, felt that certain death now awaited them in their promised homeland . . . at the hands of Nazi-supporting Arabs.

World Jewry was already distressed by the decision of leading Western nations meeting at an American-initiated conference at Evian, France, in 1938, to severely restrict the numbers of Jewish refugees they would allow into their countries. This decision, which seems extremely cruel with the hindsight of history, was actually in line with public opinion in most Western countries. The American Veterans of Foreign Wars, for example, passed a resolution just before the conference calling on Washington to suspend all foreign immigration for ten years. Nobody wanted floods of Jewish refugees, it was clear, just as the British didn't want them in Palestine to upset the Arabs on the eve of a world war.

British Mandatory authorities had let in 61,800 Jews, mostly refugees from Germany, the year before the Arab revolt broke out in 1936. But in order to help dampen the violent Arab uprising, only 12,800 immigrants were allowed in during 1938, and 16,400 in 1939, the year

World War II began. The numbers dropped even further during the war, with only 4,592 immigrants permitted to enter during 1941, and 4,206 in 1942.

As many historians have noted, the British restrictions were purely political in nature. There was certainly enough room in Palestine to accommodate many more people than were allowed in. By the start of the second World War, there were about one million Arabs and four hundred thousand Jews in the Holy Land. Today the land holds more than six million people—more than four times as many as in 1940—yet there is still plenty of room for development. The sad fact is that many Jewish lives could have been spared if they had been allowed to enter the land of their ancient forefathers before and during the war.

Jewish Zionist leaders were divided as to how to respond to the White Paper. Some, including David Ben Gurion who later became Israel's first prime minister, advocated open revolt against the British. Other, more moderate voices said such a course could lead to harsh repression of the Jews, and possibly the cancellation of all further immigration.

Before the argument was settled, Hitler invaded Poland, setting off World War II. As German forces swept through eastern and western Europe, there was no question of open Jewish revolt against the British, who were leading the fight against the Nazis. The common enemy was so evil that the dispute over the White Paper had to be put aside.

In fact, despite the sense of betrayal that local Jews felt toward His Majesty's Government, many volunteered to fight with British forces. A "Palestinian Brigade" was set up, made up mostly of Jewish men, but with some Arabs as well. The force was sent to carry out fortification work in France in 1940. Other units fought throughout the Middle East. In all, some 27,000 Jewish men and women served under British command. However, the Jewish soldiers were always carefully referred to as "Palestinians" so as not to offend the Arabs.

NOWHERE TO HIDE

The year 1942 marked the start of Hitler's systematic campaign to destroy the Jews of Europe. The demonic campaign was outlined at the secret Nazi Wannsee Conference in Berlin. The head of the German Gestapo, Reinhard Heydrich, informed the gathering of a plan for the "final solution of the Jewish problem in Europe." He presented a document detailing how the estimated eleven million Jews of Europe and Russia were to be exterminated in Nazi-run death camps. The German SS, under the command of Adolf Eichmann, was given the task of rounding up the Jews and seeing that they were executed.

Meanwhile in another part of Berlin, the Muslim Grand Mufti of Jerusalem was helping to organize an Arab military unit known as Free Arabia. After proclaiming Hitler "the protector of Islam," Haj Husseini told the Arab soldiers that their mission was to lead an army that would liberate Jerusalem from British/Jewish control. In the Holy Land, Allied forces prepared for a German ground invasion from North Africa.

The Arab fighters were to join German General Erwin Rommel, known as the "desert fox," whose forces were then sweeping into British-controlled Egypt. The city of Tel Aviv and oil depots at Haifa Port had already been bombed in 1940 by Italian planes operating out of Libya. Now, the likely prospect of a Nazi ground invasion was being seriously prepared for in the Lord's land. It was not to be.

Rommel's Egyptian advance was halted on July 1, 1942, about one hundred miles east of the Egyptian-Libyan border. Three weeks later, Nazi troops in occupied Poland began gathering up Jews living in the Warsaw ghetto to send them to "work" in the Treblinka "labor camp."

Despite their joint war effort, British Mandatory forces continued to try and stop local Jews from smuggling in Jewish refugees. In one particularly notorious case, the British refused pleas by Jewish officials in early 1942 to allow the *Struma,* a ship carrying 769 refugees, to land in Haifa. The ship, stuck at Istanbul, was then ordered by Turkish officials to sail back to its Black Sea port of departure in Romania. The next night the ramshackle vessel sank, leaving all but one passenger dead. News of the tragedy produced anti-British demonstrations in Tel Aviv and elsewhere, with posters proclaiming that the British High Commissioner for Palestine, Sir Harold MacMichael, was a murderer.

World War II left much of Europe in shambles. Starvation and disease threatened to kill those who managed to stay alive during the worst carnage in mankind's history. For surviving Jews, the scope of the horror that had befallen their people was finally coming to light. Jews in the Holy Land at first hoped that initial reports of the extent of the holocaust were exaggerated. No one could believe that such total devastation had overtaken their Jewish brethren in Europe. But as death camp survivors arrived in ships off the coast of Palestine, the stories they told confirmed the worst reports reaching the land.

Almost every Jew living in Palestine had lost relatives or friends in Hitler's hideous "final solution." The mass slaughters during the Crusades and the pogroms of the late nineteenth and early twentieth centuries were nothing compared to what had just occurred in modern, "enlightened" Europe. The seeds of anti-Semitism, planted in the public mind so many centuries earlier by several early church theologians and watered by Reformation leader Martin Luther, had finally borne their logical, if ghastly, result: a systematic attempt, led by Germany, to eliminate the Jewish people from the face of God's earth.

As so many surviving European Jews discovered they could not return to their homes, which had either been destroyed or were now occupied by others, their eyes increasingly turned toward Zion. Chaim Weizmann pleaded with British Prime Minister Winston Churchill to lift the White Paper restrictions and allow into Palestine an estimated one hundred thousand Jews living in Allied-run refugee camps. He noted that the free nations of the world were only willing to take in a small portion of the homeless Jews despite worldwide revulsion over the holocaust. Soviet communist forces now occupied Poland, part of Germany, and many other former Jewish centers, he noted, making resettlement in such places dangerous for surviving Jews. As if to prove his point, anti-Jewish pogroms broke out after the war in many parts of Poland, leaving more than 350 Jews dead by the middle of 1946. Among those killed in this postwar slaughter was the father of Israel's ninth Prime Minister, Yitzhak Shamir.

The United States, housing many of the Jewish refugees in army-run European camps, urged London to allow the one hundred thousand refugees into the Holy Land. Despite these pleas, the new British Labour Party government of Prime Minister Clement Attlee, which came to power in July 1945, refused to open the gates of Palestine to any but a few of the stateless Jews.

THE JEWS FIGHT BACK

In response, many stunned and angry Jews in Palestine joined underground groups, such as the Stern Gang and the Irgun, which had earlier been set up to fight against British Mandatory authorities. One of the underground leaders was Yitzhak Shamir, who learned that most of his family had been killed in the Nazi slaughter before the death of his father in Poland. Such discoveries, of course, only increased the determination of underground group members to fight for the setting up of a Jewish state, even if they had to use terrorist tactics to do so.

The mainstream Hagana Jewish force condemned the methods of the underground groups. They argued that Irgun and Stern Gang terror attacks, even if aimed solely at British soldiers and officials, were counterproductive, driving the British even further away from keeping the mandate commitment to set up a "Jewish national home in Palestine." Jewish cooperation, such as had been displayed during the war, was the best way to change British opinion, they believed. Hagana leaders noted that Winston Churchill repeatedly promised Zionist leaders that, despite the White Paper, a Jewish state would be set up after the Allies won World War II.

However, when it became apparent that the new British government would not keep Churchill's promise, the Hagana joined forces with the two underground groups to form the Jewish Resistance Movement. The newly united Jews sabotaged the main Lydda-Jerusalem rail line on November 1, 1945. The British responded forcefully, arresting thousands of Jews. They were particularly interested in capturing Irgun leader Menachem Begin, who became Prime Minister of Israel in 1977, placing a two-thousand-pound-sterling bounty on his head.

As Jewish refugees continued to languish in postwar European refugee camps, new British Foreign Secretary Ernest Bevin agreed to set up a joint Anglo-American Committee to recommend a solution to their plight. Committee members visited the camps and took testimony in Jerusalem from Jamal Husseini, the grand mufti's cousin and postwar leader of the local Palestinian Arab community. Husseini stood firm against any further Jewish immigration and repeated the Arab demand for the setting up of an independent Arab state over all of Palestine. He maintained that the Arabs should not be made to pay for sins committed against the Jews by "imperialist Western nations."

Zionist leader Chaim Weizmann acknowledged that the setting up of a Jewish state was not something local Arabs should be expected to welcome. But he added that the Jews did not intend to supplant the Arabs and, instead, hoped that the two peoples could live together peacefully, despite past Arab violence against Jews. Weizmann told commission members that the choice was not between absolute right and wrong, but between the lesser injustice of a small portion of the world's Arabs having to live in, or next to, a Jewish-controlled state, and the greater injustice of breaking the mandate promise to finally set up a Jewish homeland after so many centuries of wandering and persecution, culminating in the hideous holocaust.

The Anglo-American Committee voted unanimously to recommend the repealing of the White Paper and urged the British government to allow in the European refugees. Committee members suggested that a binational state under continuing overall British control be set up with Jews again allowed to purchase land. But Foreign Minister Bevin turned down the recommendations, saying their implementation would greatly offend the Arab world, whose vast oil resources were increasingly coming to light.

Five days after the recommendations were published, Britain granted total independence to Trans-Jordan, making it the seventh independent Arab state in the Middle East. Meanwhile, the 100,000 or so Jewish refugees living in crowded European camps were joined by another 150,000 Jews fleeing the renewed pogroms in Poland and communist rule elsewhere in eastern Europe.

After it became apparent that Britain still planned to

fully implement the White Paper—setting up an independent Arab state in Palestine with a Jewish minority and
no further Jewish immigration—a new round of attacks
was launched by the Jewish Resistance Movement. On
June 17, 1946, ten bridges linking the Holy Land with
neighboring countries were blown up. The next day, the
Stern Gang attacked railway workshops in Haifa, leading
to a bloody fight with British troops. Two weeks later
the British imposed a total curfew in the land and arrested
some two thousand Jewish leaders and gunmen. Jewish
Agency headquarters in Jerusalem was occupied and
searched for twelve days. Weapons were seized from
kibbutz settlements all over the land.

The strong British actions would leave local Jews totally defenseless if the proposed Arab state came into
existence, argued many Jewish Resistance leaders. Irgun
commander Menachem Begin thought that the time had
come to wage full-scale war against British Mandatory
officials. He launched his campaign by ordering the
bombing of Mandatory headquarters, located in Jerusalem's most prestigious hotel, the King David. On July
22, Irgun members disguised as Arab porters brought
milk cans full of explosives into the basement of the
hotel's southern wing, just below Mandatory offices. At
12:40 P.M. the milk cans blew up, sending shock waves
throughout the hotel and bringing down half of its southern wing. Ninety-one British, Arab, and Jewish bodies
were dug out of the rubble.

Many Zionist leaders condemned the attack, which
Begin said had been coordinated with the mainstream
Hagana. Begin insisted that a telephone warning had
been sent to British headquarters in the hotel before
the charge exploded. The Irgun attack was only meant
to destroy evacuated Mandatory offices, said Begin, not
to kill anyone. Irgun member Adina Nisan later testified
that she had called the Mandatory office a half hour

before the explosion to warn of the attack. She also said she phoned the French Consulate and the *Palestine Post* newspaper. However, Mandatory officials maintained that they had received no warning from the Irgun. Hagana leaders, deeply upset over the deaths and the damage done to the Zionist cause, severed most links with Menachem Begin's organization.

British officials ordered a new crackdown as a result of the devastating blast. More than 25,000 soldiers and policemen descended on Tel Aviv, which was placed under curfew, to search for Irgun members. After 787 suspects were arrested and placed in a Mandatory detention camp (some were later hanged), the mainstream Hagana announced it would revert to a nonviolent campaign to try and reverse Britain's stand against a Jewish state. Hagana members stepped up their attempts to smuggle in Jewish refugees from Europe and increased efforts to set up settlements in areas which Zionist leaders hoped would become part of a Jewish state. The settlements were often established in one night under the cover of darkness, protected by armed Jewish guards. The other part of the campaign was not so successful. The Royal Navy intercepted most Jewish refugee ships off the coast of Palestine, sending passengers to detention camps in British-controlled Cyprus.

News reports of battered Jewish war refugees being turned away from the very gates of the Promised Land, and then herded into British barbed wire camps on the island of Cyprus, aroused world sympathy for the latest Jewish plight. The case of the refugee ship *Exodus* was especially embarrassing for Britain. The Royal Navy used military power to intercept the ship, which was carrying more than 4,500 refugees, killing three Jews and wounding around one hundred in the process. The refugees were then sent to Cyprus and eventually back to holding camps in, of all places, Germany.

REDRAWN PROPOSALS

World outrage over British handling of the Jewish refugees forced His Majesty's Government to rethink its White Paper solution. As a result, it put forward a new plan that would divide the Lord's tiny land into four sectors. The Jewish portion would be only 17 percent of western Mandatory Palestine. The sector would not be an independent state, but an autonomous area under overall British control. The same would be true for a larger Arab sector. Jerusalem and the Negev desert would not be part of either the Arab or Jewish sectors, but would be British-administered districts.

Zionist leaders responded to the latest British suggestions by proposing that the land be divided into separate Jewish and Arab states, as had been originally proposed by the British almost a decade earlier. The Jewish Agency put forward a plan that left Bethlehem, Hebron, Nablus, and the coastal port of Jaffa in the Arab state, with the Jewish state containing the Galilee, the coastal area from Haifa to Gaza, and the Negev Desert. The city of Jerusalem would be placed under international control.

The Arabs, as usual, rejected both plans, and announced that they would launch a jihad to prevent the establishment of a Jewish state in any portion of "sacred Palestine." Grand Mufti Amin Husseini, who escaped in June 1946 from a prison in France where he was being held as a war criminal, planned the Arab-Muslim jihad from his new headquarters in Cairo. Husseini proposed that an Arab army of one hundred thousand men be quickly established and trained to invade and take over Palestine if and when the British withdrew. Local Arab opinion was divided as to whether or not this was the wisest course of action to follow. Many Palestinian Christians thought that some sort of a land division was possible, preventing an unnecessary bloodbath on both sides.

As the Arab/Jewish struggle grew hotter, the Arab nations decided in 1946 to launch an economic boycott
against the emerging Jewish state, adding that sanctions
would be enacted against any other nation or company
that dealt with the Jews. Zionist leaders were not too
upset over the first part of the boycott, expecting to do
little business anyway with hostile Arab neighbors. But
the secondary boycott of countries and companies that
refused to go along with the Arab boycott was considered
to be potentially very damaging to a fledgling Jewish
state. An office to oversee the Arab boycott was set up
in Damascus. The economic boycott, still in existence
in 1990, although without Egyptian participation, was
stepped up after the state of Israel was established in
1948.

Despite growing Arab hostility toward the Jews of Palestine, Arab League Secretary Azzam Pasha agreed in
1946 to meet with Zionist representatives Abba Eban
and David Horowitz, who tried to convince him that
war would benefit no one. The Zionist representatives
said that the Holy Land's Jewish community was willing
to sacrifice some of its hopes and dreams in order to
live in peace with the Arabs. They proposed a U.N.-guar-
anteed security arrangement for all parties.

However, Pasha rejected the Jewish peace overtures,
saying the Muslim world was duty-bound to prevent a
sovereign Jewish state from springing up in its midst.
The Arab League official admitted that the Arabs might
not be able to fulfill their pledge to destroy the Jewish
state at birth, but they would try nonetheless—with all
their might.

While the Arabs prepared for war, the Jews intensified
their struggle to drive the British out of the land. The
Stern Gang and Irgun launched a new series of attacks
against Mandatory targets. British authorities responded
with more arrests and by hanging several leading Irgun

members. Martial law was declared in Tel Aviv, cutting off the Jewish center from the rest of the land.

In Washington, President Harry Truman came out in favor of a "viable Jewish state in an adequate part of Palestine,"[2] and called upon Britain to let in weary European Jewish war refugees. Even though London had hoped to keep control of at least some parts of Palestine for strategic political and economic reasons, it finally gave in to world and local pressure and handed over the intractable dispute to the United Nations in February 1947. The British, tiring of their crumbling world empire, had finally conceded that the forces at work in the Promised Land were beyond their control.

THE REBIRTH OF ISRAEL

On May 15, 1947, the United Nations established a committee to propose a settlement of the Jewish and Arab struggle over the Promised Land. After months of deliberations, a majority of the ten nations represented on the committee recommended partitioning the land into separate Jewish and Arab states, with Jerusalem, Bethlehem, and surrounding suburbs to be an international zone under U.N. control. The partition plan was similar to the 1946 Jewish Agency plan except that the Arab state would be larger, encompassing most of the western Galilee, the hilly regions of Samaria and Judea south to Beersheba and the northern shore of the Dead Sea, and south from Gaza into the northwest corner of the Negev Desert. A majority of the Jewish state's land would lie in the arid Negev Desert.

Zionist leaders expressed alarm that the proposed Jewish state would be in three separate segments connected by small, difficult to defend passageways. (See map on page 249.) But, after much debate, they accepted the plan anyway. Britain and the Arab states lobbied hard against it. In Washington a battle raged between pro-Arab members of the State and Defense Departments, eager not to alienate Arab oil countries, pro-Zionist members of Congress, and the White House.

On October 9, 1947, President Truman spoke out in favor of the partition plan and ordered his United Nations ambassador to vote for it. The Soviet Union, apparently hoping that the Jewish state would have a socialist if not communist orientation, also supported the plan. It was approved by a vote of 33 to 13 on November 29. The Jews of the world rejoiced, while the Arabs vowed that the proposed Jewish state would never see the light of day.

It was not long before Arab displeasure with the U.N. decision was registered. On November 30, a three-day general strike was declared. Arab rioters killed seven Jews on the first day of the strike, with many more injured. By the end of December, 205 Jews and more than 120 Arabs had died. Unlike in the 1930s, the Jews were now fully armed and not dependent on British forces for their protection.

Meanwhile, several Arab countries announced that they would attack and destroy the Jewish state the moment the British pulled out of the area. Violent pogroms broke out against Jews living in Beirut and in the British protectorate of Aden in the southern Arabian Peninsula, leaving more than eighty Jews dead. Jews in other Arab countries feared that they would be the next targets of growing Arab-Muslim wrath. In London a date was set for the British withdrawal: May 14, 1948.

Fighting escalated in January 1948, with armed Arab bands quickly gaining control of most of Palestine's roads (as the British frequently looked the other way). On January 20, approximately eight hundred Syrian Arabs, who entered the area as the Arab Liberation Army, attacked a Jewish settlement in the upper Galilee. Three settlements south of the Sea of Galilee were attacked by over three hundred Arab fighters on February 17. About five thousand Liberation Army irregulars, mainly from Syria and Iraq, joined the fray in March. Fighting alongside of local Arab forces, they succeeded in capturing and closing sections of the main Jerusalem-Tel Aviv road. Mostly Jewish west Jerusalem was surrounded, cut off, and besieged. Jewish forces fought hard to reopen the roads into the city. Jerusalem's desperate Jewish residents were rapidly running out of food and water. Hundreds of Arabs and Jews died in other fierce clashes around Jerusalem during the spring. Egyptian irregulars slipped into Palestine and launched assaults on Jewish settlements and nearby roads south of Jerusalem and in the Negev Desert.

On the night of April 8, a combined Irgun/Stern Gang force killed more than one hundred Arabs in Deir Yassin, a village just above the road to Jerusalem.[3] The attack was in response to frequent ambushes launched from Deir Yassin and nearby villages on Jewish vehicles traveling on the temporarily reopened Tel Aviv/Jerusalem road. The Arabs called it a calculated massacre. Some Jewish participants later said they had "lost their heads" in the midst of battle and killed noncombatants, but they insisted that the killings came after Arab fighters feigned surrender and then opened fire on approaching Jews. Mainstream Jewish leaders condemned the killings of Arab civilians, with the Jewish Agency calling it "utterly repugnant."

In apparent revenge, armed Arabs attacked a Jewish convoy of doctors, nurses, and students four days later as they were on their way to Jerusalem's Hadassah Hospital near the Mount of Olives. Seventy-nine people were slaughtered. British forces stationed nearby did not intervene despite urgent Jewish calls for help.

By mid-April, the fighting had intensified. Palestinian

Arabs began fleeing their homes in droves. An estimated twenty thousand entered Lebanon and Syria by the end of the month. Many others went to stay with relatives in the hills of Samaria and other predominantly Arab areas. More than one hundred thousand Palestinians fled Haifa and Jaffa by the second week of May. Jewish forces captured Tiberias on April 19, and Haifa on April 23. The Jewish holy town of Safed was captured on May 11 after fierce house-to-house fighting between Jewish militiamen and some three thousand Iraqi and Syrian irregulars. Jaffa fell to Jewish forces on May 12.

The escalating fighting caused the United States and others to have second thoughts about the wisdom of the U.N. partition plan. The U.N. called for the British to delay their withdrawal until a peaceful resolution of the conflict could be formulated. Chaim Weizmann pleaded with President Truman not to hinder the setting up of a Jewish state, saying the alternative to statehood was Jewish extermination in the Holy Land. "Officials in Washington thought that the chances that the Jewish state, if proclaimed, would survive, were not very good," wrote historian Walter Laqueur.[4] In light of the proclamation by Arab League countries that they would launch a full-scale attack immediately after the last British forces withdrew, the U.S. government's assessment seemed correct.

By 1948, Mandatory Palestine had more than 1.2 million Arab residents. Some of these had come from Egypt and Trans-Jordan during the preceding decades to work in the economically booming land, where many jobs were created by the large Jewish influx. A majority lived in the area designated as an Arab state under the U.N. partition plan. Many Palestinians living in Jaffa and Haifa had moved to the two coastal towns in previous years from family homes in Judea and Samaria, taking advantage of growing job opportunities in the towns.

There were around 650,000 Jews living in the Lord's land in 1948, mostly concentrated along the coast, in the Jezreel Valley, in the upper Galilee, and in Jerusalem. The Jews had vastly inferior weapons compared to those in neighboring Arab countries. One would have thought that the Jewish state would be easily annihilated at birth by the superior numbers of Palestinian Arabs, backed by the armies of surrounding Arab countries. But it was not to be.

Historians who have conducted extensive research into the roots of the 1947–49 Arab/Israeli conflict generally agree that local Arabs at the time had little sense of Palestinian nationality, separate from their larger Arab identity. They had never been a distinct nation and had developed almost none of the infrastructure necessary to set up an independent Arab state once Britain withdrew. Some were regional Arabs who had only entered Palestine in previous decades. Local Arabs were divided politically into various factions headed by rival families, the most powerful being the Husseini clan. There had been frequent, bloody clashes between Husseini's supporters, who totally rejected the Jewish presence, and other more moderate clans, headed by the Nashashibi family. More than two-thirds of the Arabs of Palestine lived in villages controlled by local clans. Intense rivalries often sprang up between neighboring villages (which is still true today, although to a lesser extent, in Israel, the territories, and Lebanon). Education levels were low, as was political awareness. Most of those "Palestinians" who were motivated enough to resist the Jews did so mainly to *prevent* a Jewish government from gaining control of the area, not so much to *establish* an Arab state.

The Jews, on the other hand, were light-years ahead in terms of education, political awareness, and their sense of being a distinct people united in a shared history and destiny. A majority had fled for their lives from anti-Jewish violence in Russia and Europe. Their will to survive was, on the heels of the holocaust, enormous. But more importantly, they had established over the years highly centralized military and political structures in preparation for an eventual British pullout. Underground arms factories worked hard to produce weapons to stave off the anticipated Arab invasion. The Jewish community knew it would have to be fully prepared for statehood—and war—on the day of the British withdrawal if it was to stand any chance of overcoming the Arab world's jihad to crush the emerging state.

Jewish Zionist leader David Ben Gurion made the official proclamation of statehood on Friday afternoon, May 14, 1948, after the national anthem "Ha Tikva" was sung by the assembled Jews at the Tel Aviv Museum: "By virtue of the natural and historical right of the Jewish people, and of the resolution of the General Assembly of the United Nations, we hereby proclaim the establishment of the Jewish state in Palestine, to be called Israel." The Jewish dream expressed in the national anthem to again "become a free people in our land, the land of Zion, and Jerusalem" had finally come true.

After almost two thousand years of wandering and persecution, the long Jewish exile from the ancient Promised Land officially came to an end. But the struggle for an independent, sovereign Jewish state was not over. In fact, in many ways it was only beginning.

On the very evening of Ben Gurion's proclamation, as the weekly Jewish Sabbath was getting underway, Egypt, Trans-Jordan, Iraq, Syria, and Lebanon made final preparations for their preannounced holy war to annihilate the newborn state of Israel. As they did so, Palestinian Arabs continued to stream out of their homes in a refugee flight that would color and compel the Arab/Israeli conflict for many decades to come.

CHAPTER 7

ARABS AND JEWS
AT WAR

I thought it was a rather odd assignment for an American disc jockey in the midst of war-ravaged Lebanon. Surely they had no idea what a frisbee was! However, since my instructions were to demonstrate how the flying disc worked, off I went with a Voice of Hope co-worker to throw frisbees around Sidon's Ein Hilweh Palestinian refugee camp.

The brown eyes of the Palestinian children gleamed with curiosity as we walked into the camp, which is basically a neighborhood in the southern port city of Sidon. The youngsters curiously eyed the dozen or so white plastic discs stuffed under our arms. As we spread apart and began throwing our American-made frisbees, with "Courtesy of the Voice of Hope Radio Station" stamped in English neatly inside, their curiosity rapidly bubbled over into great excitement. The dozen or so children who initially came out to greet us suddenly became hundreds. All of the boys wanted to be the first to try out the newfangled toy, which was rapidly becoming the latest fad at Ein Hilweh.

After coaching several of the children on the finer points of frisbee-throwing, we walked to the nearby Voice of Hope relief truck to begin phase two of the day's excitement. Several other staff members and Voice of

Hope founder George Otis were waiting there to help hand out care packages consisting of a frisbee (which we later heard were mainly being used as plates), a blanket, some candies, and an Arabic-language Bible. Palestinian mothers and fathers soon followed their children to the truck and began clamoring for the packages. Suddenly the scene turned ugly as people started to scale the large vehicle and grab for more than one package.

Within minutes a decision was taken to move the truck, now surrounded by hundreds of shouting camp residents. Israeli soldiers standing nearby fired into the air as the large relief vehicle was slowly backed out from the midst of the crowd. International television crews filmed the chaotic scene. I and several others cleared the children out of the truck's path as it was carefully driven out of the camp. To put it mildly, our small relief effort didn't exactly turn out the way we had hoped it would.

Several weeks later, two other Lebanese Palestinian refugee camps became household words all over the world. With Israeli army encouragement, Lebanese "Christian" militiamen entered the Sabra and Shatilla camps in southwest Beirut on Thursday, September 16, 1982. The militiamen were supposed to go after Palestinian fighters who had battled Israeli forces from positions inside the camps. But the Lebanese gunmen didn't just kill their Palestinian counterparts. Many hundreds of Palestinians, several hundred of them women and children, were shot and killed. While the slaughter went on, Israeli troops—allied, if loosely, with the Christian militiamen—were stationed just outside the camps. The Lebanese militiamen, full of bitterness following the assassination of their hero, President-elect Bashir Gemayel, only two days before, had taken revenge on the hated Palestinians, whom the Christians largely blame for setting off the Lebanese "civil war" in 1975.

The massacre was fairly typical of the things that go on in Lebanon—for example, Shiite gunmen attacked the very same camps three years later, killing more than five hundred Palestinians, again many of them women and children. Nevertheless, the world was shocked. Israel bore the brunt of international condemnation even though military and government leaders said they had not known in advance that the Lebanese Christian militiamen would go after civilians as well as armed PLO fighters. Local Israeli commanders said they had heard frequent shooting in the camps, but assumed that armed Palestinian gunmen were the only targets of Lebanese militia fire. An Israeli government-ordered commission of inquiry—set up as a result of widescale public demand—reported in 1983 that Israeli leaders should have known, and probably did, that allowing Gemayel's embittered supporters into the camps was a sure recipe for disaster.

THE FIRST ARAB/ISRAELI WAR AND PALESTINIAN FLIGHT

That there are Palestinian refugees living in Beirut is, of course, the result of the 1947–49 Arab/Israeli war. Did these people flee their homes at the behest of Arab military and political leaders, as the Israelis basically maintain, or were they deliberately pushed out by the Jews, as the Arab world claims? This question lies at the center of the Arab/Israeli propaganda war, which has raged alongside the "hot wars" ever since 1948. My own informal research shows that Israeli Jews usually echo the popular idea that Arab leaders ordered the Palestinians out, while Palestinians insist that the refugee flight resulted from a deliberate Jewish plot to expel the Arabs. What is the truth?

With the release of secret papers in Israel, Britain,

and elsewhere in recent years, a clearer picture of what actually took place is emerging. The evidence shows that everyone had a hand in promoting the refugee flight, including the Palestinians themselves, but especially their leaders.

Based largely on previously unavailable information, Israeli journalist and historian Benny Morris has authored a controversial book on the topic, called *The Birth of the Palestinian Refugee Problem, 1947–1949.*[1] He writes that the Palestinian refugee flight basically began as a result of the Arab war launched against the emerging Jewish state. The Jews neither planned nor initially encouraged it. Moreover, the first evacuation wave was, for the most part, neither encouraged nor discouraged by surrounding Arab states and local Arab leaders.[2]

During the first few months after the outbreak of hostilities in early December 1947, the majority of those who fled were wealthy Arabs seeking temporary shelter elsewhere—until things settled down a bit. Many were Christians who were unenthusiastic about the holy war being launched against the Jews. As the fighting intensified in early 1948, most of those leaving were again seeking only to escape for the duration of the battles, believing that the Arab countries would surely be victorious in their forthcoming invasion. The flight of prominent Palestinians encouraged many other Arabs to leave their homes.

According to Morris, the picture changed somewhat after the April Deir Yassin killings, with fear of the Jews becoming a secondary motive for flight. The Arab media trumpeted and exaggerated the episode for propaganda purposes, but this also had the effect of scaring many Palestinians, even though mainstream Jewish leaders condemned the killings. Irgun and Stern Gang members were not unhappy with the growing Palestinian panic, writes Morris, believing that the Jewish state's chances of survival would increase if fewer Arabs remained within its designated boundaries. At the same time, both Arab and Jewish military commanders ordered the evacuation of towns and villages to clear the path in anticipation of major battles in mid-May as Arab armies launched their pre-announced full-scale jihad.

Street battles between Jewish and Arab forces in several major cities, especially Haifa, Tiberias, and Jaffa, sped up the Palestinian flight. Local Palestinians felt demoralized when most of their leaders fled the scene at the first sign of a Jewish victory. This in turn led to further flight. Arab military disorganization, coupled with occasional looting and rapes committed by irregular Syrian and Iraqi forces, contributed to a general breakdown of Arab morale. Even more fled for safety.

On Saturday morning, May 15, Tel Aviv was bombed by Egyptian aircraft, signaling the start of the full-scale Arab assault against the newly born Jewish state. Trans-Jordanian King Abdullah, who had hopes of annexing the "Arab portion" of partitioned Palestine, attacked from the east.

To the north, Syria, Lebanon, and Iraq launched their armed assaults with the aim of throwing the Jews out of Tiberias and Haifa. The Israelis were hard pressed on every front, since the invading armies had air power, artillery, and armor, all of which the Jews still lacked (British Mandate officials did not allow the Jews to import weapons). The Syrian Army, assisted by Iraq, attacked north and south of the Sea of Galilee, capturing several settlements. In the Galilee panhandle, Lebanese soldiers briefly took control of a Jewish settlement in the Naphtali hills and surrounded another. Fighting was especially intense around the Sea of Galilee.

Cairo's forces slowly penetrated up the Gaza coast toward Tel Aviv, capturing kibbutz settlements along the way. After several weeks of fierce fighting, the Egyp-

tian advance was halted twenty miles south of Tel Aviv
with the aid of the first Israeli fighter planes, newly arrived
from, of all places, Czechoslovakia.

Arab/Jewish battles raged north and south of Jerusalem
and around the Old City. The Trans-Jordanian forces,
known as the Arab Legion, were especially tough soldiers
since the Legion was set up and commanded by the
British. Jewish fighters were quickly forced to abandon
several settlements north of Jerusalem, and four others
in the Etzion Bloc southeast of Bethlehem. Once again
the Tel Aviv-Jerusalem road was closed, this time by
the Arab Legion, forcing the Israelis to build a temporary
bypass to reach besieged Jews in west Jerusalem. Abdullah's forces next captured the Old City, but could not
overrun Jewish west Jerusalem.

To the surprise of almost everyone, the Arab offensive
ran out of steam in early June. Analysts say the combination of extremely high Jewish fighting morale (the Arabs
had, after all, pledged to throw them into the sea), and
disorganization and low motivation amongst the Arab
forces contributed to the change of tide. As it became
apparent that they were not succeeding in their holy
war of annihilation, the Arabs agreed to a United Nations-
sponsored twenty-eight-day truce. It took effect on June
10.

Naturally enough, the fierce warfare in all parts of
the Promised Land forced a new wave of Palestinian-
Arab flight. Benny Morris writes that, contrary to popular
Israeli opinion, the Arab states did not urge Palestinians
to flee the offensive, except in a few instances. But such
advice was hardly necessary, he notes, since Palestinian
civilians, like people anywhere, were not eager to get
caught up in full-scale warfare. Likewise, Morris found
no evidence to support the Arab charge that the Israelis
pushed out Palestinian villagers as a deliberate policy
of expulsion, but in the midst of battle, "it was under-

stood by all concerned that, militarily, in the struggle
to survive, the fewer Arabs remaining behind and along
the front lines, the better."[3]

At the same time, Israeli leaders began to realize that
the mass evacuation would help solve one of the new
state's main projected problems—the presence of a large
Arab minority that could aid outside Arab forces in future
attacks upon Israel. In all, somewhere between 200,000
and 300,000 Palestinians became refugees during this
period, joining many thousands who fled prior to April
1948.

When fighting resumed on July 8, Israel's army, which
had received new equipment during the twenty-eight-day
truce, went on the offensive, capturing more of the Galilee
and the strategic towns of Ramle and Lydda, southeast
of Tel Aviv. Attempts by some of the estimated 100,000
Israeli soldiers—one-sixth of the Jews of Israel (many
were basically civilians who had been handed guns and
quickly taught to shoot them)—to capture the Old City
of Jerusalem were unsuccessful. The Arabs, again seeing
that they were getting nowhere, agreed to another cease-
fire, to begin on July 18.

During the ten days of fighting, another twenty to thirty
thousand Palestinians became refugees. Many of them
were from the towns of Ramle and Lydda (the latter
located next to the strategic international airport) whose
defense was suddenly abandoned by the Arab Legion.
Military analysts say King Abdullah probably decided
that the towns were beyond the area he could successfully conquer and annex to his kingdom. Ramle and Lydda
had been central Arab staging grounds for attacks on
the Tel Aviv-Jerusalem road. Israeli officials, convinced
that control of the towns was essential to the new state,
ordered the residents to evacuate their homes. Morris
writes that this was the first and largest deliberate expulsion ordered by the Israelis during the war.

Arab irregular forces did not accept the July cease-fire, and fighting continued in many areas. In mid-October full-scale warfare resumed. The Israelis managed to cut off Egyptian forces south of Jerusalem and open the coastal road south of Tel Aviv. The Negev Desert town of Beersheba was captured on October 21, as was the entire upper Galilee by October 31.

With the Arab armies clearly defeated, Egypt agreed to indirectly negotiate an armistice agreement in early January 1949. The U.N.-mediated armistice was signed in February. Agreements with Lebanon and Trans-Jordan soon followed. Negotiations with Syria, which continued to launch attacks on Israel, were more difficult, but an armistice was finally signed in July of that year.

During the final battles of 1948, another 100,000 to 150,000 Palestinians became refugees. Some of these, especially Muslims living in the Galilee region, were ordered out of their homes by the Israelis. Most Galilee Christians and Druze (a religious sect derived from Islam) were allowed to remain in their towns and villages. Israeli leaders were, by this time, eager to have as few Muslims as possible in the Jewish state since they feared that the holy jihad would be resumed (as it was) by the Arab nations at some point in the future, with Palestinian Arabs, especially Muslims, likely to act as an internal "fifth column" against Israel.

Benny Morris concludes that the Palestinian refugee flight was caused by a combination of factors, all of them set into motion and overshadowed by the fierce fighting initiated by the Arabs. "What happened in Palestine/Israel over 1947–49 was so complex and varied, the situation radically changing from date to date and place to place, that a single-cause explanation of the exodus from most sites is untenable."[4]

The United Nations reported that 726,000 Palestinian Arabs had become refugees before and during the war.

The Israelis put the number at around 600,000, and the Arabs at about 1,000,000. Some 150,000 Arabs remained in their homes in Israel. It is important to note that nearly two-thirds of the Palestinian refugees had not left the Holy Land, but went to areas designated by the U.N. partition plan as parts of the proposed Arab state. About 38 percent fled to the West Bank, according to U.N. statistics, while another 26 percent went to the Egyptian-controlled Gaza Strip. The next largest group, 14 percent, fled to Lebanon, with 10 percent entering Syria and another 10 percent crossing over to Trans-Jordan (some of these were returning to family homes). Only about 1 percent settled in Egypt.

Thousands of Palestinians counted by the U.N. as refugees, especially many who fled from coastal cities to towns and villages in Judea and Samaria, actually returned to family homes. Israeli officials said such Palestinians could not be truly considered as refugees. This is the main reason for the lower Israeli refugee estimate. U.N. officials also suspected that more than 150,000 people who registered as refugees, especially in Trans-Jordan, were actually Arab peasants who already lived outside of Palestine.

The historical evidence suggests that, while the Israelis deliberately expelled some Palestinian Arabs following months of bitter fighting, most left of their own volition or at the behest of local Arab commanders. More importantly, if the Arabs had not been certain of their ability to destroy the Jewish state—rejecting the United Nations partition plan and launching local attacks and then a four-front army assault—the plan could have been carried out with little or no violence and no forced refugees. Many Palestinians might have chosen to move to the new Arab state, and they would have most likely done so with full compensation. Various relocation schemes for those wishing to move had already been discussed at the United Nations, the Jewish Agency, and in Washington. The Palestinian refugee flight was tragic, as is their continuing plight today. But the historical record shows that pinning the blame solely or largely on Israel, as the Arabs, communist countries, and many others have done ever since, simply is not accurate.

By the time armistice negotiations got underway in 1949 (see map on page 250), the Israelis had decided to allow only a token number, if any, of the Arab refugees to return to their homes. It was judged too dangerous to allow such a return, at least until passions cooled in the region. Israeli leaders hoped that the refugees could be permanently resettled in Judea, Samaria, and Gaza— the areas designated for an Arab state by the United Nations, or in the other countries to which they had fled. The United States and the U.N. pressed Israel to take back at least a third of the Palestinians. However, after the loss of some four thousand soldiers and two thousand civilians, or about 1 percent of the total Jewish population of Israel (equivalent to around two million Americans in the Vietnam War), Israeli officials were not willing to let potentially fifth-column Palestinians into the now predominantly Jewish nation.

Israel quickly realized that the Arab nations, reeling from their defeat, had no intention of resettling the Palestinian refugees in permanent housing, even though the United Nations, the United States and others offered to help them do so. The refugees were instead to become the main propaganda weapon in the ongoing Arab struggle to destroy the Jewish state. The Egyptians feared that resettling Gaza Arabs inside Egypt would lead to greater instability in the country. On the other hand, Cairo was unwilling to turn the Strip over to Jordanian King Abdullah, who was strongly disliked by Egyptian leaders, or to grant the area "independence." Abdullah was dead set against allowing the Palestinians to set up an independent state along his western border in Judea and Samaria. Anyway, the Palestinians did not want a state there, holding out instead for the total destruction of Israel. The Lebanese were too preoccupied with their own problems to worry about the Palestinians. The Syrians had no interest in doing anything which might make life any easier for the "Zionist invaders."

Keeping the refugees in increasingly cramped camps would provide a steady stream of disgruntled young men ready and eager to fight for the "liberation of Palestine." Their continuing homelessness would also provide constant propaganda ammunition against the very existence—in the heart of the Arab/Muslim world—of mainly Jewish Israel. And besides, the United Nations would take care of the medical and food needs of refugee camp residents, lifting the burden off of Arab treasuries. Despite these factors, Jordan did eventually resettle many of the estimated seventy thousand refugees who fled east across the Jordan River—the only Arab country to do so. Today, a majority are fully integrated and fairly prosperous citizens of Jordan.

In early 1950, Jordanian King Abdullah annexed the districts of Judea, Samaria, and east Jerusalem, although only two nations, Britain and Pakistan, recognized his move. In order to reduce Jewish claims to the area, the King dropped the biblical names Judea and Samaria and announced that the annexed land would be known as the West Bank of the Kingdom of Jordan, since it was located beyond the west bank of the Jordan River. At the same time, Abdullah was holding secret talks with Israeli leaders in order to try and work out a permanent peace settlement between the two neighboring countries. He was assassinated for his efforts in 1951. A Palestinian militant who opposed his "traitorous talks with the enemy" shot and killed the king as he toured Muslim shrines on the Temple Mount.

JEWS AT THE CENTER OF THE WORLD

As the Arab Palestinians were fleeing, thousands of Jews, mainly from Europe, Asia, and North Africa, began pouring into the newborn State of Israel. Most were temporarily housed in tent camps, others in homes and apartments which had been abandoned by fleeing Arabs. Anti-Jewish persecution and occasional rioting which broke out in a number of Arab countries in 1947 and continued through 1948 and 1949, led hundreds of thousands of Jews to abandon their homes and flee to Israel. Many of the more than one-half million Arabic-speaking Jews who sought refuge in Israel during the late 1940s and early 1950s were forced to leave their possessions behind, arriving in the country completely destitute. Although the Jewish state was financially strapped, the new immigrants, many of whom could truly be called refugees, were absorbed into the country. By the end of 1951, 690,000 Jewish immigrants had made their way to the Promised Land, more than doubling Israel's May 15, 1948, Jewish population. The number of Jewish arrivals was roughly equal to the number of Palestinian Arabs who had fled.

By 1970, nearly 600,000 European Jews had immigrated to Israel. The vast majority of them, over 80 percent, came from six east European countries which fell under Soviet-communist control after World War II. The largest group, 229,779, emigrated from Romania, the country which violently threw off its communist dictatorship in 1989. Over 150,000 came to Israel from Poland. Thousands of Jews also arrived from China, the Soviet Union, India, Iran, North and South America, southern Africa, Australia, and New Zealand. Jews were literally returning to their ancient ancestral homeland from the uttermost parts of the globe. At least eighty-six countries contributed Jews to the new nation during Israel's first two decades.

Forging a united society with people from so many diverse cultural backgrounds was not easy, to say the least. Arabic-speaking Oriental Jews complained of discrimination at the hands of the European Ashkenazi "elite." Like their pre-state European cousins, most had suffered some degree of persecution before immigrating to Israel, leaving many emotional scars to overcome. The threat of annihilation was ever present with the Arab world periodically renewing its jihad war against the Jewish state. Between the "hot" wars, the military threat was kept alive by frequent sniping and cross-border terror attacks from the Gaza Strip, the West Bank, and the Golan Heights. Many Jews were killed by this constant war of attrition, 967 alone between 1951 and 1955.

Despite the many obstacles, a remarkably united Israeli society has been forged in just a few decades. Much of the credit for this can be traced to shared army duty, which acts as a great force of integration between the various Jewish communities. Israel's armed forces quickly became the strongest in the Middle East, reducing fears that the Arab world would eventually succeed in its war of destruction. Mutually shared burdens helped to create a relatively stable society, free to pursue nation-building in the midst of a sea of Arab hostility.

Jews from Arab countries have slowly moved up the ladder of social success, with such Jews and their offspring the majority of all Israelis in the mid-1980s (although they will probably be the minority once again due to the huge influx of Ashkenazi Soviet Jews which began in late 1989). Many of them hold leading positions in business and government, including David Levy from Morocco, who became Foreign Minister in 1990. Israel's most popular entertainer in the 1980s was Ofra Haza, of Yemeni background. At any rate, intermarriage between different immigrant groups, and time, is leading to the emergence of the truly "Israeli Israeli," a native Hebrew speaker with little or no ethnic distinction, and very much at home in the Middle East.

Serious economic problems have plagued the Jewish state since its inception, mainly because of Israel's need to maintain such a disproportionately large military machine. Fighting the various wars has severely strained Israel's economy. The fact that most Israeli men must spend at least one month a year doing military reserve duty is another serious financial drain. Israel's overly socialized and bureaucratic system of government, patterned too closely on east European models, has also blocked economic progress, although a more open free-enterprise system is now coming into place. These factors, plus the constant fear of terrorism and never knowing when the next war will begin, have caused many Israelis—estimates say up to a half a million—to move overseas since the 1950s. Many so-called *yordim* (literally "those who go down" from Zion) say they intend to return after making their fortune in greener, mostly American pastures, although only a small percentage have made it back home so far.

SINAI—ISRAEL'S SECOND WAR

Constant cross-border attacks from Egyptian-supported Palestinians in the Gaza Strip, which left more than four hundred Israelis dead in the early 1950s, and a threatening Egyptian-Syrian military alliance led to Israel's second major war, the 1956 Sinai Campaign. However, it was actually more of a superpower contest than an Arab/Israeli conflict.

The Soviet Union, fighting a rather hot Cold War with the United States for regional influence, began sending arms to Egypt via Czechoslovakia in 1955. The United States and western Europe were at least as concerned about the Soviet move as was Israel, since the strategic Suez Canal runs through Egyptian territory. After the arms deal was signed, Washington withdrew an offer to help Egypt build a dam on the upper Nile River. The move infuriated Egyptian strongman Gamal Abdel Nasser, who responded by nationalizing the canal.

The fiery Egyptian leader, whose speeches were peppered with both Marxist and Muslim slogans, was already perceived as a great threat in Israel before the decision was taken to join British and French forces in a campaign to return the Suez Canal to Western control. Nasser had ordered his navy to blockade the Israeli port of Eilat in 1954, closing Israel's outlet to the Red Sea. He also banned all Israeli shipping through the canal, effectively cutting off Israeli exports to the southern hemisphere. Next he signed a military pact with Syria, while telling the world in frequent, bombastic speeches that he would lead the Arab states in a renewed attempt to annihilate "the Zionist entity." All the while Nasser was massively beefing up his armed forces in the Sinai peninsula.

Israeli forces, in coordination with Britain and France, attacked Egyptian positions on October 29, 1956. In a prearranged move, the two European superpowers joined the assault the next day. Egyptian defenses quickly crumbled as Israel seized the Gaza Strip and the Sinai Peninsula. But the United States was unhappy with the attempt to forcibly retake the Suez Canal, fearing all-out war with the Soviet Union. The Soviets had threatened to use force if a U.N. General Assembly Resolution for an immediate cease-fire was not heeded. Under American pressure, a cease-fire went into effect on November 6. A special U.N. force was created to separate the warring armies in the Sinai. Within several months the Israelis withdrew from the conquered territory, finally pulling out of the Gaza Strip in March 1957.

Although Nasser had lost the war, he emerged as the hero of the Arab world for successfully holding onto the Suez Canal. He vowed to renew the military struggle against the "Zionist-imperialist state" at an appropriate time in the future. As the so-called "Nasserite Movement" spread across the Arab world, Israeli leaders became more and more alarmed. They responded by continuing to build up the Israeli Defense Forces, and by beginning work on a secret nuclear weapons program, with French assistance. Meanwhile the Soviets and their communist-bloc allies stepped up military support to Egypt and Syria, who continued to sponsor cross-border raids into Israel by Palestinian gunmen known as *fedayeen.*

THE PLO

In 1964, Nasser helped to set up an organization which would later become a major player in the Arab/Israeli conflict. The first official Arab League summit meeting, held in Cairo in January, decided to back the establishment of an organization to represent all Palestinian Arabs in "the struggle to liberate Palestine." Echoing the pre-state Zionist practice, Palestinian delegates held a Congress in east Jerusalem during May to implement the Arab League decision. The result was the Palestine Liberation Organization.

The first PLO leader, Ahmed Shukeiri, pledged at the Congress that the PLO would aid the Arab nations in throwing the Israelis into the sea. The PLO was to be the roof organization for various Palestinian paramilitary and civilian groups, most of them assisted by the Kremlin and its allies. Yasser Arafat, head of the largest armed group, *al-Fatah* (Arabic for "the victory" and also the name of a chapter in the Koran that celebrates Muhammad's capture of Mecca) became overall PLO leader in 1969.

The Arab states, often at each other's throats over the years, continued their frequently intense rivalries by sponsoring various subgroups within the PLO. The

Egyptians backed the setting up of the Marxist Popular Front for the Liberation of Palestine, headed by George Habash. The Syrians sponsored the Palestine Liberation Front, led by Ahmed Jabril, which briefly joined forces with Habash's group. Not wanting to be left out, Iraq backed the Popular Democratic Front for the Liberation of Palestine, headed by Naif Hawatmeh. The various PLO subgroups have at times clashed violently with each other, and more often with Arafat's mainstream Fatah movement.

Israelis saw the PLO as another vehicle in the ongoing Arab attempt to drive them out of the region. They had good reason to think so. The Palestinian Congress of May 1964, adopted a founding charter for the Palestinian movement which called for Israel's total destruction. The PLO Charter still officially remains in effect. Here are some of its main points:

Article 1. Palestine is the homeland of the Palestinian Arab people and an integral part of the great Arab homeland. . . .

Article 3. The Palestinian Arab people possesses the legal right to its homeland, and when the liberation of its homeland is completed, it will exercise self-determination solely according to its own will and choice.

Article 6. Jews who were living permanently in Palestine before the beginning of the Zionist invasion will be considered Palestinians. [In other words, Jews living in the land before the first aliyah wave of the 1880s can stay after the land's "liberation."]

Article 8. The phase in which the people of Palestine is living is that of the national struggle for the liberation of Palestine. [The article then calls for unity and the suspension of internal rivalries, ending with the statement that the Palestinians "comprise one national front which acts to restore Palestine and liberate it through armed struggle."]

Article 9. Armed struggle is the only way to liberate Palestine and is therefore a strategy, and not tactics. The Palestinian Arab people affirms its absolute resolution and abiding determination to pursue the armed struggle and to march forward toward the armed popular revolution, to liberate its homeland and return to it. . . .

Article 10. Fedayeen action [paramilitary and terrorist attacks by armed Palestinians] forms the nucleus of the popular Palestinian war of liberation. [The article then calls on all Arabs to support groups launching such "actions."]

Article 15. The liberation of Palestine, from an Arab viewpoint, is a national duty to repulse the Zionist, imperialist invasion from the great Arab homeland, and to purge the Zionist presence from Palestine. Its full responsibilities fall upon the Arab nation, people and government, with the Palestinian Arabs at their head.

Article 19. The partitioning of Palestine in 1947 and the establishment of Israel is fundamentally null and void, whatever time has elapsed. . . .

Article 20. The Balfour Declaration, the Mandate Document, and what has been based upon them are considered null and void. The claim of a historical or spiritual tie between Jews and Palestine does not tally with historical realities . . . Judaism, in its character as a religion of revelation, is not a nationality with an independent existence.

The Palestinian Charter also contains assurance that the holy places of Christianity and Judaism will be protected after the "liberation"; it calls for broad international support for the struggle; and it declares Palestinian neutrality in the various internal Arab conflicts.

The covenant ends with Article 33: "This Covenant cannot be amended except by a two-thirds majority of all members of the National Council of the Palestine Liberation Organization in a special session called for this purpose."

THE SIX DAY WAR

Three years after the founding of the PLO, the Arab world, led by Gamal Nasser, renewed its jihad against Israel. The result was similar to the first attempt to wipe out the Jewish state in 1948—the Israelis ended up with more territory than they started out with. In fact, the June 1967 Six Day War left Israel in control of the entire West Bank, the Gaza Strip, the Sinai Peninsula and the Golan Heights just above the Galilee panhandle. Of greatest importance to most Israelis, Jewish forces had also captured Jerusalem's Old City. Jewish sovereignty had returned to the area of King David's city, including the ancient Temple Mount, for the first time in over two thousand years.

The war was preceded by a period of rapidly escalating hostile rhetoric and actions on the part of Egypt, and attacks from Syria. Ever since 1948, Israeli settlements in the north had been assaulted by Syrian forces and Palestinian fedayeen. The frequency of attacks increased during 1966, with five Israelis killed and around twenty wounded. Syrian soldiers lobbed artillery shells and fired machine guns and rifles at Israeli settlements, such as Kibbutz Hagoshrim, in the Hula Valley below the Golan Heights. Syrian infiltrators planted land mines in fields and along roads, and Syrian artillery fire was directed at Israeli boats on the Sea of Galilee.

The attacks were stepped up even further in the spring of 1967, with frequent tank battles between Israeli and Syrian forces. On April 7, Israeli planes—most of them purchased from France which was then Israel's main foreign source of weapons—struck at Syrian artillery positions. Six Soviet-supplied Syrian Mig jets were shot down in subsequent dogfights. The Syrians responded on April 8 by lobbing two hundred heavy mortar shells on Kibbutz Gadot, located on the Jordan River just next to Syrian front lines. The shelling completely destroyed the settlement.

Nasser was meanwhile banging the drums of war ever more loudly. On May 14, he mobilized his armed forces of around 240,000 men for what he said would be a decisive attack upon Israel. Two days later he demanded that United Nations peacekeeping forces leave the Sinai peninsula and began moving his army across the Suez Canal. Under increasing pressure, the U.N. agreed on May 19 to withdraw its international force, while Cairo radio announced that the Arabs now had a chance to "deal Israel a mortal blow of annihilation, to blot out its entire presence in our holy land."[5] Three days later Nasser ordered his navy to repeat the 1950s blockade of the Israeli Red Sea port of Eilat, a move which Israeli officials, in accordance with international law, considered an act of war.

The entire Arab world was called upon to support the Egyptian-Syrian attempt to wipe out the Jewish state. Mutual defense pacts were signed between Egypt and Jordan on May 30, and between Egypt and Iraq on June 4. Forces were mobilized in Jordan, Saudi Arabia, Kuwait, Iraq, Algeria, and Lebanon. Israeli leaders quickly noted that they were potentially facing almost three times as many soldiers, three times as many tanks, and over three times as many warplanes as they had at their disposal. Even more alarming was the presence of Soviet and other

East Bloc forces aiding Egypt and Syria. Tension reached fever pitch during the last week of May, when Syrian, Iraqi, Jordanian, and Lebanese soldiers were moved to forward positions close to Israel's borders.

The Arab nations refused to listen to international pleas that they halt their movement toward war. With Israeli soldiers heavily outnumbered along the borders, the Israeli cabinet decided that the Jewish state's best hope for survival was to strike the first blow. On the morning of June 5, Israeli warplanes launched a lightning attack on Egyptian aircraft stationed at more than fifteen bases throughout Egypt, nearly wiping out Nasser's entire air force. The Six Day War had begun.

After two days of fierce battles with Jordanian forces— who began shelling Israeli positions on June 5 from east Jerusalem despite Israeli pleas to King Hussein to stay out of the war— Israeli troops captured the walled Old City of Jerusalem. Israeli soldiers had been hampered somewhat in battling to enter the city by strict orders not to harm any Christian or Muslim holy places. With tears in their eyes, emotional Jewish soldiers touched the ancient Western Wall of the Temple Mount, which had been off limits to all Jews since Jordan captured the Old City in 1948. Israeli leaders toured the nearby Jewish Quarter, largely destroyed during the Jordanian conquest nineteen years earlier. Officials surveyed the remains of ruined Jewish synagogues and homes, promising to immediately begin the quarter's reconstruction.

By June 10, Israeli forces had occupied the Sinai Peninsula, the annexed West Bank of Jordan, and the Syrian Golan Heights. Several hundred thousand West Bank Palestinians and some from the Gaza Strip fled east during the fighting, greatly swelling the Palestinian refugee population in Jordan proper. Some of the refugees later returned to their homes.

The overwhelming Israeli victory stunned the Arab

world. The Soviet Union, deeply embarrassed by its client's disastrous defeat, broke off diplomatic relations with Israel. The Israelis, who had only one week earlier faced the real prospect of annihilation, were, to say the least, ecstatic over the war's outcome, and especially over the reuniting of Jerusalem. But there was much grief over the loss of 766 soldiers and the wounding of 2,500 others.

The Six Day War left the Jewish state in control of land more than three times the size of Israel, with an Arab population of over a million people. How Israel could rule such a large area with a hostile population was of immediate concern to Israeli leaders. The government of Prime Minister Levi Eshkol wasted no time in stating its readiness to hand back at least most of the captured territories, providing the Arab states finally agreed to halt their twenty-year jihad against Israel. But vanquished Arab leaders, meeting in Sudan in September 1967, declared that they would not negotiate, recognize, or make peace with the "Zionist entity."

Soon after the meeting in Sudan, the United Nations passed Resolution 242 which called on Israel to withdraw its forces from "territories occupied in the recent conflict." The Resolution also called for "a just settlement of the refugee problem" and for all Mideast nations to be permitted "to live in peace in secure and recognized borders." The Israelis said they would comply with the resolution only after the Arab states agreed to recognize Israel's permanent existence.

Israeli leaders soon began a limited settlement program in portions of the captured territories, to the dismay of the Arab world. The program was undertaken as part of the Allon Plan, named after deputy Prime Minister Yigal Allon. The plan stated that Israel would eventually pull out of the Sinai Peninsula, the Gaza Strip, and the West Bank, except for certain portions considered vital to Israel's security. Israel would retain control of most of the strategic Jordan Valley and the first mountain ridge west of it, along with east Jerusalem and some areas south of the city where Jewish settlements existed until 1948. The rest of the West Bank would become a Palestinian-Jordanian state. A large corridor located around Jericho would connect the state with Jordan proper. Egypt would regain control of the Gaza Strip and most of the Sinai Peninsula. Arab leaders rejected the plan, calling again for the complete annihilation of the Jewish state. The government then went ahead and began to construct settlements in areas which the Allon Plan designated as essential for Israel's security.

THE WARS OF ATTRITION AND YOM KIPPUR

Nasser backed up his rejectionist stand by launching renewed military attacks against Israeli forces stationed east of the Suez Canal. Hundreds of Israeli soldiers were killed in the almost daily bombardments, which lasted for over three years. The Israeli air force responded by launching raids deep inside Egyptian territory, taking on Soviet pilots several times in the process. The so-called "War of Attrition" finally ended on August 17, 1970, with Israeli and Egyptian forces still dug in on opposite sides of the canal.

The full-scale Arab jihad was renewed on Saturday afternoon, October 6, 1973. But this time, Arab leaders kept quiet about their intentions before launching a surprise attack. In Israel it was Yom Kippur, the holiest day in the Jewish calendar and a day when most people, even many who are basically nonreligious, abstain from eating food. Television and radio are off the air and private vehicles stay off the roads. The quiet of the holy day was suddenly shattered around noon as sirens began wailing throughout the country, alerting everyone that another Arab/Israeli confrontation was about to begin. Men everywhere rushed off to their military units. At 2 P.M. Egyptian and Syrian forces attacked simultaneously with all of their armed might. The Yom Kippur War had begun.

The Soviet Union had fully resupplied the Syrians and Egyptians with the latest weaponry, including close to a 1,000 warplanes and over 4,000 tanks. When the battle got underway, Israel had less than 500 planes and about 1,700 tanks. Israel's 300,000 soldiers faced a combined Egyptian/Syrian force of over 800,000, with more on the way from Iraq, Morocco, and Algeria. Later Saudi Arabia and Kuwait sent token forces to aid the Syrians. Iraq and Jordan added more than 300 tanks to Syria's already large force of around 2,000.

For the first time, the Arabs had the Israelis on the run. The Jewish army was pushed back on both the narrow Golan Heights and in the Sinai Desert. But after several weeks of bitter fighting, and despite an immediate and large-scale resupply effort by the Kremlin, the Israelis, with delayed help from America, once again overcame seemingly insurmountable odds and routed their opponents. Israeli casualties were high: 2,378 soldiers dead and many more injured.

Despite their loss, the Arabs were satisfied that they had proven that Israel was not an invincible military machine. Government officials in Jerusalem found themselves engulfed in a political storm as accusations flew as to who was responsible for not foreseeing the combined Arab attack. In Idaho, I was closely following the tide of battle on radio and television, wondering what was really behind this Arab/Israeli—and superpower—struggle at the center of the world.

CHAPTER 8

FROM OPTIMISM TO DESPAIR

Less than three months after the Yom Kippur War ended, I was sitting in the same stuffed pillowchair where I first heard of the war's outbreak, pondering my brother Tim's testimony of "rebirth" in the Messiah, which he had shared with me several times, the last over the Christmas holidays. Beside the pillowchair was a book I had never read: the Bible. Tim had given it to me for Christmas.

At a certain point during that January 4, 1974, evening I quietly asked the God of Abraham to reveal himself to me—if he indeed existed. I'd already experienced the reality of the "other world" through friends who engaged in certain occult practices, but it had definitely been the dark side of that world. Now I wanted to know what (or should I say who?) was on the good side.

My Christian faith helped me to get a clearer picture as to why people all over the globe were closely following the latest chapter in the Arab/Israeli conflict. I hadn't realized that millions of Christians see the Jewish state as a prophetic timeclock, pointing the way toward the end of the world and the return of the Messiah. I knew that most Muslims view Israel as an usurper, a stealer of holy Muslim land, but I assumed that the Islamic concept of holy war went out with the Middle Ages. It was already apparent to me that Jews all over the world, on the heels of the holocaust, looked to Israel as a special sanctuary for Jewish people everywhere.

However, it quickly became evident that the main reasons for such intense world interest in the ongoing Mideast crisis were not religious, but economic. As the Yom Kippur War raged, Arab petroleum exporting countries decided to support the struggle against Israel by sharply reducing their supply of oil to the West. A total oil embargo was enacted against the United States and the Netherlands, and partial embargoes against other lands. European nations were hardest hit by the move, since most of them imported more than two-thirds of their oil from the Middle East. The Arabs intended to press demands that the West, especially Americans, put pressure on Israel to withdraw from the territories captured in the 1967 war. The United States and Canada, less dependent than Europe on imported Mideast oil, did feel the pinch.

The Arab oil nations soon discovered that they could substantially push up the price of their precious commodity by restricting supplies. The international petroleum companies didn't seem too displeased by the price increases, which left more money in their pockets as well. With long lines forming at gasoline stations in many parts of the globe, the Israelis were indeed pressured to give in to Arab demands that a Palestinian state be set up in the West Bank and Gaza Strip. Israeli leaders responded as they had just after the Six Day War: They would only consider going back to the pre-1967 borders if all Arab states agreed to officially end their ongoing war of annihilation.

The Palestine National Council met in Cairo in June 1974, to discuss what moves the PLO should take in the wake of the 1973 war and subsequent oil embargo. Yasser Arafat told the delegates that the Ramadan Campaign (the Arab name for the war which occurred during the Muslim holy month of Ramadan) was only the "beginning of the advance of the Arab nation." He compared the Arabs' relative success in the war to the Muslim warrior Saladin's victory over the Crusaders, adding that the Arab advance "will only end in Tel Aviv."[1] On June 8, Palestinian delegates formally adopted a ten-point plan, known to Israelis as the "phased plan," which basically calls for the dismantling of Israel in stages. Key articles of the plan include:

Article 2. The Liberation Organization will employ all means and first and foremost armed struggle, to liberate Palestinian territory and to establish the independent combatant national authority for the people over every part of Palestinian territory that is liberated. . . .

Article 4. Any step taken toward liberation is a step toward the realization of the Liberation Organization's strategy of establishing the democratic Palestinian state specified in the resolutions of previous National Councils.

Article 8. Once it is established, the Palestinian national authority will strive to achieve a union of the confrontation countries with the aim of completing the liberation of all Palestinian territory. . . .

In short, the phased plan calls for the setting up of a PLO-controlled state in the West Bank and Gaza Strip. This "independent combatant national authority" would then work to set up "the democratic Palestinian state" over *all* of Palestine, in other words, over Israel as well as the captured territories, in line with the PLO's founding Charter. The Arab world would be asked to back militarily the final moves toward full liberation. Israel, naturally enough, did not enthusiastically welcome the new plan. Soon after the plan was adopted, Arab leaders meeting in Morocco decided to recognize the PLO as "the only legal representative of the Palestinian people." In November 1974 the United Nations granted the PLO full observer status.

Israelis felt increasingly isolated in the mid-1970s as billions of Arab petrodollars flowed back into Western economies—vastly increasing Arab power and influence. Various African states, assisted agriculturally by Israel over the years, broke off diplomatic relations in exchange for Arab promises of aid, which was not always forthcoming.

The low point of this period for Israel was the passage by the United Nations in November 1975, of a resolution equating Zionism with racism. A majority of 72 nations, including the entire communist bloc, supported the Arab-sponsored resolution, with 35 opposed and 32 abstaining. The resolution was meant to delegitimize Israel's very existence by condemning the movement which led to the Jewish state's rebirth. Israel's U.N. ambassador pointed out that despite many years of war and hostility, Arab citizens of Israel have full voting rights and almost unlimited freedom of press and speech, unlike the citizens of most of the states which supported the resolution.

A political revolution occurred in Israel in May 1977. The Labor Alignment, a coalition of moderate and left-wing political parties which had governed Israel since 1948, was thrown out of office and replaced by the right-of-center Likud party headed by Menachem Begin. The Likud party, which won 43 seats to Labor's 32 in the 120-member Israeli parliament, the Knesset, was able to form a government with the support of several centrist parties, plus two religious parties which had earlier supported Labor-led coalition governments. Begin's election victory came on the heels of several scandals which rocked the Labor movement. The Likud party has either led or been part of every Israeli government since 1977.

Labor leaders prophesied that the chances of peace with the Arab world would be further reduced under Begin, who opposed any Israeli withdrawal from the territories captured in 1967. However, such predictions proved to be premature. One Arab leader had already decided that his country's future would best be served by ending the state of war with Israel.

CAMP DAVID PEACE ACCORDS

Egyptian President Anwar Sadat had kicked out his Soviet patrons in the mid-1970s and was looking for Western aid to help rebuild his economy, shattered by the 1973 war. His sudden arrival at Ben Gurion Airport in November 1977 was like a dream come true for most Israelis. Sadat's historic decision led to the first—and so far only—peace treaty between an Arab state and Israel. It also led to his assassination by members of the Egyptian Islamic Jihad group, an offshoot of the Muslim Brotherhood Movement (an Islamic fundamentalist group to which Yasser Arafat belonged while a student in Cairo). The Brotherhood continues to this day to support the abrogation of the peace treaty and a resumption of the holy war against Israel.

Egypt, Israel, and the United States signed the Camp David Peace Accords on September 17, 1978, after thirteen days of grueling negotiations at American President Jimmy Carter's Maryland retreat. One accord spelled out the peace settlement between Egypt and Israel, while the other dealt with the larger Arab/Israeli conflict. The latter said that regional peace talks should be based on United Nations Resolution 242. It called for implementation of a plan giving Palestinians self-governing autonomy in the West Bank and Gaza Strip while a final overall peace settlement was negotiated by Israeli, Palestinian, Egyptian, Jordanian, Syrian, and Lebanese representatives. An elected Palestinian council would have full self-governing authority in the territories, except in security matters, while a final settlement was negotiated.

The Arab world reacted harshly to the Camp David Treaty, as did the Soviet Union. Every Arab state severed relations with Cairo, which was kicked out of the Arab League. Sadat was charged with treason for having made peace with "the Zionist enemy." The PLO totally rejected the autonomy plan, saying it would settle for nothing less than a fully independent PLO state in every inch of "liberated Palestine." Although Jordan's King Hussein quietly signaled that he would dearly love to follow Sadat's example, his hands were tied by warnings from his powerful northern neighbor, Syria, that he would be overthrown if he made peace with Israel. The Jordanian leader undoubtedly vividly remembered the Jerusalem assassination in 1951 of his grandfather, Abdullah, which he personally witnessed.

Sadat and Begin didn't even try to reach agreement on the crucial issue of Jerusalem, recognizing that their respective positions were miles apart. Instead, Begin handed Sadat a letter declaring that Israel considers all of Jerusalem to be its permanent, indivisible capital city. Sadat in turn gave Begin a letter declaring that east Jerusalem, including the Old City and its Temple Mount, is an indivisible part of the Arab world which must be returned to Arab sovereignty.

TERROR FROM THE NORTH

The Israeli people were in an optimistic mood when I arrived in the country in November 1980. Finally there was some light at the end of what had so far proved to be a long, dark tunnel. The peace treaty with Egypt had just been signed two years before, and many were hopeful that a formal accord with Jordan was not far off. The absence of the Arab world's most powerful nation from the war camp might mean the end of the constant cycle of Arab attacks. True, I didn't meet one Israeli who wasn't pained to see the barren, but beautiful, Sinai Peninsula revert to Egyptian control as part of the settlement, but most thought its loss was more than worthwhile in exchange for lasting peace.

There were just a couple of flies in the optimistic ointment—the Palestinians and Syria. Everyone knew that an explosion would probably occur one day in Judea, Samaria, and the Gaza Strip, where Israel's growing presence and often squalid living conditions, made worse by a high birth rate, produced hundreds of thousands of young, disgruntled soldiers for the Palestinian cause.

The chances that Jordan would resume full control over its self-declared "West Bank" as part of a future peace treaty with Israel seemed remote after the Arab decision to recognize the PLO as the sole representative of the Palestinians. There was little evidence that either Jordan or Egypt was eager to take on the Gaza Strip with its teeming refugee camps. Syria was supremely hostile to the Egyptian peace move, declaring it would continue the military struggle against Israel until the Jewish state was obliterated. At any rate, the chances that Israel would give back the small, but strategic Golan Heights to Syria seemed to disappear after the Knesset extended Israeli law to the area in 1981.

However, it was in Lebanon that the flies in the ointment were most apparent. The Syrians had entered the troubled country as "peacekeepers" after fighting broke out between various Lebanese factions and Palestinians in 1975. Syria now controlled two-thirds of the country. Syrian strongman Hafez al-Assad resisted calls from fellow Arab leaders, and most Lebanese Christians, to pull his soldiers out of the Land of the Cedars. Assad also heavily backed several PLO militia groups operating in southern Lebanon, although he was hostile toward Arafat's mainstream Fatah group.

The most pressing problem facing Israel in the early 1980s was the frequent rocket attacks on its northern towns and settlements, launched mainly by the PLO from south Lebanon. The attacks originated in the PLO's south Lebanon mini-state, which stretched from southern Beirut to the ports of Sidon and Tyre and east to the Syrian border. The PLO zone was established after the organization was thrown out of Jordan in the early 1970s following an unsuccessful PLO attempt to overthrow King Hussein. The ever-worsening internal fighting in Lebanon left the south's mostly Shiite Muslim residents powerless to prevent the PLO from taking over their towns and villages, even though few wanted to see the Palestinian fighters in control of the area.

Israel responded in 1978 to the growing PLO presence by helping south Lebanese Christians and Shiites set up an Israeli-patrolled border enclave—the south Lebanon "security zone"—sandwiched between the Israel/Lebanon border and an area to the north patrolled by United Nations peacekeeping forces. The U.N. forces had been sent to the area in the mid-1970s to help prevent terror squads from penetrating into Israel. Still, such squads occasionally pushed through, leading to the idea of setting up a buffer zone that would increase protection for northern Israel and for south Lebanese residents who were becoming frequent targets of attack by the PLO and its allies.

As I mentioned in Chapter 2, I was personally well-acquainted with the fear and disruption caused by the sometimes heavy PLO shelling of northern Israel. I also knew of another, even deeper fear which shaped the lives of Israel's Galilee citizens—the fear of a Palestinian terrorist attack.

My Hagoshrim "kibbutz parents" (everyone on my Project Kibbutz team was assigned a family to visit with regularly during the year) told me about one such attack that affected them personally. Close friends lived on nearby Kibbutz Misgav Am located in the Naphtali hills near the border with Lebanon. Their two-year-old daughter was killed when PLO terrorists crossed the border on April 7, 1980. After sneaking into the kibbutz under the cover of darkness, the five heavily armed Palestinians took over a building housing four young children, two babies, and their adult female companion. The terrorists ordered the woman to calm down the frightened, weeping youngsters. But she was unable to comfort one of the young girls, who kept on crying. At that point, the leader of the terrorist band used the butt of his gun to club the child to death. The PLO terrorists, who belonged to Arafat's Fatah group, announced that they would only release their kibbutz hostages if fifty Palestinian prisoners were immediately set free from Israeli jails. At mid-morning, Israeli soldiers stormed the house, killing all five terrorists. One soldier lost his life in the assault, but the remaining five children and the adult hostage were unharmed.

The Misgav Am attack was just the latest in a series of violent terror assaults launched by Palestinian squads from Lebanon. Since 1974 the attacks had left nearly one hundred Israelis dead. On April 11, 1974, three terrorists penetrated the border and attacked an Israeli apartment building in Kiryat Shmona—in the same neighborhood where I later resided. The terrorists slaughtered sixteen civilians (eight of them children) along with two soldiers, before being killed by Israeli security forces.

Just over one month later, another three-man terror squad belonging to Naif Hawatmeh's PLO faction slipped over the border in the middle of the night, this time into the town of Ma'alot. The terrorists sneaked into an apartment building and murdered an Israeli family in their beds. Later they killed two Arab women passing by on their way to work. Finally, the Palestinian squad seized the Ma'alot high school. After holding nearly one hundred Israeli teenagers and several adults hostage for most of the day, soldiers stormed the school, shooting to death the three Palestinian terrorists. As they did so, the terrorists lobbed hand grenades at their youthful prisoners, killing twenty teenagers. About seventy others were wounded. In all, ten terror attacks in the north and center of Israel during 1974 left fifty-nine people dead and hundreds wounded.

The Jewish state suffered its worst terror outrage on March 11, 1978. Thirteen Fatah commandos set sail from south Lebanon and landed on Israel's Mediterranean coast near Kibbutz Magen Michael, south of Haifa. There they seized control of a taxi and two civilian buses after shooting dead a female American tourist on the beach. Eleven terrorists were eventually killed, a few when one of their comrades set off an incendiary bomb in the bus. The lives of thirty-three Israeli civilians and two soldiers were taken by Arafat's men. A year later, four Fatah terrorists seized hostages in an apartment in the coastal border resort of Nahariya, which was also frequently shelled by the PLO from Lebanon. Three Israeli civilians and a policeman were killed before police shot and killed two of the terrorists. Another attack was launched against the town during 1979, leaving three more Israelis dead.

Undoubtedly the most widely reported terrorist attack outside of Israel occurred at the 1972 Summer Olympic Games in Munich, West Germany. The building housing Israeli athletes was taken over by eight armed PLO gunmen, all members of Arafat's Fatah faction. With viewers around the globe glued to their television sets, German forces stormed the dormitory, killing five terrorists and capturing three others. But inside eleven young Israeli athletes had been murdered by their captors. The three captured Fatah terrorists were released from jail one month later, after Palestinian gunmen demanding their release hijacked a German Lufthansa airplane.

Arafat's Fatah group, splinter PLO factions and several Palestinian breakaway groups conducted many other terror attacks along the Israel/Lebanon border, elsewhere in Israel, and abroad. The overseas attacks usually had international communist and Arab backing, along with occasional support from non-Arab terror groups like the Japanese Red Army, whose members had killed twenty-six people at Ben Gurion airport in a 1972 operation coordinated with the Popular Front Palestinian group. Most of the attacks were planned in Lebanon.

Ironically, almost all of the overseas casualties were neither Israelis nor Jews. The U.S. Ambassador to Sudan and his deputy were gunned down in 1973 on what American intelligence officials said were orders from Arafat. Planes were hijacked, airports shot up, restaurants and synagogues blown up. Hundreds of people were killed in these attacks which the terror groups said were legitimate, nationalist acts in line with the Palestinian Charter declaration that armed struggle is the only way to liberate Palestine. Inter-Palestinian killings between rival group members left many Arabs dead as well.

THE LEBANON WAR

By 1982, most Israelis had had enough of Palestinian terror attacks around the world, not to mention infiltrations and bombings of northern Israel from Lebanon. Israeli leaders decided to launch a "clean out" operation against the PLO mini-state in southern Lebanon from where most of the terror assaults were either planned or launched.

After a Palestinian terrorist belonging to the PLO-breakaway Abu Nidal group shot and critically wounded

Shlomo Argov, Israel's Ambassador to Britain, on June 3, 1982, Prime Minister Menachem Begin convened his cabinet. After a brief discussion, Begin decided to order air strikes against Palestinian targets near Beirut. The PLO responded by renewing full-scale shelling of northern Israel, halted the previous summer after American mediation. The Israeli Premier asked his cabinet ministers to authorize "Operation Peace for Galilee," a military campaign designed to dislodge the PLO from south Lebanon.

I wasn't aware of Argov's shooting, or that Israeli jets had struck Palestinian positions, when I arrived at Kiryat Shmona's nearly empty central bus station on the evening of June 4. I did note that the few Israelis who rode with me into town closely followed news reports over the radio. But the reports were in Hebrew, which I still did not understand very well, and I didn't bother to ask anyone what was going on. I caught another bus to the small border town of Metulla where I was to spend the night at the home of Voice of Hope manager Chuck Pollack before crossing over into Lebanon to work at the station the next morning.

Before too long I discovered—with a bang—what was happening. As the nearly empty bus passed an apple grove just outside Metulla, a loud explosion filled the air. The sound was quite familiar to me. Stunned, I looked up at my fellow passengers to catch their reactions. They seemed calm even though all realized a Soviet-built Katuysha rocket had just landed not far from the bus. As we entered Metulla, rockets began falling like hailstones all around us. (We later learned that the PLO was using a newly delivered North Korean multiple launcher that could fire forty rockets at a time.) The bus driver kindly let me off right in front of Chuck's house. As I disembarked, a rocket landed on the sidewalk only fifty feet in front of the bus—in fact, probably just next to where it would have been if we had not stopped.

I found Chuck alone at home, busy talking via two-way radio to the station across the border. "Why don't you join the others in the bomb shelter?" he suggested, as calmly as if he was directing me to the bathroom.

"Not until you tell me what's going on!" I demanded.

"Oh, its just the war we've all been expecting," he replied, turning his attention back to the radio conversation.

The first Israeli war casualty occurred within an hour. A local man, driving on the very road I had just traveled on, died when shrapnel from an exploding PLO Katuysha struck him in the neck.

Prime Minister Begin thought he was authorizing a limited operation to push the PLO out of southern Lebanon. His defense minister, Ariel Sharon, had other ideas, which were apparently soon accepted by Begin. The former general and hero of the Six Day War wanted the PLO entirely out of Lebanon, followed by the installation of a friendly Christian government in Beirut which would sign a formal peace treaty with Israel. Of course, such goals would mean the Israeli operation would have to be much larger than originally conceived. And so it was.

Fortunately, I wasn't yet news director at the Voice of Hope when Israeli forces poured across the border the first week of June. There was a lot of news to report—too much, in fact, to properly keep up with. And much of the news happened literally just outside our doorstep. However, we didn't necessarily report everything we saw. It was, after all, wartime.

The main Israeli route into the Bekaa Valley, where Israeli forces took on the Syrians, ran right past the station. During one of my evening newscasts I reported that "Beirut radio stations say Israel is reinforcing its tank and armor forces in the southern Bekaa Valley." I wondered with amusement how clearly my listeners could hear the loud rumble in the background as Israeli tanks and armored vehicles slowly made their way past the station on their way to the Bekaa Valley!

Many of the air battles between Israeli and Syrian jet fighters took place in our neighborhood. One would suddenly hear a loud explosion and glance up to see smoke pouring from a warplane—most of them Soviet-built Syrian Migs—which would then come tumbling out of the sky. The remains of one such jet landed just a few hundred yards behind the station. Charbel Younis, the Voice of Hope's Lebanese chief engineer, ran out with several other staff members to see if anything could be salvaged. They found the tail-end of the plane still very much intact and hauled it up to place on display in the radio station's foyer. A picture of the station's Syrian trophy later appeared in *Newsweek* magazine.

Charbel was especially pleased to discover certain parts inside the tail that he needed to repair the station's radio transmitter. "I ordered these parts a long time ago from the States," announced the portly engineer with a big grin stretched across his face, "and finally they've arrived—via air mail from Moscow!"

Charbel's comment struck me as a bit odd in light of the fact that someone had obviously just lost his life in the shoot down. Yet I soon discovered that the only way many Lebanese could cope with the ugly violence and intense hatred in their country was to try to keep their sense of humor alive.

The original Israeli goal of expelling the PLO from south Lebanon was accomplished with lightning-like speed, with the Israelis pursuing the PLO up the coast toward Beirut. The leader of the Israeli-funded and trained Free Lebanese Forces militia, Major Saad Hadad, who spoke regularly over the Voice of Hope to friend and foe alike (to the latter in words not usually heard on a religious radio station, which led to some moral qualms among us Westerners at the station), was wel-

comed with roses and kisses as he toured local Christian
and Muslim villages and towns—finally freed from the
hated PLO grip.

By mid-June the battle had moved to Beirut, with quiet
prevailing in the Bekaa Valley after a cease-fire went
into effect between Israeli and Syrian forces on June
11. Peace had also come to the south for the first time
in many years. Israeli tour buses quickly appeared on
south Lebanese roads taking excited visitors to see the
sights of the recent fighting. Joyous south Lebanese residents who had not ventured very far from their homes
since the mid-'70s were busy visiting friends and relatives
all over the area. Lebanese friends invited me to join
them in festive meals. How good it was to eat the traditional, elaborate Lebanese dishes free of worry that PLO
shells might come raining down at any moment! Lebanese families north of the border enclave—frequent re-
cipients of return Israeli and south Lebanese militia shelling—also undoubtedly enjoyed their new-found peace.

MANY VERSIONS OF THE TRUTH

But the situation was anything but a picnic in the
rest of Lebanon. As fighting continued around Beirut,
world opinion turned sharply against Israel. For the first
time in her short history, Israel appeared to be the aggres-
sor, surrounding and cutting off one of the Arab world's
leading cities. Widespread media reports describing "indiscriminate" Israeli shelling of Beirut brought international condemnation, even from Washington. Menachem
Begin's government in turn charged that much of the
press coverage was one-sided or exaggerated, coming
from journalists living under the thumb of the PLO and
Syria.

Having spoken to many people who were in the Lebanese capital at the time, I believe Begin had a fair basis

for his charge, even though Israel was certainly besieging west Beirut in order to flush out PLO, Syrian, and other anti-Israeli forces. For example, colleagues from Jerusalem relate that they were with a group of Christian journalists and others who visited Beirut during the fighting. While at a Maronite monastery on a hill overlooking the city, someone in the party turned on his radio to hear the BBC correspondent report that "Beirut is in flames as a result of indiscriminate Israeli shelling." However, the visitors could clearly see that very few fires smoldered in the city, which had been calm for many hours.

Had the BBC correspondent recorded his report while sitting in the Commodore Hotel, where most journalists hung out, based on information fed him by young Palestinian stringers who had an obvious interest in exaggerating reports of Israeli shelling? Or did he just *think* he saw flames everywhere, not having the clear view that the Jerusalem visitors had? Or was it an old report, being played over again by the BBC? Whatever, it did not reflect the reality the group saw with their own eyes that day in Beirut.

New York Times correspondent Thomas Friedman, who was stationed in Beirut during the siege, admitted that intimidation played a role in shaping what foreign journalists reported. "No discussion about the reality of Beirut reporting would be complete without mentioning a major reporting constraint journalists there faced: physical intimidation," wrote Friedman in his book *From Beirut to Jerusalem.*[2]

He added that, in his opinion, Syria and its Palestinian allies posed the biggest threat, noting that agents operating for them shot and killed several Western and Arab journalists during the 1970s and early 1980s. "The situation got so bad that many Lebanese were afraid to even mention the word *Syria* in public."[3] Friedman doesn't add the obvious: Journalists must have had the same reservations in their news reports—if they valued their own skins!

The award-winning American journalist reports that "the main PLO factions, the Phalangists (the main Christian militia), and the various Muslim militias were less direct, and much less touchy than the Syrians, but no one had any illusions that they would tolerate much seriously critical reporting."[4] Although Friedman mentions the east Beirut-based Christian forces in the same breath with the PLO and Muslim militias, he earlier notes that most foreign journalists were based in *west* Beirut, controlled by Syria and its Muslim and PLO allies. Therefore, the greatest intimidation reporters faced obviously came from anti-Israeli groups.

Friedman tells his readers very candidly that "for any Beirut-based correspondent, the name of the game was keeping on good terms with the PLO," after admitting that "the Western press coddled the PLO and never judged it with anywhere near the scrutiny that it judged Israeli, Phalangist, or American behavior."[5] And no wonder! The *Times* bureau chief recalls that he asked for an interview with Yasser Arafat in the midst of the Israeli siege in July 1982. Arafat's spokesman insisted that Friedman's colleague Bill Farrell conduct it, since Friedman is a Jew. The spokesman finally changed his mind, but not before telling Friedman that "I have asked our office in New York for a complete assessment of all your reporting on us." The young correspondent admits that the remark caused him great paranoia as it would anyone who values his life! After receiving the assessment, the PLO spokesman told Friedman that his reporting was not good enough. The tense encounter between the two men ended with the spokesman telling a Palestinian stringer who worked for the *Times* that "we know he's not bad. We just need a little more from him."[6]

As a journalist working in southern Lebanon during the war, I often read and heard what I knew to be one-sided or exaggerated reports on the fighting, none of which were ever in Israel's favor. Naturally I had sympathy for my colleagues in west Beirut, having faced some intimidation myself from leftist Lebanese and PLO groups. Yet I had to also empathize with Israeli frustration over exaggerated media coverage. I knew that the average reader and listener overseas had no way to verify fairly accurate Israeli charges that the Beirut press often slanted the news in order to please Syria and its PLO and leftist Muslim allies.

Still, unfair reporting does not change the by-now-obvious fact that Israel not only lost international prestige by besieging Beirut, but also failed to make any long-term political or military gains as a result. While Sharon's goal of expelling the PLO from the entire country was widely supported in Israel, even by many in the Labor Party, his confidence that a lasting peace treaty was achievable between Israel and Lebanon was a pipe dream at best, since "Lebanon" was by 1982 basically two countries: one dominated by Maronite Christians, and the other by Syria through its Palestinian Druze, Shiite, and Sunni Muslim allies. While the Christian side might—and in 1983 did—sign an American-mediated peace treaty with Israel, the Muslim side, under Syria's thumb, would obviously oppose it, which it did, leading to the treaty's abrogation several months later. Had Israel pushed the Syrians entirely out of Lebanon, a lasting peace accord might have been possible. Sharon probably would have pursued this goal if not for United States opposition. From day one America pressured Israel to refrain from attacking Syrian positions, apparently afraid that an all-out Israeli assault could drag the U.S. into a confrontation with Assad's Soviet backers.

As the siege of Beirut continued, Israeli public support for the war weakened. Charges flew that Ariel Sharon had deceived the government and the people as to his ultimate intentions in Lebanon. Prime Minister Begin admitted that a total PLO expulsion from Lebanon had not been originally envisaged by his cabinet when it approved Operation Peace for Galilee. Still, he went along with Sharon's move to Beirut, agreeing with his Defense Minister that prospects for peace in the region would improve if the PLO was no longer dominating any part of the country. Most Lebanese that I spoke with at the time, including many Muslims, were hopeful that the PLO would indeed be pushed out of their homeland, along with the Syrians, whose ongoing and overwhelming presence was increasingly resented.

Palestinian fighters and Syrian troops began evacuating Beirut in late August after several months of heavy artillery exchanges with Israeli forces. Portions of the once-great capital city lay in ruins. Palestinian refugee camps from which PLO fighters had operated were largely destroyed. PLO gunmen fled to Syrian-controlled territory north of Beirut (the Israelis basically let them escape).

A multinational force made up of American, French, and Italian Marines oversaw the separation of hostile Lebanese forces in the city after the PLO evacuation. Finally, following several months of intense battles and many casualties, relative calm returned to Beirut, and the process of repairing the war damage got under way.

In Washington the Reagan Administration, upset that its ally had sunk so deep in the Lebanese mud, was busy all summer devising new proposals to end the Arab/Israeli conflict. The Reagan plan was unveiled on September 1. It proposed a Palestinian "entity" in the West Bank and Gaza Strip, linked to Jordan. Jewish settlement activity would be frozen, with the final status of the settlements to be determined by negotiations, along with the future of east Jerusalem. The plan did not support the establishment of an independent Palestinian state, and it opposed Israeli annexation of the territories.

Prime Minister Begin was not exactly thrilled with President Reagan's plan, still hoping local Palestinians would negotiate on the basis of his Camp David autonomy plan. He rejected the Reagan Plan on September 2. Arab leaders, meeting in Fez, Morocco, one week later, also rejected the proposal. They called instead for: a total Israeli pullout from all areas captured in 1967, including east Jerusalem and the Golan Heights; the complete dismantling of all Jewish settlements; and the establishment of a PLO-controlled Palestinian state with Jerusalem as its capital. The Fez resolution was the death knell of Israeli hopes that Jordan would once again play a governing role in the territories as part of an overall peace settlement. The PLO welcomed the Fez Summit statement.

As political moves intensified, Israeli forces were busy digging in opposite the Syrians in the Bekaa Valley. The Kremlin was busy doubling the number of Soviet "advisors" in Syria to about five thousand. To compensate for not actively backing its ally in the earlier fighting, the Soviets also delivered substantial quantities of new missiles and planes. Occasional skirmishes took place over the next several years in the Bekaa, but both well-equipped armies seemed eager to keep away from renewed full-scale fighting. With a fresh show of Soviet support, Syria was not about to budge from Lebanon—Israelis or not. Assad had long maintained that Lebanon was part of "greater Syria." The Syrian strongman did not accept the French Mandate creation of Lebanon out of "western Syria," nor for that matter the existence of either Jordan or Israel in what had traditionally been known, especially to Muslim Arabs, as "southern Syria."

Heavy clashes broke out around Tripoli, north of Beirut, in 1983 between Arafat's gunmen and Syrian-backed Palestinians headed by Abu Musa. President Assad had apparently decided that he too would like to see Arafat's PLO fighters out of Lebanon, with only Palestinians loyal to him remaining behind. He was upset that Arafat had dared to discuss the Reagan Plan with his foe to the south, King Hussein. The PLO leader was becoming too moderate for Assad, but unfortunately not nearly moderate enough for Israel. With strong Syrian support, Abu Musa's men defeated Arafat's fighters in late 1983. Hundreds of rival Palestinian gunmen and civilians were killed in the clashes. On December 23, Arafat left Tripoli for Tunis, his new headquarters.

A growing number of Israelis wanted to emulate Arafat and get out of Lebanon as quickly as possible. The perception was rapidly spreading that little could be done to bring stability to the fractured, medieval-like country. Internal political pressure to withdraw increased substantially after Israeli military headquarters in Tyre was blown up by suicide bombers in November 1983, leaving sixty-one soldiers dead. Syrian-supported saboteurs claimed responsibility for the attack which left Israeli military morale at an all-time low in the increasingly hated land of Lebanon.

United States Marines meanwhile made final preparations to leave Lebanon after suffering a great tragedy in October. I was on an airplane returning from a two-week vacation in London when a truck packed with explosives blasted the Marines' main barracks in Beirut, killing 241 American servicemen. U.S. officials said the attack was most likely carried out by Syrian and Iranian-supported Lebanese terrorists. I arrived at the station to discover I would be broadcasting details of a horrible terror attack involving my own countrymen. We spent the next few days reporting the sad news and trying to minister some good news to survivors who had lost buddies in the explosion. It was especially at such times that I was grateful to have the opportunity to broadcast the Lord's message of hope to hurting people in war-torn Lebanon.

UP TO JERUSALEM!

Not long after the Marines withdrew from Lebanon, I decided it was time for me to pull out as well. My last day on the air was in February 1984. Although I had grown to love the country, I felt it was time to pursue an earlier goal: to study Hebrew in Jerusalem. I had already been offered a job in the Holy City as an overseas correspondent for IMS News, a Christian news network based in Washington, D.C. No longer would I see the Golan Heights from my living room window, or get caught in traffic jams with Israeli tanks and army trucks heading north to the Lebanese border. The constant background tension always present along Israel's northern border would be exchanged for the bustle of city life in Jerusalem. I arrived on April 1, eager to unload my Volkswagen and begin a new chapter of my life in the Promised Land.

It was not long before I realized that the Arab/Israeli conflict is also played out violently in Jerusalem, the City of Peace. On April 2, three Palestinian terrorists suddenly rushed out of a sporting goods store on Jaffa Road and King George Street—Jerusalem's busiest downtown intersection—tossing hand grenades and shooting pistols at people walking and driving nearby. One Israeli was killed and fifty-nine people were wounded, including four Palestinian passers-by and ten European tourists. Police killed one of the terrorists at the scene and captured the other two.

Although my debut radio report for IMS was about terrorism, most of the stories I sent during 1984 and

1985 were related to the Israeli army pullout from Lebanon and the rapidly deteriorating Israeli economy, hit hard by the war.

As the months wore on, popular opinion in Israel increasingly supported an immediate withdrawal from what had commonly become known as the "Lebanese quagmire." The cost of keeping soldiers in Lebanon helped fuel the inflation rate, which soared to an incredible 450 percent during 1984. Although a majority of the six hundred Israeli soldiers who had been killed by October of that year died during the first few months of the war, roadside bombs and other acts of sabotage continued to take their toll.

The Israeli National Unity Government, a coalition formed after Israel's two main parties, Labor and Likud, came out basically even in elections held during the summer of 1984, voted to withdraw Israeli forces in stages. The last remaining soldiers said farewell to the area north of the security buffer zone in the spring of 1985.

Another major story which I covered during this period was an extremely controversial Arab/Israeli prisoner exchange. On May 20, 1985, Israeli leaders announced to a stunned nation that they had agreed to swap 1,150 Arab terrorists imprisoned in Israeli jails for three Israeli soldiers being held captive in Lebanon. Among the 1,150 were perpetrators of some of the worst terror attacks against Israel. The lopsided exchange—an expression of the high value Israel places on each and every soldier's life—was denounced by many politicians as a blatant surrender to terrorism, even though all welcomed the soldiers' release.

Charges of sellout were repeated just over a month later when Lebanese Shiite terrorists hijacked an American TWA jet and forced it to land in Beirut. The hijackers demanded the release of an additional 766 Arab prisoners being held in an Israeli detention center. Israeli leaders complied with the demand, prompting more charges that they had lost their will to fight terrorism. Possibly as a result of the outcry, Israel refused to release fifty Arab prisoners as demanded by terrorists belonging to Abul Abbas' PLO faction, who seized the Italian ship *Achille Lauro* while it was cruising the Mediterranean during October.

The TWA hijacking story, naturally of great interest to Americans, prompted CBS-affiliated Boston radio station WEEI to ask if I would send regular reports on the drama. I also supplemented WEEI's network coverages of the *Achille Lauro* seizure, and continued to send reports on other Mideast happenings until 1987.

BUILDUP TO BREAKDOWN

The longer I lived in Jerusalem, the more Palestinian Arabs I became acquainted with. Among them were Christian and Muslim shopkeepers in the Old City. Palestinian moneychangers helped me exchange my hard-earned dollars for daily deteriorating Israeli shekels (one changed money frequently, but in as small an amount as possible during those days of hyperinflation). Good friends of mine, an American Christian couple who worked at a Bethlehem evangelistic center, introduced me to quite a few Palestinian young men, both Christians and Muslims, including one who became my new Volkswagen mechanic.

The young Palestinians I befriended described in detail some of the difficult problems they had to wrestle with. Although officially Jordanian citizens, they are basically stateless people—surrounded by Israelis and yet not citizens of Israel; using Jordanian currency and passports, and yet not living anymore in Jordanian-controlled territory. I understood their frustration at having to get Israeli approval for almost any act of consequence, including travel abroad. I felt their anger and hurt at being the objects of constant suspicion in the eyes of soldiers who frequently patrolled the town where Jesus was born almost two thousand years ago. I sympathized with them over the humiliation they felt when stopped and questioned while driving or riding into their own hometown— often by soldiers not exactly the epitome of politeness. I listened quietly as they expressed their grief over the death and imprisonment of loved ones participating in the often violent struggle against the Israeli occupiers.

While fully appreciating their dilemma, I nonetheless urged my Palestinian friends to consider the apparent truth that violence only leads to more violence. I pointed out that their personal stories, while painful and sad, are also a part of the wider Arab/Israeli conflict, which has led to loss of life and hardships for many Jews as well. Root responsibility for their admittedly bad situation should not necessarily be pinned only on the Israelis, I suggested, and maybe hardly at all. While some of my Palestinian friends, especially born-again Christians, did agree that violence is not the answer to their perplexing problems, I frankly found very few who would entertain the notion that internal Palestinian and external Arab actions over the years might have contributed substantially to their stateless situation.

Most Palestinians and Israelis, along with local and foreign journalists, sensed that an explosion was coming in the West Bank and Gaza Strip long before the Palestinian uprising broke out in December 1987. The Palestinian population of the areas was mushrooming, largely because of the high Muslim birth rate. The areas captured by Israel twenty years earlier (excluding the Golan Heights) had also become home to almost 75,000 Israeli Jews living in more than two hundred settlements, a majority of them built since 1977. Most of the West Bank settlers were living in what amounted to urban suburbs of Tel Aviv and Jerusalem. The vast majority had not moved to the new bedroom communities for ideological reasons, but because housing was more affordable than in the big cities. Clashes occurred frequently between Jewish settlers—especially the 15 percent or so who lived in outlying settlements—and Palestinians.

Labor leaders had only allowed settlement in certain areas in accordance with the Allon Plan, despite the belief most of them hold that Israel has a legal right to settle in all portions of what was Mandatory Palestine.[7] But Likud leaders promoted Jewish settlement throughout the territories, although heavily populated Arab areas were usually avoided. Despite the fact that the settlers were only a small percentage of the overall population, and for the most part living on hilltops and other areas that had been empty of Arab inhabitants, local Palestinians realized that any Jewish presence strengthened Israel's hold on the territories and made a future total withdrawal unlikely. While Labor leaders spoke of territorial compromise and at least a partial pullout, the Likud Party clearly had no intention of evacuating any portion of the Gaza Strip, or Judea and Samaria, as Likud leaders used to call it even before "West Bank" became a misnomer after Jordan in effect rescinded its annexation of the area in 1988.

Likud leaders, along with many in the Labor Party, believe that the Arabs forfeited any legal claim over the territories when they rejected the United Nations partition plan in 1947. Israel's legal right to remain in the areas is strong, they maintain, since Jews were permitted to settle throughout Palestine, including in the hills of Judea and Samaria, under the original British Mandate, approved by the League of Nations. Several places, especially east Jerusalem and Hebron, have long held Jewish communities, they note, adding that Jerusalem, Bethlehem, Hebron, and Nablus (biblical Shechem) were Jewish towns long before Arabs settled in them. Another factor which strengthens Israel's right to hold onto the West Bank, say Likud leaders and others, is that the area was captured during the Six Day War after Jordanian forces launched attacks from there upon the tiny Jewish state, as they had in 1948.

Israeli government legal experts reject the term *occupied territories* since the West Bank and Gaza Strip did not legally belong to sovereign nations when they came under Israeli control. The areas were under Turkish control until the British pushed out the Turks in World War I, they point out. Britain then controlled Palestine until Israel assumed sovereignty over part of the area in 1948. The other portions are disputed, they note, with Israel's claim over them quite strong since it is based on the League of Nations Mandate and the Arab rejection of the partition plan. Jordan's annexation of Judea and Samaria was not recognized by the Arab states or the larger world community. Egypt didn't even attempt to claim sovereignty over the Gaza Strip, which it controlled at the time of the Six Day War. Referring to the areas as "occupied territories" implies that they will someday revert to the previous nations which held sovereignty over them. Does that mean Turkey will regain control, they ask, or possibly Great Britain? Since the answer is obviously no, the areas should at most be referred to as "disputed territories."

Palestinians obviously reject these Israeli positions. Zionism was an illegitimate movement from the beginning, as stated in the PLO Charter and confirmed by the 1975 U.N. equation of Zionism with racism. Judaism is a religion with no nationalistic traits, and therefore, Jews have no claim on the soil of Palestine. Every inch, not only the West Bank and Gaza Strip, is Arab territory.

Despite these widely held views, many Palestinians

are now ready to accept that Israel does in fact exist, if not that it has a *right* to exist, but certainly not that Jews have any right to settle in the West Bank, including east Jerusalem, or the Gaza Strip.

It was from east Jerusalem that King Hussein launched the 1967 Jordanian attack which led to the capture of his "West Bank." The subsequent Israeli annexation of east Jerusalem did not automatically convey citizenship on Arab residents of the city, but did entitle them to choose that option and to vote in municipal elections and travel freely throughout Israel (their vehicles have the same yellow license plates as Israeli Jews and Arabs, while the Palestinians in the territories have blue plates). After Menachem Begin came to power, several new Jewish suburbs were built around the city, mostly on land captured from the Jordanians. The growing Jewish presence naturally upset many Palestinians, especially those living in villages adjoining the new suburbs. By 1991 some 120,000 Jews resided in neighborhoods constructed on land captured from Jordan in 1967.

By the time the Israelis were making final preparations for the state's fortieth birthday celebrations in May 1988, the Arab population of the West Bank and Gaza Strip had swollen to around 1.5 million. Another 140,000 lived in annexed east Jerusalem. Out of the estimated 850,000 people in the West Bank (the last official census was taken in 1985), some 90,000, about 12 percent of the population, were living in nineteen United Nations-run refugee camps. Most Palestinians resided in usually comfortable, but often crowded, homes located in the many towns and villages which dot the hills. Farming was the largest single occupation, followed by services and construction. The economy was heavily tied to Israel's with many people working in Israel or for Israeli companies operating in Judea and Samaria. The situation was similar in the Gaza Strip except that a much higher percentage of the population, around 200,000 out of 650,000 people, were living in eight crowded and run down refugee camps.

Israeli attempts over the years to improve the refugee's living conditions had met with both Palestinian and international resistance. The Israeli government launched a discreet camp rehabilitation program in 1972 aimed at resettling Palestinian families in new, modern apartment buildings and houses built near the camps. The United Nations, the PLO and various Arab countries attacked the program, charging that Israel was only trying to upgrade housing and ease overcrowding in the camps in order to lessen political pressure on it to withdraw from the territories. Israeli leaders admitted that this was one motivating factor, but said the camp residents would at least have better living conditions until an overall Arab/Israeli peace settlement could be worked out.

World resistance to the Israeli resettlement plan—coupled with PLO warnings to local Palestinians not to take up the offer—meant the program barely got off the ground. Yet some eight thousand families did move from Gaza Strip camps to new Israeli-financed housing between the years 1976 and 1978. However, most of the area's refugees continued to live in squalid, overcrowded camps. The largest camp, Jabalya, housed some sixty thousand people. It was there that hundreds of angry Arabs clashed with Israeli soldiers on December 9, 1987, signaling the start of a new phase in the holy war for the Promised Land.

CHAPTER 9

HOLY WAR OF STONES

I found myself increasingly bored with my work as a radio correspondent for IMS News after the Israeli withdrawal from most of Lebanon. Economics never interested me at all, yet Israel's dreadful financial situation forced me to focus almost exclusively on this very topic (although the 1984–85 Israeli Operation Moses airlift of thousands of black Ethiopian Jews to Israel provided some relief). As my boredom grew, I began thinking that it would be nice to go back to the States for half a year or so to get reacquainted with family and friends. After nearly seven years in the turbulent Middle East, I definitely needed a break.

Just as I started to make travel arrangements, a former co-worker at the Voice of Hope told me that his employer, the U.S.-based Christian Broadcasting Network, was looking for an additional newswriter for their nightly English-language newscast. The program was broadcast over CBN's Middle East Television (METV), located in southern Lebanon. The offer, which included training in video editing, seemed challenging. I had never before worked in television. I joined the METV Jerusalem news bureau in June 1987, deciding I would put off my visit to America for at least a year.

The METV bureau employed Americans, Canadians,

and other Westerners who produced the nightly news in English. Lebanese Christians, along with a number of Israeli Arabs, Druze, and Palestinians, turned out an Arabic-language newscast. As I prepared my first news report for METV in early July, my mind kept wandering back to the early years of the television station and the role I played in keeping viewers glued to their sets in anticipation of the next . . . index card! Chuck Pollack had asked our Project Kibbutz team to come up with some nicely lettered index cards announcing the name of the new station (then under Voice of Hope ownership and called the "Star of Hope"), along with other pertinent information, such as where local Lebanese citizens could get their teeth fixed!

My teammates and I labored over the project with great love and care, knowing that our cards could potentially build up a great audience, ready for the soon-coming day when facilities were completed to actually start broadcasting television programs! Huddled together in Hagoshrim's recreation room, we were thrilled when our own personal index card made its debut on the TV screen.

Six years later, my voice was about to be heard nightly on the former Star of Hope, which had in the meantime become one of the most popular television stations in the region, reaching several million viewers in Lebanon, Syria, Israel, and Jordan.

As 1987 wore on, METV's nightly news reports contained increasing evidence of an impending explosion in the West Bank and Gaza Strip. The program carried details in April about the Palestinian firebombing of a Jewish car from the Samarian settlement of Alfei Menashe. The bomb left an Israeli woman dead and two of her children severely wounded, one of whom died in July. In response to the incident, angry Jewish settlers called for greater army protection along the roads. On August 2 we covered the slaying of a high-ranking Israeli military policeman, shot and killed by Palestinian gunmen who surrounded his car while it was stalled in heavy traffic in Gaza City. The entire Gaza Strip was subsequently sealed off for several days while a massive search was conducted for the killers.

Our main story during September was the formal ending of a nearly three-year state of war between Yasser Arafat's PLO fighters (who had slipped back into Lebanon—without their leader) and Lebanese gunmen belonging to the Shiite Amal militia. More than twenty-five hundred people, many of them Lebanese and Palestinian civilians, had been killed in the savage struggle, and some three thousand others wounded. The so-called "Camps War" began when the Lebanese Shiites, who felt threatened by the PLO's return to its former military positions in Beirut and south Lebanon, attacked Fatah outposts in several Palestinian refugee camps. The cease-fire agreement was a major psychological boost for the Palestinians, deeply embarrassed by the fierce inter-Arab bloodletting.

Also during September, we reported on a border infiltration attempt by a coalition of leftist Lebanese and Palestinian groups backed by Syria. Three Israeli soldiers were killed when their patrol came upon the infiltrators not far from Kibbutz Hagoshrim. Soon afterward an Israeli soldier, a Dutch convert to Judaism, was brutally murdered in the Galilee. In early October an Israeli secret service agent was shot and killed in the Gaza Strip by members of the Islamic Jihad movement. Within a week of the Gaza killing, a Jew walking through Jerusalem's Old City was stabbed to death by Palestinian assailants.

The most important pre-uprising morale booster for the Palestinians occurred on November 24. An airborne hang-glider, piloted by Syrian-backed Palestinians, sailed over the Israel/Lebanon border and quietly landed not far from Hagoshrim. The Palestinians made their way to a nearby army base where they killed six Israeli soldiers and wounded eight others before being killed themselves. The attack was hailed as a great victory by Palestinians both inside the territories and abroad. The once seemingly invincible Israeli Army, whose image was so badly tarnished in Lebanon, was proving to be quite vulnerable even inside of the Jewish state.

THE PALESTINIAN UPRISING

By early December almost any spark could have set off the violent explosion that occurred in the Gaza Strip on December 9. Three days before, an Israeli shopper was stabbed to death in Gaza City. The Strip had been a favorite shopping area for many Israeli bargain seekers, especially for those needing auto repairs and spare parts. The following evening, December 7, a private Israeli vehicle was involved in a traffic accident with a van carrying Palestinians from the Jabalya refugee camp. The accident left four of the van's Arab passengers dead.

Rumors soon spread that the Israeli vehicle had deliberately collided with the van in order to kill Palestinians in revenge for the December 6 stabbing (a charge the Israeli driver called absurd). Disturbances broke out on December 8 and large-scale rioting a day later. Israeli army reinforcements rushed in to join the vastly outnumbered soldiers who regularly patrolled the camp. One Palestinian was killed and sixteen others wounded before some semblance of calm was restored. The following day, December 10, violence spread to other parts of the Gaza Strip, and then to the West Bank. The uprising's flame had been lit.

The Palestinian revolt, often referred to as the *intifada* (an Arabic word meaning "shaking off" of Israeli rule), caught the army off guard. Israel's highly trained fighters, who fourteen years earlier had proved capable of repulsing a two-front surprise attack backed by the Soviet

Union, suddenly found themselves confronting not enemy soldiers, but young adults, teenagers, and sometimes even pre-teens armed mainly with stones, broken
bottles, and an occasional firebomb.

Of course such objects, along with building blocks
and sharp metal objects, could and did injure many Israeli
soldiers and civilians, and even killed a few. Yet it was
still morally and militarily impossible to fight Palestinian
civilians as one would the Syrian or Egyptian armies.
This fact frustrated both the soldiers and their commanders—all the way up to Israeli Defense Minister Yitzhak
Rabin, an old soldier himself who had served as prime
minister in the mid-1970s.

Rabin knew that Syria's Hafez al-Assad had not hesi-
tated to brutally murder some fifteen to twenty thousand
of his own citizens in 1982 when Muslim fundamentalists
staged a revolt in the northern Syrian city of Hama. He
remembered that King Hussein had ruthlessly crushed
a PLO rebellion against Jordanian rule in 1970, leaving
untold thousands of Palestinians dead. The Defense Minister publicly recalled that thousands of Palestinians had
died in inter-communal and PLO-Shiite battles in Lebanon during the 1980s. But none of these previous exam-
ples of how the Arab world deals with its internal disputes
mattered, said Rabin, because Israel was a democracy,
and a state heavily influenced by the moralistic principals
of Judaism. The ways and means of Israel's neighbors
would not be applied by Rabin or his superior, Prime
Minister Yitzhak Shamir.

Shamir's mid-December prediction that the uprising
would end soon failed to materialize. In fact, the rioting
intensified, and Palestinian casualties mounted. Few
world leaders called for the Palestinians to end their
violent revolt; many apparently felt it was justified. But
almost all condemned Israel for using live ammunition
against the protesters.

In the face of growing international criticism, Rabin

ordered new, less lethal riot-control measures in early January 1988, measures he hoped would reduce Palestinian deaths. The death toll from army gunfire did indeed drop. But to many observers, including Israeli critics, the new measures, which permitted beating stone and petrol-bomb throwers caught running away from pursuing soldiers, seemed to partially resemble the methods used by Israel's Arab neighbors.

Whatever his intentions, Rabin's "might and beatings" policy only led to a greater worldwide outcry against Israel, particularly after several Palestinians were beaten to death. The defense minister and senior army officers quickly realized that they had not sufficiently spelled out the limits of permitted physical force, leaving it up to young, often frustrated soldiers to decide how many blows were enough. The beatings policy was modified, and a number of soldiers were court-martialed for excessive use of force (most claimed they were only obeying orders). However, cases of Palestinians being physically abused by soldiers and security personnel continued long after the policy was changed.

Within several weeks of the uprising's outbreak, the PLO was taking charge of the popular rebellion by means of the Unified Leadership of the Palestinian Uprising, a coalition of Arafat's Fatah movement, the Syrian-aligned Popular and Democratic Front PLO groups, and the outlawed Palestine Communist Party. But it was apparent to Israeli leaders that the divided PLO was not the primary force behind the uprising, which had spread to all parts of the West Bank and Gaza Strip by mid-December. The main propellant was the Palestinians' own pent-up frustration and anger over their continuing statelessness, directed primarily at Israel, but also, at least privately, against the always-feuding PLO and Arab states who had failed over two decades to make any progress toward pushing the Israelis back into their pre-1967 borders.

ISLAM LEADS THE REVOLT

The first Palestinian groups to harness and direct these emotions were two Gaza Strip-based Muslim fundamentalist movements: Islamic Jihad and the Muslim Brotherhood Movement. The groups quickly declared the spreading revolt to be the latest phase of the jihad against Israel and began mobilizing support for the rebellion from mosques throughout the Strip.

The small but militant Islamic Jihad, founded in 1979 in the wake of the Islamic revolution in Iran, openly engaged in terror attacks against Israelis. The more moderate Muslim Brotherhood Movement, active in the Holy Land since the 1940s, had actually been aided by the Israeli government in its campaign to bring Islam to Gaza's Palestinians. The number of mosques in the strip had doubled to approximately 180 in the three years prior to the uprising, partially due to financial assistance from the Israeli government's Religious Affairs Ministry. Israeli analysts say the aid was handed out largely in an attempt to strengthen the Islamic movement in the area, thus hopefully weakening support for the more secular and leftist PLO.

Several Israeli experts on Islam warned officials that they were playing with fire in aiding the Muslim fundamentalists. In the end, they predicted, Islam would prove to be a more potent and intractable force than the PLO or other mostly secular Palestinian groups. The Islamic element had always loomed large in past Arab resistance to the state of Israel and could become the dominant force once again, especially in light of the Khomeini-inspired Muslim fundamentalist resurgence. They said Islamic militancy had been on the rise throughout the Middle East ever since the 1967 Six Day War. Nasser's humiliating defeat at the hands of Israel had dealt a severe blow to the Egyptian leader's basically secular pan-Arab movement, and to the idea that secularist governments could crush the Jewish "infidels." The experts noted that the Egyptian-based Muslim Brotherhood Movement, founded in 1928 and suppressed by Nasser, had never renounced its aim of destroying the Jewish state. The group had only declared a "truce" with Israel in order to educate the masses for the day when full-scale jihad was formally resumed.

Even though Palestinian Muslims almost all belong to the dominant Sunni wing of Islam, the Israeli experts warned that the Iranian Shiite Muslim revolution was having a deep impact on many Palestinians who admired the fervent religious devotion shown by Khomeini's followers. Palestinian Muslims were also thankful for the Iranian leaders' frequent pledges to confront the "Zionist occupation of the Muslim holy land"—with special mention always given to the sacred mosques in Jerusalem.

Many Palestinians were also encouraged by Khomeini's support for the Hizbullah, or Party of Allah, Movement which frequently attacks Israeli forces and their Lebanese allies in Israel's security zone. The movement, whose members are mostly poor Lebanese Shiites from the Bekaa Valley and South Beirut, had been set up after the 1982 war under the supervision of Khomeini's Iranian Revolutionary Guards. To show their support for the uprising, hundreds of Hizbullah fighters, backed by Shiite gunmen from the Amal Movement, simultaneously attacked eight South Lebanese Army outposts on December 21, 1987, the same day that one of the first uprising general strikes was being observed in the territories. Hizbullah and allied groups are widely believed to have been behind the kidnapping in Lebanon of several dozen foreigners, including Americans, during the latter half of the 1980s.

By mid-1988, the Fatah-dominated "Unified Leadership" realized they had strong competitors in the Islamic groups. They launched a campaign to convince local Palestinians that the PLO was as dedicated to Islamic values, including holy war, as any other liberation movement. Uprising leaders pointed out that many PLO officials, including Yasser Arafat, are observant Muslims in good standing. Arafat was one of the first foreign visitors to fly to Tehran after Khomeini seized power, they noted. On top of this, the PLO, at a 1981 Islamic summit conference held in Saudi Arabia, had enthusiastically endorsed a thirty-eight-nation proclamation of "full jihad" against Israel, with Arafat personally urging a "general mobilization for jihad."

The PLO leader repeated his support for jihad in a fiery, anti-American speech given in Khartoum, Sudan, on October 15, 1985 (just after the seizure of the *Achille Lauro*), saying that "the will of the Arab nation is the will of Allah, and therefore, the Arab nation will be victorious." Islam had always played an important role in the PLO's struggle to liberate Palestine, argued uprising leaders, noting that Islamic teachings were the soil from which much of the PLO's thinking and policies sprang.

AN ISLAMIC COVENANT

PLO leaders were particularly worried over the growing power of a militant offshoot of the Muslim Brotherhood Movement called the Islamic Resistance Movement. The group, formed shortly after the uprising began, is popularly known by the acronym *HAMAS,* Arabic for "zeal." And zeal the group has indeed displayed! HAMAS leaders formally adopted jihad against Israel as their central tenet. Islamic Resistance leaders stated clearly that they considered the Palestinian uprising as the first step in the renewed Islamic holy war to "liberate every part of Palestine," not just the West Bank and Gaza Strip.

In August 1988, HAMAS published its founding charter.

The forty-page document, which many saw as an Islamic Palestinian alternative to the PLO's official charter, was widely distributed in the territories. An audio cassette version was also handed out, mainly to illiterate Palestinians.

The HAMAS Covenant begins with several verses from the Koran which condemn the Jews for their unbelief in Allah. Former Egyptian Muslim Brotherhood leader Imam Hassan al-Bana is then quoted: "Israel will exist and continue to exist until Islam eliminates it, just as it eliminated what preceded it" (a reference to the defeat of the Crusader Kingdom).

Next comes the Covenant's main introduction, spelling out the structure and goals of the Islamic Resistance Movement which "links arms with all warriors of the jihad for the liberation of Palestine." It calls for "Arab and world Islamic assistance, support and commitment" in the effort to destroy Israel, because "our war against the Jews is a great and serious undertaking which requires mobilization of all resources . . . until the enemy is overthrown."

The Covenant's thirty-six articles detail the Movement's holy war program. Here are some of the HAMAS Covenant's main points:

Article 6 says HAMAS is "working to unfurl the banner of Allah over every inch of Palestine." It then goes on to promise that total Islamic control will not hurt non-Muslims, who will be "protected" by the Muslim authorities as they were down through the centuries.

Article 7 states that HAMAS is a "link in the chain of jihad against the Zionist invasion." It "looks forward to the fulfillment of Allah's promises in the not-too-distant future." The Article ends with a well-known Islamic *hadith,* or Muslim oral teaching, attributed to the prophet Muhammad: "The day will come when

Muslims will fight the Jews and kill them, to the degree that the Jew will hide behind rocks and trees which will call out to the Muslim and tell him, 'Servant of Allah, a Jew is hiding behind me. Come and kill him!' "

Article 8 endorses martyrdom in the name of the holy jihad: "Allah is the ultimate objective of HAMAS, his messenger Muhammad its touchstone, the Koran its constitution, jihad its path, and death for the sake of Allah its chief interest."

Article 11 spells out the official HAMAS position regarding the present and future status of the Holy Land: "The Islamic Resistance Movement considers that Palestine is Islamic *Waqf* (religious trust) land assigned to the Muslims until the end of time. It may not be renounced or conceded, whether in whole or in part . . . This is stipulated in the Islamic *Shira* (law). Palestine is to be treated like all lands forcibly conquered by the Muslims."

Article 13 states that "initiatives, so-called peaceful solutions, and international conferences to solve the Palestinian problem contradict the principles of the Islamic Resistance Movement. Renouncing any part of Palestine is equivalent to renouncing part of the religion . . . There is no solution to the Palestinian problem except through jihad. Initiatives, proposals, and international conferences are a waste of time and entirely useless. Such conferences are no more than the appointment of infidels as judges over Muslim land. When have infidels ever dealt justly with the faithful?" The article then paraphrases a relevant passage from the Koran: "The Jews and Christians will never be satisfied until you join their communities" (Sura of the Cow, 120). Israeli analysts say Articles 11 and 13 are direct condemnations of the PLO's phased program, which calls for a Palestinian state in the territories as the first step in the overthrow of the Jewish state.

Articles 14 through 19 call upon Muslim educators to instruct the Muslim masses about the need for all-out jihad against Israel. The articles also detail the role of women in the Islamic jihad. The Islamic mother is encouraged to stay at home and "educate her children to obey the religious precepts, as preparation for the task that awaits them in the holy struggle."

Articles 20 and 22 reveal the deep prejudices and anti-Semitism which form the basis of much of the continuing widespread Palestinian opposition to the existence of Israel in any part of "sacred Palestine." The former begins with a call for the "Islamic spirit" to "prevail throughout Muslim society, to counteract the scheming enemy with his Nazi conduct." It says that "Jewish Nazism" does not "spare women or children," and aims to destroy Palestinian livelihood.

Article 22 echoes more traditional forms of anti-Semitism, ironically in terms that mirror the very Nazi movement HAMAS tries to equate with modern Israel: "The enemies . . . have labored to amass astounding and influential material wealth, which has been exploited to realize their dream. They have used their wealth to gain control of the world media, news agencies, the press, broadcasting stations, etc." The Jews are said to have been "behind the French and Communist revolutions," and have "used their wealth to set up clandestine organizations to destroy society and serve the interests of Zionism." Such groups are said to include "the Freemasons, the Rotary, Lions Club, and Bnai-Brith. All these organizations engage in espionage and destruction."

After gaining control of the "imperialist states," the Jews are said to have "instigated World War I" in order to secure the Balfour Declaration from Britain. Next they "set up the League of Nations in order to rule over the world." The "world Jewish conspiracy" also "caused World War II" as a "prelude to setting up their state." After the war they "gave the instructions to establish the United Nations," again "in order to rule the world." The Jews "pull the strings of any war that is waged anywhere in the world," but will be finally overthrown when "Islam comes into its own." The fact that Israel is barely getting by financially—struggling with high infla- tion and unemployment—and that the United Nations regularly condemns Israel in the strongest terms seems to have somehow escaped the authors of the Islamic Resistance Covenant, along with the fact that the "Jewish- controlled world press" has been increasingly critical of Israel in recent years.

The final fourteen articles pledge HAMAS support for all "sister organizations" struggling to "liberate Pales- tine," including the PLO, which is called the movement's "father, brother, kinsman and friend." Surrounding Arab states are urged to "open their borders to the warriors of the jihad." The Jews must be defeated because they seek to "destroy society and values, to annihilate con- science and virtue, and to liquidate Islam." Egyptian lead- ers are condemned for making peace with Israel under the tutelage of the "imperialist, Crusader West," and Palestinians are warned that they shall "incur the wrath of Allah and end up in hell" if they do not fully support the holy jihad struggle.

During the first few months of the uprising, the PLO and Israeli authorities virtually ignored the HAMAS and Islamic Jihad movements. However by mid-1988, the Uni- fied Leadership was forced to take notice as the two movements, especially HAMAS, proved to have the sup- port of many Palestinians in the Gaza Strip, along with growing numbers in the West Bank.

Several general strike days called by HAMAS were

widely observed, and HAMAS pamphlets giving "guidance" to the uprising began to appear regularly alongside of frequently issued Unified Leadership communiques. Tension mounted between Islamic militants and PLO supporters, some of whom are secular Marxists, leading to violent clashes in Bethlehem and other locations. As HAMAS continued to increase in strength, Israeli officials banned the organization in May 1989 and arrested many of its leading figures.

THE WILL OF THE PEOPLE

Although a devout Muslim himself, Yasser Arafat probably was not very pleased by the results of a poll conducted by Bir Zeit University in the West Bank and published in the *Jerusalem Post* newspaper on April 14, 1988. Pollsters asked a scientifically selected cross-section of Palestinians what sort of state they wished to see established in place of Israeli military rule. The results showed that 59 percent of West Bank Palestinians want to be citizens of an Islamic theocratic state. Only 33 percent, or one in every three, supported the establishment of a democratic state, while the remaining 7 percent favored a state based on communist or socialist principles. The results would undoubtedly have been much more pro-Islamic if the poll had also been conducted in the heavily fundamentalist Gaza Strip.

My own informal survey of Palestinians in the territories agrees with the poll's findings. The average Palestinian Arab is a religiously observant Muslim who has little interest in democratic values—generally seen as Western, foreign concepts. Academic, business, and other leaders (often highly educated) hold a more pro-democracy view. They have seen Israel's freewheeling democracy in action and many of them would like to emulate it.

But the likes of Hanna Siniora, a Christian east Jerusalem newspaper publisher frequently interviewed by the
Western media, or Bethlehem Mayor Elias Freij, the leading Palestinian Christian politician; or even Faisal Hussein, a prominent and controversial PLO supporter who
is related to the former Palestinian Muslim leader Haj
Amin Husseini, have relatively little influence over the
average Palestinian in comparison to local Muslim
preachers or radical Palestinian leaders, such as Naif
Hawatmeh and George Habash. I think many of my Jerusalem-based colleagues would agree that peace between
Israel and the Palestinians probably could have been
negotiated long ago if these men, and especially the
two prominent Christians, were truly representative of
how the average Palestinian thinks.

The results of the Palestinian poll didn't surprise me
for another reason. Western-style democracy is not practiced in any other Arab nation, so why should it be the
centerpiece of any future Palestinian state, as the PLO
says it will be? It is true that most Arab countries have
legislative bodies whose members are elected by the
people, but the governments are actually run by un-
elected kings, sheiks, presidents, or by elected leaders
who run unopposed, such as Egyptian President Hosni
Mubarak. Why expect the "state of Palestine" to be any
different? Islamic fundamentalists calling for a theocratic
state and Israel's destruction won almost half the seats
in Jordanian parliamentary elections held in 1989 (the
first in twenty-two years), posing a threat to both King
Hussein's autocratic rule and Israel. Why expect more
moderate candidates to be elected in the West Bank
and Gaza Strip?

Media interest in the Palestinian uprising peaked in
March and April of 1988, just as I began working as a
regular reporter for CBS Radio. I was only on the job
one day when Khalil al-Wazir, widely known as *Abu Jihad,*

or "father of the holy war," was assassinated at his seaside home in Tunis. Wazir was said to have been the "military commander" of the uprising. The April 16 death of the second-ranking PLO leader—undoubtedly gunned down by Israeli agents—led to widespread and heavy Palestinian rioting. More than a dozen Palestinians lost their lives that day and scores more were injured.

The number of violent protests dropped substantially in the weeks following the killing, causing Israeli leaders to predict that the Palestinian revolt was coming to an end. However, violent clashes increased after King Hussein declared on July 31 that Jordan would no longer play any role in its West Bank, in effect cancelling his grandfather's annexation of the area. The move revived Palestinian hopes of establishing an independent state there and in the Gaza Strip.

Clashes escalated even further after Palestinian schools in Judea and Samaria, closed in January as the uprising spread to all parts of the territories, were re-opened by Israeli officials in the fall. Within several months the schools were shut once again. Israeli officials said they were being used by PLO-trained youth activists, the *Shabiba,* to recruit youngsters for violent anti-Israeli activities. Palestinian teachers conceded that this was indeed often the case. The schools gradually reopened in 1990 after many Palestinian parents pressured uprising leaders to order the Shabiba to do their recruiting somewhere else.

Although world attention was shifting to the American presidential elections, ongoing *glasnost* reforms in the Soviet Union, problems in China, and other topics, the Palestinian uprising against Israeli rule continued to receive substantial coverage by the world press throughout 1988. My reports for CBS Radio were almost exclusively about the ongoing revolt.

Violence at the Temple Mount in Jerusalem's Old City

was of special interest to my editors in New York. Many Fridays were spent with media colleagues on top of a building overlooking the Temple Mount plaza. The rooftop afforded us a clear view of the frequent demonstrations staged by Muslim worshipers who gathered for Friday prayer at the Islamic holy site. Our pictures and reports of Israeli police and paramilitary soldiers shooting tear gas, and occasionally rubber bullets, at protesting Palestinians featured prominently around the world.

As we waited each week for the prayer service to let out, I often felt like a spectator at the ancient Roman Coliseum—waiting to see if blood would flow. If it did, we had a story. If not, we went away feeling that we had wasted our time.

As the uprising moved into its second year, many increasingly weary Palestinians demanded that the PLO negotiate some sort of settlement to the Palestinian/Israeli dispute, despite the HAMAS warning that talking to Israel about peace was traitorous. This sentiment was echoed by many Israeli Jews, distressed by reports of soldiers who seemed to be losing their cool in putting down the ongoing rebellion. On the Arab side, the pressure came mainly from middle-class Palestinian businessmen who were suffering great financial loss as a result of the ongoing conflict.

Many shopkeepers secretly defied the uprising leadership's order to close down their businesses every day at noon. Like my Old City moneychanger, they quietly received customers in the afternoons and on general strike days behind shuttered exteriors, despite occasional threats and firebombings from young Shabiba activists. Several businessmen said privately they suspected that communist elements in the uprising leadership were out to crush the "merchant class" because it was "too close to Israel."

Some Palestinian shopowners were forced to sell out as the intifada, with its frequent general strikes called for by the Unified Leadership and HAMAS, continued. Their shops, including many in the so-called "Christian Quarter" of Jerusalem's Old City, were often sold to Islamic fundamentalist businessmen offering generous sums of money. Most of the Christian Quarter's businesses are now owned by Muslims, who comprise about half of the Quarter's resident population.

The Reagan administration was obviously not pleased that its main Mideast ally was portrayed nightly on American television screens as an apparently oppressive military regime ruthlessly killing and wounding unarmed women and children. While continuing to pledge basic American support for Israel, the State Department nonetheless joined Britain, France, China, the Soviet Union, and many other nations in frequent denunciations of Israeli anti-uprising practices. At the same time, Secretary of State George Shultz rushed off to the Middle East to try and get Palestinian/Israeli peace negotiations off the ground. But everyone knew that such talks would have to wait until after the November 1988 U.S. and Israeli general elections.

"PEACE . . . PEACE . . ."

As election victors George Bush and Yitzhak Shamir busily put together their new governments, Yasser Arafat convened the Palestine National Council in Algiers. The PNC meeting was attended by several of Arafat's main PLO rivals, including George Habash and Naif Hawatmeh. Despite some bitter arguments between members of the Syrian-backed factions and Arafat's Fatah supporters, a declaration was approved proclaiming the "establishment of the State of Palestine in the Israeli-occupied territories, with holy Jerusalem as its capital."

Representatives of the "state" would negotiate peace with Israel based on "all relevant United Nations resolutions," presumably including Resolutions 242 and 338 which call for an Israeli withdrawal from areas occupied in 1967. However, the negotiations would be "based on Resolution 191," the original 1947 U.N. partition plan. In other words, the peace talks would begin with the Palestinians demanding that Israel withdraw not only from Judea, Samaria, and the Gaza Strip, but from adjacent areas allotted to the proposed Arab state which were captured by Israel in 1948. The proclamation added that all Palestinians who fled their homes in 1948 and 1967, and their offspring, have a right to return to them.

Exactly forty-one years after local Palestinian leaders and the larger Arab world completely rejected the United Nations partition plan and launched a war of annihilation against the newly declared Jewish state, the PLO was finally ready to accept the two-state solution. The move, said Arafat, signaled a Palestinian recognition of the existence of Israel. Habash disagreed, telling reporters that no such recognition was intended by PNC delegates. He pointed out that no move had been initiated to amend the PLO's Founding Charter, which calls for Israel's total destruction. Speaking to reporters in Paris one month later, Arafat declared the charter to be "inoperative." However, Habash and other PLO leaders again demurred, denouncing the statement as so much hot air. They pointed out that Article 33 states that only a two-thirds vote by PNC delegates can change any part of the PLO's charter.

The Palestine National Council's acceptance of negotiations based on U.N. resolutions was welcomed throughout the world, although most western democracies were not enthusiastic about the statehood declaration. Arafat's subsequent announcement in December that he would order a halt to all PLO terror attacks—which led the

Reagan administration to begin official talks with the PLO—was also hailed by governments everywhere, many of whom had already "recognized" the nonexistent Palestinian state.

The reaction to these events in Israel was hardly enthusiastic. Prime Minister Shamir was joined by his coalition Labor Party colleagues in denouncing the PNC declaration of Palestinian statehood. Shamir said the declaration was designed to put a halt to the Arab/Israeli peace process since the Palestinian side had declared a final outcome in advance that was totally unacceptable to Israel. The prime minister maintained that if *Israel* did the same thing—by announcing for example that it would annex the territories no matter what was decided during peace negotiations—the world would be in an uproar. But when the *Palestinians* declare statehood as the final outcome, the world overwhelmingly accepts and even welcomes the move. Israeli leaders also rejected the restatement of the official PLO position that all Palestinian refugees and their progeny have a right to return to Israel. Most Israelis agree that an influx of even a portion of what could be several million Palestinians would spell the end of the Jewish state.

Israeli officials and political analysts said the PNC declaration did not necessarily mean that the PLO had given up its goal of destroying Israel. In fact, Arafat's second in command, Salah Khalaf, better known as Abu Iyad, said on December 18, 1988, that the PLO's phased plan was still operative. He told the Kuwaiti newspaper *al-Anba* that the PNC statehood declaration meant "First a small state, and then with the help of Allah, it will be made large and expand to the east [i.e., Jordan], west, north and south." He told the paper that he was "interested in the liberation of Palestine, step by step." Khalaf reiterated this position on January 1, 1991, during a news conference in Amman, Jordan, saying, "We accept the formation of the Palestinian state on part of Palestine, on the Gaza Strip and the West Bank. Now we must start from that part, and we will liberate Palestine inch by inch."

Arafat's statement on terrorism was received skeptically by Israeli officials, and even by many left-wing politicians who support negotiations with the PLO. Government leaders pointed out that Arafat pledged to continue the armed struggle against Israel, meaning armed terror bands would not halt their frequent attempts to try and penetrate Israel's borders from Lebanon and elsewhere. The PLO leader maintained that such assaults were not terrorism but legitimate acts of self-defense. Attacks by PLO underground cells against Jews both inside Israel and in the territories would also continue, said Arafat, as would the PLO-led uprising. Israeli officials stated that these positions would hardly help move the peace process forward.

The "armed struggle" did in fact continue during 1989. Palestinian gunmen, mainly from Syrian-backed PLO factions, repeatedly tried to infiltrate into Israel from Lebanon, with several attempts also made from Jordanian and Egyptian territory. Several of the actions were undertaken by Arafat's Fatah group. A heavily armed, five-man Fatah squad was intercepted after crossing into Israel from the Negev desert on December 5. A number of Israeli soldiers were killed during the various infiltration attempts, as were most of the Palestinian infiltrators. Underground PLO cell members killed or wounded several Jews inside Israel, and others in the territories. Bombs were placed in various places injuring a number of Jews, and forests were burned by PLO-paid arsonists.

The worst terror attack inside Israel since the 1978 coastal road bus massacre occurred on July 6. A Palestinian man from the Gaza Strip forced an Israeli bus off the main Tel Aviv/Jerusalem highway, killing sixteen

Jews, including two Canadians, and wounding himself and over two dozen other passengers. The Palestinian saboteur said he was a supporter of the fundamentalist HAMAS Movement and had decided to steer the bus down a steep ravine in order to contribute to the jihad struggle.

Meanwhile, the Palestinian uprising went on, with the total Arab death toll reaching five hundred by midsummer. More than ten thousand others had been wounded, many by rubber or plastic bullets. Several dozen Israeli Jews had been killed by Palestinians, a majority of them civilians. Hundreds of others had been injured, many of them badly burned by petrol bombs. Thousands of Palestinians had been jailed, and more than sixty deported to Lebanon. Many of those imprisoned had not been formally charged with a crime or undergone trial. Israeli officials said public trials would lead to the revelation of sensitive security information. Palestinian leaders shot back that many prisoners were jailed for purely political reasons, adding that some had been tortured.

Israeli settlers could often be found in the news as the uprising rumbled along. Many took the law into their own hands to counter what they charged was inadequate protection by the Israeli Army. Settlers' cars were often the target of stones and petrol bombs, leaving hundreds injured and several dead. The Jewish settlers' reactions—or what the government and army leaders at times termed overreactions—became a hot Israeli political topic, especially after some settlers went on the rampage in Arab villages to avenge local Palestinian attacks.

Yasser Arafat was not the only one talking about peace in the midst of the continuing violence. The new Israeli National Unity Government put forward a Four-Point Peace Plan in May 1989. The proposal, drawn up largely by Defense Minister Rabin, featured Palestinian elections to choose representatives who would negotiate peace with Israel. Only Palestinians who live in the territories would be eligible to run, meaning the PLO could not field candidates from abroad. The elected Palestinians would also play a part in governing the territories while peace talks continued. The Israeli initiative also called for a public reaffirmation of the Camp David Peace Accords by the United States and Egypt, an official end to the formal state of war and economic boycott against Israel by all other Arab nations, and an international effort to resolve the Palestinian refugee problem.

The PLO basically rejected the Israeli plan, which was endorsed by the new Bush administration. The move was part of a growing PLO shift back to more hard-line positions which prevailed before the November 1988 PNC conference. In August 1989, Fatah delegates convened in Tunis to discuss the ongoing uprising and the PLO's "peace strategy." Fatah delegates approved a final resolution that called for "intensifying and escalating armed action and all forms of struggle to eliminate the Zionist Israeli occupation of our occupied Palestinian land." The State Department said the resolution raised "questions about the PLO's commitment to accommodation, understanding and peace."

Prime Minister Shamir's Likud party concluded that the PLO was officially withdrawing from the comparatively moderate positions espoused by Arafat the previous winter. Several Likud leaders, including Housing Minister David Levy and Industry Minister Ariel Sharon, said that the occupied Palestinian land mentioned in the Fatah resolution undoubtedly included *all* of present-day Israel along with the West Bank and Gaza Strip. If so, the largest and most moderate wing of the PLO was apparently openly re-embracing the PLO charter's call for the total destruction of the Jewish state. The two ministers pressed Shamir to abandon his elections proposal, saying it would only lead to a Palestinian state headed by Arafat.

To many observers, including myself, the Palestinian uprising didn't seem to be bringing the prospects of a Palestinian state any closer, as most Palestinians originally hoped it would. In fact, just the opposite was the case as far as I could tell. Every bullet that entered a Palestinian body created that much more hatred for Israel. The destruction of several hundred homes, where Palestinians charged with various crimes lived; the deportation of more than sixty intifada leaders; the frequent curfews and "search and arrest" operations; the armed Jewish settlers who sometimes seemed to be aching for a fight with their Arab neighbors—all this and more was reducing Palestinian "goodwill" toward Israel, which wasn't exactly bubbling over even before the uprising began.

Israeli endearment toward the Palestinian Arabs was certainly not reinforced by such acts as the firebombing of an Israeli bus near Jericho, which left a mother and several of her children burned to death; the slaying of three elderly Jews in downtown Jerusalem by a knife-wielding Palestinian yelling, *"Allahu akbar!* Allah is great!"; the knifing to death of at least ten other Jews, mostly in Jerusalem; the torching of forests, fields, factories, and hundreds of automobiles; or the destruction of the Jerusalem-bound bus. Such violent actions left people on both sides much more polarized, with the Israelis less willing to hand back land to the Palestinians than they were before the uprising began in December 1987.

Frankly, I have often wondered if a total break in Israeli-Palestinian relations is not exactly what the PLO is striving for. Surely Arafat and his followers know that urging Palestinians to attack Israelis and their possessions only leads to harsher Israeli countermeasures, which in turn leads to greater Palestinian bitterness and hatred toward Israel. This results in more Palestinian attacks, and then in further Israeli countermeasures, ad nauseam. The Israelis—historically the victims of frequent persecution and attempted genocide—will never seriously negotiate with someone in the process of attacking them, no matter what he says to the press in Paris or elsewhere. Was Arafat too thick to grasp this, or did he have other motives for urging on the violent uprising?

Many Israelis argued that a major bloodbath would result if their army simply pulled out of the territories, leaving rival Palestinian factions to fight it out. This argument seemed to gain credibility as the uprising entered its second year.

Internal Arab bloodletting, widespread in the Arab revolts of 1936–1939, surfaced once again. In fact by the middle of 1989, one out of every two Palestinian deaths was at the hands of fellow Arabs. More than one hundred Palestinians, or about one in five killed during the uprising up until then, had been slain by Arab executioners. The number jumped to around 150 by the end of the year, and 250 by mid-1990. The deaths were for the most part extremely brutal, with axes and knives the usual weapons used. Hands and heads were often severed along with other body parts. Decapitated bodies, some naked, were strung up on telephone poles to act as a warning to anyone who would dare cooperate with Israel. By 1990 a majority of Palestinian uprising deaths were from intercommunal killings.

The dead, in what journalists quickly dubbed the "intra-fada," were usually accused of collaborating with Israeli authorities. My own research and that of other journalists found that only a portion actively cooperated with the authorities to help put an end to the uprising. A few were killed because they expressed reservations over the direction the intifada took; others were murdered by personal enemies using the cover of the popular revolution to mask their crimes. Still others were slain by members of rival Palestinian groups waging a war to gain local hegemony. For some, "collaboration" meant they sold drugs or engaged in prostitution, crimes said to weaken the Palestinian community and thus strengthen Israeli control. Several Christian pastors in Bethlehem and elsewhere were accused of collaboration because they refused to endorse Palestinian violence. Toward the end of 1989 the local uprising leadership, which had earlier echoed Arafat in applauding "collaborator" killings, issued new "guidelines" to "popular committees" in order to reduce the number of killings.

YOUTHFUL HEROES

Media coverage of the uprising during its first two years often focused on the many Palestinian children and teenagers killed or injured by army gunfire. Human rights groups said more than 150 children, most of them in their teens, were shot dead or killed by tear gas by the end of 1989. The army put the number at less than half that, saying many of those counted as having died from tear gas inhalation were not even exposed to such gas.

Army investigators pointed out that since all those killed in the uprising, especially children, are hailed as "martyrs and heroes," with their pictures plastered all over local walls, the incentive to blame any death on Israel is great, even if they result from illnesses or other causes. Another incentive, said Israeli analysts, is the money which the PLO pays to any family who "offers up its sons and daughters to the glorious cause," as one uprising leaflet put it.

Israeli Army commanders insisted that children were often deliberately put in the front lines of violent demonstrations, since intifada leaders knew that soldiers had orders to try and avoid hitting them. Several uprising leaflets did encourage children to join in the fray, and Palestinian youngsters usually seemed to be in the forefront of violent confrontations which I witnessed.

Israeli officials charged that human rights groups and Western aid agencies operating in the territories naively believe anything told them by Palestinians. Such groups should realize that the uprising is another form of Arab warfare against Israel, they said, adding that propaganda is a vital part of any modern conflict.

I can't judge the accuracy of accounts about incidents I have no firsthand knowledge of. But I have found over the years that many Palestinians do have a tendency to exaggerate, especially when reporting alleged Israeli abuses. Most are aware that published or broadcast reports of Israeli brutality harm Israel whether the charges are completely true, exaggerated, or totally false. Beyond this, Arab society as a whole is inclined toward hyperbole, as noted by many Westerners who have closely studied the Arab world. Certainly Palestinian terror groups have shown this tendency. Attacks that end in the deaths of most or all of the terrorists are usually labeled as huge successes, with the number of victims killed greatly exaggerated. An example of this was Abul Abbas' claim that his men killed five hundred Israeli soldiers during a raid on Israeli beaches in 1990, when in fact no Israelis were killed.

As the 1980s came to an end, the Arab-Muslim/Israeli dispute seemed as intractable as ever. Syria, Libya, and non-Arab Iran continued to speak of the total destruction of the "Zionist entity." Syrian President Assad was busy building up his formidable army—and reportedly stockpiling chemical weapons capable of devastating the tiny state of Israel. Iraq had tested a new long-range missile in December 1989 and was known to be producing chemical weapons—with the help of Western, and especially German, companies—and seeking to acquire or produce nuclear bombs. Iran was waging war against Israeli forces in Lebanon through its Lebanese Shiite Hizbullah proxies. Libya, also reportedly producing nerve gas and acquiring long-range missiles, was pouring money into various terror groups operating in Lebanon and elsewhere.

Jordan, Saudi Arabia, and other more moderate Arab nations spoke of the possibility of accommodation with the Jewish state, but did so while acquiring the most advanced weapons systems available on the world market. Only Egypt had actually made peace with Israel, but it was a cold peace, at best. Some Palestinian groups spoke of a "two-state" solution to the conflict, but many others—both secular Palestinians and Islamic fundamentalists—said the cremation of Israel was, and would always be, their only goal. As the decade ended war, not peace, seemed to be on the horizon. And all agreed that the next major Arab/Israeli war would probably make the previous ones look like mere military exercises.

CHAPTER 10

THAT
ELUSIVE
PEACE

To say the least, the first year of the new decade strongly reinforced the perception I had at the end of 1989: the Arab/Israeli conflict was once again moving more in the direction of war than peace.

Attempts to implement Israel's peace plan stalled after the collapse of the National Unity Government in March 1990. The emergence in June of a right-wing coalition government headed by Yitzhak Shamir seemingly further reduced the prospects of peace between Palestinians and Israelis. America's dialogue with the PLO was suspended following Yasser Arafat's refusal to renounce a raid onto Israeli beaches in May by heavily armed gunmen belonging to Abul Abbas' PLO faction. American Secretary of State James Baker expressed frustration with both the PLO and Israel, telling Congress that both parties could "call us" when they are "serious about peace." Even friends who had ridiculed my concerns as vastly overblown began to believe that another Middle East war was brewing when Saddam Hussein threatened in early April to wipe out half of Israel with chemical weapons.

"I swear to Allah that we will let our fire eat half of Israel if it tries to wage anything against Iraq," Saddam said on Baghdad radio, after charging that Israel was planning to use nuclear weapons against him. Since Israel had threatened to do no such thing (although government leaders had several times warned all Arab countries that a chemical attack upon Israel would be met by a response "one hundred times greater"), officials and military analysts began to worry seriously what Saddam was up to.

The ruthless "butcher of Baghdad" had used chemical weapons against his own Kurdish citizens and Iranian soldiers. He had also personally killed or ordered dead some of his opponents and a number of his closest friends and advisors. Was he actually preparing to launch deadly chemical missiles at Tel Aviv or other Israeli cities?

Did Saddam really believe that Israel planned to attack his chemical weapons and rocket-making facilities? Did he fear a repeat of Israel's 1981 air force raid that destroyed a nuclear reactor under construction near Baghdad?

Several days before issuing his threat, the Iraqi strongman stood beside Yasser Arafat in Baghdad, reviewing a military parade in honor of "Land Day," which annually commemorates the killing of six Arabs by Israeli policemen in 1976. At the parade, Saddam pledged to help secure the "liberation of Palestine," telling Arafat, "I can see the day when I and you, hand in hand, march to victory in Palestine." The PLO leader responded enthusiastically, telling Saddam that "we will enter al-Quds [the Islamic name for Jerusalem, meaning "the holy"] victorious and will raise our flag on its walls. You will enter with me, riding on your white stallion."

More ominously for Israel, Arafat pledged that Iraqi long-range missiles would be used to liberate holy Palestine. The moderate-sounding peace pronouncements of 1988 were no longer being uttered by the PLO leader; they were now replaced with more traditional calls to war.

Saddam stepped up his war rhetoric in June 1990,

saying he would launch his missiles if Israel bombed targets in any Arab country, not only his own. American intelligence reports said Iraq was building about fifty missile sites within range of Israel. The chances of an armed clash were enhanced by a growing military and political alliance between Iraq and Jordan. Joint ground and air squadrons were set up by the two countries in the spring. Israel warned that any significant movement of Iraqi forces into Jordan would be considered an act of war.

Israeli leaders expressed alarm over the increasingly hostile Arab rhetoric, saying it was ominously reminiscent of statements made just before the 1967 and 1973 Arab/Israeli wars. The Israeli government took the repeated Iraqi war threats quite seriously, with Defense Minister Moshe Arens noting that "what the Iraqi dictator has threatened to do in the past, he has done."

Saddam's war rhetoric sent renewed shivers down Israeli spines when Iraq invaded its southern neighbor, Kuwait, on August 2. Israeli analysts said the move proved that the ruthless "butcher" is not afraid to use his enormous military power against perceived regional enemies, be they Arab, Iranian, or Israeli.

Saddam's attempts to link his invasion and annexation of Kuwait with the Arab/Israeli dispute gained momentum in October, after seventeen Palestinians were killed by Israeli security forces on the Temple Mount.

Israeli officials responded to Iraq's "linkage" strategy by pointing out that Israel had occupied the West Bank, Gaza Strip, Sinai Peninsula, and Golan Heights in a war of self-defense. The Arabs had used the areas captured since 1948 to launch repeated attacks against Israel, they noted, and were massing large armies and equipment there when the Six Day War broke out. Kuwait, on the other hand, posed no territorial threat to Iraq.

By popular demand, the Israeli government decided

in early October to distribute gas masks and other protective equipment to all Israeli citizens—Jewish and Arab—and to foreigners living or studying in Israel. The widely publicized campaign helped calm fears of an Iraqi gas attack, while virtually killing off what remained of dwindling tourist traffic to Israel.

The Palestinian uprising continued during 1990, but at a more subdued pace than in the previous two years. There was a brief upsurge of clashes between Israeli soldiers and Palestinians in May after an apparently deranged Israeli civilian shot and killed eight Palestinian workers near Tel Aviv, and in October following the Temple Mount tragedy.

The overall Palestinian death toll from Israeli army gunfire reached around seven hundred by the end of 1990 (figures vary depending upon whom you ask), with more than forty dead from Israeli civilian fire. Palestinians had killed about forty Israeli civilians and twenty-two soldiers and policemen. The Associated Press said 324 Palestinians had been killed by fellow Arabs by the end of the year as the "intra-fada" intensified.

The HAMAS Movement picked up additional Palestinian support as the year wore on, especially after Saddam's calls for holy war in August and September, and after the violence at Islam's third holiest site in October. In April, HAMAS leaders demanded that their movement be allotted up to half of the seats in the Palestinian National Council. PLO leaders rejected the demand. Following clashes in the summer between PLO and HAMAS supporters, the PLO was forced to recognize HAMAS' growing appeal by agreeing to honor all HAMAS-called general strike days.

Widespread popular Palestinian support for Saddam Hussein dealt further heavy blows to the already dwindling prospects for progress in the Arab/Israeli peace process. Israeli peace activists expressed open shock at the depth of Palestinian support for the Iraqi leader, with some saying that the clock apparently had been turned back to the days when Israel's total destruction was the Palestinians' chief goal.

Yasser Arafat said on September 3 that it was natural for the Palestinian masses to support Saddam. "To those who ask about the Palestinian position, we ask 'Where is Israel in this war?' We can only be in the camp hostile to Israel and its imperialist allies who have mobilized their sophisticated war machine," said Arafat in an interview with the PLO's news agency in Tunis.

SOVIET FLOODGATES SWING OPEN

Largely as a result of fast-moving changes in the Soviet Union, Soviet Jews began pouring into Israel in large numbers during 1990—to the great dismay of Arafat, Saddam Hussein, and the rest of the Arab world. Israeli officials said more than one million Soviet Jews had applied for permission to immigrate to the Jewish homeland by mid-1990. About 185,000 arrived in Israel during the year.

Arab leaders, including Egypt's Hosni Mubarak, met in Baghdad in May and issued a statement condemning "the transfer of Jews to Palestine and the other occupied Arab territories." Israeli leaders said less than half of 1 percent of immigrating Soviet Jews were settling in the territories (around 2 percent if east Jerusalem Jewish suburbs are included). They said the summit statement reflected Arab anger that any Jews at all were immigrating to Israel, or to "Palestine," as the Arab leaders put it.

The original "Zionist invasion" began with Russian Jews moving to Palestine, said various Arab leaders as the new aliyah wave gathered momentum.[1] Rising Jewish numbers will lead to stepped-up Israeli attempts to extend Zionist control over the entire Middle East, they maintained, and therefore the Arabs must prepare for war to oppose "expansionist Zionist threats." Yasser Arafat "proved" this point after a special U.N. debate held in Geneva in May 1990, by holding up an Israeli ten-agorot coin (worth about five cents) that he claimed contains a "map" outlining Zionist plans to conquer Jordan, Lebanon, parts of Syria, Iraq, and Saudi Arabia. Israeli coinmakers said the supposed map was in reality the eroded contours of an ancient Jewish coin surrounding a seven-branch menorah.

THE PARIAH STATE

With the apparent ending of the East-West Cold War and the winding down or cessation of conflicts in much of the rest of the world, the Arab/Israeli dispute continues to simmer, threatening once again to boil over into a full-scale war. World opinion seems to have concluded that Israel is largely to blame for the continuing peace impasse. Polls show that support for the Jewish state declined in all Western nations as the Palestinian uprising wore on, although east European nations, newly released from the Kremlin's iron grip, bucked the tide by restoring long-severed relations with Israel.

While obviously welcomed by Israeli leaders, the east European moves cannot even begin to compensate for the erosion of west European, and even more importantly, American support for the small east Mediterranean country. Israeli businessmen trade mainly with western Europe and the United States, and American financial aid has kept the Israeli economy—heavily drained by huge military expenditures—from total bankruptcy.

According to several surveys taken in the U.S. and elsewhere, Christian evangelicals continue to over-whelmingly support Israel's right to exist. But the traditional feeling of warmth and sympathy for the Jewish state is declining. The rise in recent years of dominion, or reconstructionist, theology which generally reflects the "replacement" view that the church has completely taken over Israel's role in God's plan for humanity, has added significantly to the growing evangelical move away from Israel. Polls show that mainline Protestant and Roman Catholic support, never as strong as evangelical backing, has eroded even further. Critical voices are also heard more and more in the worldwide Jewish community, always Israel's staunchest supporters.

The tiny Jewish state, so popular in the West and with much of the church in the 1950s and '60s, is seemingly becoming a pariah, an embarrassment, even to her most tenacious Christian and Jewish admirers. Have events in the Middle East over the last decade finally proved that Christian backers of Israel are way out of line, as many dominionists and others maintain, or do her supporters still have a leg to stand on?

My answer to that question should be obvious by now. Jacob's children have a right to live in the mostly Muslim Middle East, I believe, on moral, legal, and biblical grounds. Yet supporters of this contention must be the first to acknowledge that Israeli Jews are human beings, prone to the same sins and selfishness as the rest of humanity—including Christians. Far too much has been expected from Israel by her supporters, and even by many detractors. She has too often in the past been placed on a pedestal and judged by unrealistically high standards.

But now, in my opinion, the nation of Israel is being driven into the ground by an overly critical world—a world still smelling of the smoke of Jewish bodies burning in the ovens of Christian Europe.

It seems to me that many Christians and Jews, especially Americans, have held an overly sentimental view of Israel and have, therefore, been disappointed when Israelis have not lived up to preconceived expectations. Some Israeli Jews have hoped that Israel would be a "light to the Gentiles," but most have no ambition but to survive in a hostile world. Israel's behaving like a typical Mideast nation should surprise no one. Israel is, after all, a nation in the Middle East—one whose very right to exist is constantly questioned. Still, Israeli self-criticism, self-restraint, and human rights standards are far ahead of other regional states, such as Syria, Lebanon, Iraq, and Libya.[2]

THE ANCESTRAL FAITHS

Of course, Israel's friends cannot and should not ignore the fact that there were Arabs living in the Holy Land before large-scale Jewish immigration began in the 1880s. Most Palestinians, especially those who fled or were expelled from their homes during the war of 1947–49 and again in '67, are still suffering today. The "Palestinian problem" will not go away by simply denying that it exists, or by ignoring it.

Yet friend and foe alike should also be prepared to concede that there may *not* be a man-made solution to the intense Arab/Israeli conflict. This is basically the conclusion I have come to after a decade of studying the conflict, not in some classroom, but in the places where it is played out every day. I've discovered, as have others before me, that the dispute is basically *religious* at its core.

Most of the books I have read on the Arab/Israeli conflict either play down or ignore the intense religious struggle at the center of the dispute. The average author tends to make the mistake of seeing many of the leading Jewish and Arab actors as largely *secular* people. While this may be true on the surface, the fact is that Jewish-Israeli society and thinking is heavily influenced by Judaism, as Arab society is overwhelmingly by Islam. Yitzhak Shamir, like other Israeli prime ministers before him, may not have a deep personal faith, as may also be true of Hafez Assad and King Hussein. But all are heavily influenced by the religious concepts held dear by many, if not most, of their citizens.

While Israeli Jews are definitely less religious overall than their Arab cousins, Judaism still plays a significant role in people's everyday lives. Israelis are married and buried by orthodox rabbis. Most major holidays such as Passover, Rosh Hashanah (the Jewish New Year), Yom Kippur, and the Feasts of Weeks (Pentecost) and Tabernacles are straight out of the Bible. Many of Israel's most popular folk songs, sung enthusiastically by even the most atheistic Jews, come from biblical passages. It is no coincidence that most major state ceremonies, including military inductions, are held at the Western Wall. Having lived in Israel for over a decade, I can attest that Judaism's influence here is far greater than most casual observers might imagine.

Islam plays an enormous role in the lives of Muslim Arabs, whether they are deeply observant or not. Islamic holy days are national holidays. Allusions to the Koran pepper everyday speech. The call to prayer from tall mosque minarets is a familiar sound to all Arabs, from cradle to grave.

Islam is not only the religion of most Arabs; it is their shared cultural heritage. The dominant Mideast religion has also been the major factor in the Arab world's rejection of the Jewish state of Israel. Several Arab leaders have reportedly told their Western counterparts that their efforts to make peace with Israel have been greatly constricted by the religious beliefs and prejudices of their Muslim citizens. On the other hand, basically nonreligious leaders like Saddam Hussein have often found Islam quite useful in overcoming internal and external affairs.

It is not only modern analysts who underestimate the religious dimension of the Arab/Israeli dispute. Many of the earliest Jewish immigrants, familiar with the latest medical and agricultural methods, naively believed that local Arabs would welcome their move to Palestine, or at least not resist it. The largely secular and socialistic northern European and Russian immigrants simply did not have an adequate understanding of Islam, although they were more familiar with replacement theology in Christianity.

At the same time many Zionist leaders, preoccupied with the Jewish need for a homeland in the face of vicious anti-Semitic pogroms, down-played or ignored the fact that hundreds of thousands of Arabs, most of them devout Muslims, were already living in the Holy Land.

While the role of the Jew in God's economy is still debated by Christians, the Koran leaves no room to doubt that Allah is finished with them as a sovereign people. As I have already mentioned, it was inconceivable to Muslims that the eternally subjugated dhimmi Jews would once again have control over Jerusalem. If Islam were required to wage jihad against the Christian Crusaders until they were pushed out of Jerusalem, then certainly war would be doubly waged against any Jewish attempt to regain sovereignty over *al-Quds*. This was, and remains, the root cause of the decades-old violent Arab resistance to a Jewish state near the center of the Muslim world.

Had Islam not mandated such resistance, and had replacement theology not been so dominant in the ancient established churches of the region, the Arabs would have undoubtedly been more sympathetic toward early Jewish immigrants fleeing violent pogroms. Still, one could not have expected them to welcome unconditionally the arrival of hundreds of thousands of foreign Jews, even though all realized that Judaism sprang up in the Holy

Land. After centuries of rule from Istanbul, nobody was too excited at the prospect of being a minority citizen of a Jewish state.

And yet, some empathy for incoming Jews would have at least been a possibility if cultural prejudices, based on religious biases, had not been so strong. Many historians have written that Arab hostility against the proposed Jewish national home was greatly enhanced by British and Jewish insensitivity and arrogance toward the Arabs of Palestine. There is little doubt that European Christians and Jews saw their way of life as superior to that of local Arabs—an understandable view in light of Europe's relatively advanced social, political, and health systems.

Still, we must remember that Arabs first expressed strong opposition to the proposed Jewish state before Britain had issued the Balfour Declaration or had any role in Palestine, and before many Jews had moved there. It was the *idea* of a sovereign Jewish state, more than Jewish or British actions, that produced loathing in many Palestinian Arabs. Actual encounters with British officials, soldiers and immigrating Jews only moderately enhanced the strong antagonism toward Christians and Jews that was already deeply inbred in most Muslims.

Palestinians and other Arabs argue that the League of Nations had no right to vote a special status for Palestine when affirming the San Remo mandates for creating sovereign states in the Middle East. I strongly disagree. Palestine was sacred to Muslims and Christians precisely because it was first holy to Jews. Islamic Arab warriors occupied the Holy Land by force, ending Christian control of such ancient historic sites as the Temple Mount and Abraham's Tomb. Centuries earlier, the Jews had largely been pushed out—against their will—by the Romans. The League of Nations rightly recognized that the Holy Land is a unique place, still sacred to millions of Jews and Christians, as well as to Muslims. Members of the two older religions—especially the wandering, persecuted Jews—legitimately expected the League of Nations to treat Palestine differently. If Muslims had conceded that the Holy Land demanded special treatment (as did Lebanon), the Jewish/Arab strife of the twentieth century might have been averted.

While the new immigrants didn't speak often of their people's ancestral religion, the well-established and overwhelmingly observant Jewish communities of Jerusalem, Hebron, and elsewhere had lived and worshiped in the Holy Land for centuries. Local Arabs certainly knew that religious Jews still regarded Jerusalem as the centerpiece of Judaism, even if the faithful had been scattered to the remotest parts of the earth. Many must have realized that Zionism was not a new Jewish movement, but only a new expression of a very old Jewish yearning—to return to the hills and valleys of the Promised Land, *Eretz Yisrael.*

EVERLASTING LAND COVENANT

The religious struggle over the Lord's land centers on who has the God-given right to possess it. Polls show that an overwhelming majority of Israeli Jews, even most who don't regularly attend synagogue, believe in the existence of the God of Israel. Many of these are convinced that the Bible teaches that God gave them title to the land forever. Muslims, and most Christians who subscribe to replacement theology, strongly disagree. As we saw in the Muslim fundamentalist HAMAS charter, the Holy Land is seen by observant Muslims as part of the Islamic heritage forever bequeathed to Islam by Allah. The Roman Catholic and Eastern Orthodox churches have traditionally viewed the land as a Christian heritage, as demonstrated during the Crusades.[3]

What does the Bible say? In Genesis 17, God promises

to give Abraham and his descendants the land of Canaan for "an everlasting possession" (v. 8). He does so after telling Abraham that he will be "the father of many nations" (vv. 5–6). Then God clarifies that his covenant promises will be passed on through the descendants of Isaac (v. 19), although he reassures Abraham that Ishmael's descendants will also become a great nation (v. 20).

On his deathbed, Isaac's son Jacob tells his son Joseph that God had appeared to him at Luz in the land of Canaan, saying, "Behold, I will make you fruitful and multiply you, and I will make of you a multitude of people, and give this land to your descendants after you as an everlasting possession" (Gen. 48:4). God's eternal land covenant to Israel is recalled in Psalm 105:

He has remembered His covenant forever,
The word which He commanded to a thousand generations,
The covenant which He made with Abraham,
And His oath to Isaac,
And confirmed it to Jacob for a statute,
To Israel for an everlasting covenant,
Saying, "To you I will give the land of Canaan
As the allotment of your inheritance." (vv. 8–11)

To those who believe in God, and that the Bible is his word, these foundational promises seem to reveal clearly the Most High's intention to give "the land of Canaan" to the tribes of Israel forever. Of course, the Scriptures are full of warnings of what will happen to the Jews if they disobey God's commands, including being thrown out of the Promised Land. Twice the Jews have been scattered from the land as a result of sin. Yet throughout the Hebrew Bible, or Old Testament, God promises to regather the descendants of Jacob to their ancient ancestral homeland in the "last days," just before he fully establishes his kingdom on earth. Many regathering promises were fulfilled in the return from the seventy-year Babylonian Exile. But others, such as the one recorded in Isaiah 61:4, speak of the Jews returning and rebuilding their nation after "the desolation of many generations," in other words, after a very long exile. Still other Scripture passages speak of Jews returning from the four corners of the earth, which did not occur in the Babylonian return but is happening in our day.

Yet even if the Jews have been given a permanent divine title to the Holy Land, there is no biblical reason why Arabs and others cannot also live in it. Various peoples resided in Israel and Judea along with the Jews in ancient times. Modern Jewish Zionist leaders assumed in the beginning, undoubtedly naively, that most Arab residents would not be too unhappy to become citizens of the emerging Jewish state. It was thought that some might want to move to neighboring lands in order to live in an Arab-controlled state, but most would be content to stay where they were.

Among Christians and Jews who do believe that God forever promised the land to the Jews, some argue that the current ingathering is not the one spoken of in the Bible. The end-time prophecies, they say, indicate that the Jews will only come back to the land after the Messiah either comes or returns. It seems to me that this argument is irrelevant to the question of whether or not the Jews have a God-given right to live in the Holy Land. If the land was promised to Jacob's Jewish descendants as an "everlasting possession," then it still rightfully belongs to them, even when they are scattered from it.

Apart from this, as a Christian I find it hard to believe that the re-creation of a sovereign Jewish state in our century—which was accomplished against incredible odds—is just an accident of history or a "Western imperialist plot," of no meaning to God or mankind. Either the sovereign Lord who determines the boundaries of nations (Acts 17:26) has allowed the establishment of Israel in our time, or he is not sovereign after all.

Can Christians, Jews, or even Muslims reading of God's promises to and love for Jacob's descendants, see the creation of a Jewish state after almost two thousand years of exile that culminated in the holocaust as simply a historical accident? Is there no prophetic significance to the fact that the Jewish people, scattered as foretold all over the earth, once again have sovereignty over Jerusalem, their beloved ancient Holy City? No one, not even the Arabs, can deny that the long desolate, sparsely populated land of Israel, which the Romans renamed "Palaestina" to erase all Jewish association, has been transformed into a major agricultural center with beautiful forests and cities over the past one hundred years. Visitors coming from Egypt and Jordan often comment on the lushness of the land compared to those neighboring countries. Is it just an accident—a chance, purposeless event—that the Jews have even made portions of the desert blossom?

JEWS, ARABS, AND JERUSALEM

To call the Jewish migration to the Lord's land "the greatest crime of the century," as the Arab nations generally do, ignores the history of humanity over the past one hundred years. Mass migrations have taken place all over the globe. Large-scale refugee flights have also occurred in many places, especially in Asia and Africa. For example, the 1980s Afghan refugee exodus of several million Muslims was considerably larger than the Palestinian flight, yet little is heard about it. The Palestinian flight was not even in the century's top ten in terms of overall size.

National boundaries in Europe, Africa, and much of Asia have been either created or redrawn many times during the 1900s, usually as a result of war.

The Arabs, like other peoples, were promised an independent state or states by the victorious European powers who helped liberate them from Ottoman control during World War I. They now have not one but seventeen states stretching from the west coast of Africa to Iran.[4]

After centuries of oppression and persecution in Muslim and Christian regions, the Jews were also promised a national home in the Mideast, a proposition basically agreed to by Arab/Muslim leader Faisal Hussein and endorsed by the League of Nations and later by the United Nations. While many Jews did not see the need for such a state a hundred years ago, almost all did so after the fires of the holocaust were finally put out.

Jews immigrating to Palestine did not "steal Arab land" as is so often charged, but legally bought what they could, as Arieh Avneri fully documents in his book *Claim of Dispossession*. It is true that much Arab-owned property was seized by Israeli authorities in 1948 and 1949 and many abandoned villages, usually partially destroyed, were either completely razed or rebuilt for Jewish settlement. Palestinians understandably reacted with much anger and bitterness when they learned, in many cases, that their homes either no longer existed or were being occupied by Jews.

But the Israeli land seizures must be placed in their historical context, as is usually not done by Palestinians and their advocates. It was the Arabs who initiated a self-declared total war of destruction against the fledgling Jewish state after turning down the partition plan and refusing, as is generally still true today, to recognize that the Jews might have a legitimate right, and certainly a need, for a sovereign homeland in their beloved Holy Land. If the Arabs had agreed to a land partition, there would have been no war, no refugees, and no land seizures. Socialist and Western-oriented Jewish leaders like David Ben Gurion—keenly aware that world support was vital for the new state—were not about to initiate military action to drive Palestinians from their homes and farms. It was in the midst of the 1948 and 1967 wars, waged by a number of Arab states against the vastly outnumbered Jews, that Palestinian land was seized. Unpleasant as it may be, it must be noted that land is often taken by victors in war, especially if the other side initiated the conflict and threatens to do so again in the future. The United States did not expand by land purchases alone, nor has any other nation in recorded history.

It is also important to remember that Jewish properties and other assets were seized all over Europe before and during World War II and from parts of the Arab world as Jews fled to the newly established state of Israel. Plundered Jewish wealth in Arab lands has never been compensated for, although West Germany paid war reparations to most holocaust survivors. The more than one hundred thousand Jews who fled Iraq in the early 1950s were only allowed to carry one small suitcase with them, and could take out of the country no more than the equivalent of 140 American dollars. The Iraqi government seized all of the remaining Jewish assets, which were substantial. The Jews of Europe and parts of the Arab world lost their property and valuables because of unprovoked attacks upon them, or they were forced to give them up in order to buy safe passage from hostile Arab lands. Palestinian refugees lost their assets in the course of wars initiated by their leaders and surrounding Arab states.

Yet even if one accepts the Jews' biblical right, or at least practical need, to return to the Promised Land, the pictures and stories of suffering Palestinians grip the heart and mind. I have witnessed Palestinian agony firsthand. Many are my neighbors, my business contacts, my friends. I have visited their war-ravaged camps in Lebanon, and watched them battle Israeli soldiers patrolling crowded camps in the West Bank and Gaza Strip. I have interviewed local Palestinian leaders and regularly read translations of their east Jerusalem-based press. The Palestinians are not just statistics or "terrorists" to me, but real flesh-and-blood people who have legitimate needs and desires like anyone else. Many of them have poured out their problems and feelings to me, and I have listened with an open heart. A person would have to be extremely callous not to realize that these people are really hurting.

The Palestinian Arabs are definitely victims—but not primarily of the Israelis. They are, in my opinion, mainly the victims of an often-violent religion based on a corruption of the Bible. While I have great love and respect for the Muslims as people made in the image of God, I cannot but grieve for them as prisoners of a religious system, based on the Koran and Hadith, which exalts warfare and almost mandates hatred, or at least scorn, of the Jews. Of course, many Muslims, Palestinian and otherwise, are basically fine people who shun violence. But this is in spite of what their holy book and oral tradition teaches, not because of it. Many Palestinian Christians also disdain the Jewish people and Judaism, based on selected biblical passages and church tradition. But at least they have no scriptural basis—unlike Muslims—to wage war against Jews.

It was Haj Amin Husseini's use of Islamic motifs which cemented Palestinian Arab opposition to the emerging Jewish state in the 1920s and '30s. And Islamic teachings, above all else, inspired the entire Arab world to wage or support wars of annihilation against the Jewish state in 1948, 1967, and 1973. Although many PLO founders were Marxists or atheists, deeply rooted religious prejudices against the Jews are clearly reflected in the PLO's founding charter.

If Islam's supreme prophet Muhammad personally killed Jews, as most Palestinian Muslims believe, then what were they to do to the Jewish "infidels" who were building a nation in the midst of the Arab-Muslim world, and who subsequently captured some of "their" holy sites during the 1967 war? Such actions seemed to contradict Islam's God-given role as conqueror and ruler of the entire Middle East.

Many Muslims have a hard enough time accepting that Christian shrines are allowed to exist in the Holy Land, since Christians follow the "abominable" practice of worshiping Jesus. How then can they ever accept the fact that the doubly rejected Jews now control the traditional site of Muhammad's ascension to heaven, the holy Mount in Jerusalem's Old City? This seems to call into question the validity and truthfulness of Islam itself.

Yet the Temple Mount is not Judaism's third holiest site, as it is Islam's. I recently observed a Muslim saying midday prayers near my home south of the Old City. I noted that he was facing *away* from the Temple Mount which I could clearly see behind him. He was praying toward Islam's holiest site, the Kaaba Shrine in Mecca, Saudi Arabia. But religious Jews pray facing *toward* the Temple Mount, which is far and away Judaism's holiest site. Many people think that the Western Wall is Judaism's most sacred shrine, but it is the Mount itself which is holy to praying Jews. They gather at the Wall to pray that God will soon reveal the chosen Messiah and allow the construction of the third Jewish Temple on the sacred Mount. Then, they believe, the prophecies recorded in the books of Isaiah and Micah will be fulfilled, that "in the last days" the "mountain of the house of the Lord [*Har ha Biet*] will be established as the chief of the mountains," with all nations and peoples streaming up to it (Isa. 2:2–3, Micah 4:1–2). Until such a time, observant Jews are forbidden to walk around on the Mount lest they accidentally tread over, and thus desecrate, the site of the ancient Holy of Holies.

Just as no Arab leader could ever agree to recognize

permanent Jewish control over the Mount's holy mosques, so no Israeli leader could ever voluntarily concede Jewish sovereignty over the spot which has been at the center of Jewish hearts for three thousand years. Polls show that a majority of Israeli Jews would agree, under certain circumstances, to an Israeli withdrawal from most of the territories captured in 1967, thereby giving up control of such Jewish holy sites as Joseph's Tomb in Nablus, Abraham's Tomb in Hebron, and Rachel's Tomb in Bethlehem. But east Jerusalem, especially the Old City's Jewish Quarter and nearby Temple Mount, is another matter. While a majority might agree to an arrangement whereby Islam is guaranteed permanent control over the Mount itself, many Orthodox Jews and Israeli nationalists would strongly resist such a move, probably violently.

Indeed, the struggle for control of the Temple Mount and the rest of the Old City is the central point of contention in the Arab/Israeli conflict—a fact often obscured in the day-to-day media coverage of the latest happenings in the conflict. It seems to me that the American President, his Secretary of State, the British Prime Minister, and all other world leaders can talk until they're blue in the face about the need for progress in the Mideast "peace process." But political pressure alone cannot change the fact that Islam—the world's fastest-growing religion with nearly one billion followers—will never willingly accept permanent Jewish sovereignty over any portion of "sacred al-Quds," and especially over the Temple Mount and adjacent Muslim areas of the Old City. Just as clearly, Israeli Jews will never willingly hand back control of the Old City and its Western Wall and Temple Mount.

Of course, many Israeli Jews couldn't care less about holding onto the Temple Mount for religious reasons. Either they view Judaism in a more universal sense—

no longer needing a "sacred spot"—or they are not religious at all. But even for many such people, the Mount seems to be a powerful and important, although frequently subconscious, symbol of their national and personal identity. This is probably the reason an Israeli pullout from east Jerusalem, and especially the Old City, is considered unthinkable to most Israelis.

During my ten years in Israel, I have yet to come across a peace proposal that contains even a plausible solution to the intensely emotional holy war being waged by both Muslims and Jews over the ancient Old City of Jerusalem. The Muslim world, still bristling with humiliation over the loss of the area in 1967, wants a total end to Israeli sovereignty . . . period. This view is shared by moderate, pro-Western Egypt and by radical Libya and Iran (although the latter two want Jewish control eliminated over all of Jerusalem, and all of Israel, for that matter).

Israeli Jews, remembering that they were completely barred from even approaching the gates of the walled Old City from 1948 until 1967, believe that continued access to the Western Wall will only be assured if they retain absolute control of the area. Most are prepared to fight, if they must, to retain such control.

Another major obstacle to a peaceful solution of the Arab/Israeli conflict is deep Israeli suspicion that nobody really cares whether or not Israel survives as a distinct nation, let alone has access to Jerusalem's Old City. In fact, Israeli friends tell me they suspect that many non-Jews would be quite happy if a violent "final solution" led to their demise as a nation.

While a majority of Israelis do not really care about holding on to religious sites in Judea and Samaria outside Jerusalem, they do see at least portions of the area as strategically vital to Israel's defense. A number of military analysts maintain that Israel does not need such a territorial buffer zone anymore, since any future fullscale Arab/ Israeli war will most likely be largely fought by missiles and jets. But many others argue that the area is still essential to Israeli security. They say such a war would probably begin with a surprise chemical missile attack upon civilian and military targets, followed by a ground assault. If many Israeli soldiers and civilians were killed in a surprise chemical attack—a distinct possibility if the heavily populated coastal plane were hit—then a follow-up ground attack could be fatal, even if Israel used chemical or nuclear weapons in response.[5] In such an event, Israel's full-time and reserve army would need every inch of territory up to the Jordan River in order to halt a ground invasion.

Israelis keenly remember how easily Hitler discarded his prewar "peace" commitments as soon as it suited him. Even left-wing activists of the "progressive peace camp" (who are generally not religious) tell me they realize that Israel cannot agree to the minimal Palestinian and Arab withdrawal demands without taking great military risks. Thus, even a liberal Labor Party-led government is not likely to rush into a peace treaty, despite the threat of war. In light of Jewish history and continuing threats from Arab leaders like Saddam Hussein, one can hardly blame Israelis for wanting to carefully check out every angle before agreeing to potentially suicidal concessions.

But shouldn't Israel be able to make peace with the Palestinians and other Arabs since she was able to do so with Egypt in 1978? It was relatively simple to resolve Egyptian/Israeli differences. Although Egypt used the Sinai Peninsula as a staging ground for two attacks against Israel, the desert area was not considered absolutely vital for Israeli security. The substantial financial aid which the United States pledged to give both countries in order to shore up the peace, and in Israel's case, to partially compensate for the loss of Israeli-developed Sinai oil wells, was an obvious incentive. But the main reason why the Camp David Peace Accords were signed was that the two sides agreed not to really deal with the thorny religious-based issue of east Jerusalem, nor of the other captured territories near Israel's heartland. Anwar Sadat knew he could not seriously address those concerns and still get back the Sinai.

It is quite obvious that the alternative to a peaceful resolution of the Arab/Israeli struggle is continuing violence and warfare. Nearly everyone, including most Israelis, recognizes that the Palestinians will not rest until their stateless status is resolved. It doesn't matter that Palestinian statelessness may be largely due to their leader's having "never missed an opportunity to miss an opportunity," as former Israeli Foreign Minister Abba Eban put it. Although it is undoubtedly true, it is irrelevant to argue that the Palestinians would have long ago been citizens of their own state if they hadn't rejected the British and United Nations partition plans, or subsequent Israeli peace proposals. The frequently heard Arab argument that the West solved its own "Jewish problem" by creating Israel also does very little to bring the dispute to a peaceful resolution.

But all should recognize that religiously based conflicts are especially difficult to resolve. The late Iranian leader Ayatollah Khomeini taught that Satan created "that cancerous tumor" Israel, with Allah's approval, as a judgment on backslidden Muslim nations. When Muslims, especially decadent Western-inspired leaders, repent of their wicked ways, then Allah will destroy the "infidel" state. To say the least, this view—widely believed by Palestinians—greatly impedes efforts to establish a lasting peace between the Muslim world and Israel.

If the powerful Arab/Israeli struggle were basically an ideological one, such as between communism and capitalism, a peaceful resolution could probably be achieved. We have witnessed the fall of discredited communist governments in eastern Europe, and we are even seeing the unraveling of communism in its "mecca," Moscow. Although *like* a religion in many respects, communism is ultimately open to change because it is acknowledged to be a belief system based solely on the teachings of human beings. However, Islam and Judaism are long-established *religions,* and therefore not subject to sudden abandonment by most observant followers. The average Muslim is fully convinced that Allah revealed Islam, the final religious truth, to Muhammad through the Angel Gabriel. Religious Jews are just as convinced that the God of Israel established their nation and religion through his covenants with their forefathers. Western leaders caught up in the excitement of a "new world order" must remember that Abraham, Moses, and Muhammad are revered as prophets of God by millions of people, not simply as philosophers or politicians whose teachings and ideas can be easily put aside.

THE LORD'S TINY LAND

Even if the overall Arab/Israeli conflict was not basically religious in nature, the Israeli/Palestinian dispute would still be extremely difficult to resolve. The reason is simple—two peoples are struggling to control a very small piece of earth. It is hard for many Westerners to conceive just how tiny the land in question is. It is on average only 50 miles from Israel's western Mediterranean Sea border to the Jordan River. This extremely narrow land is at least much longer than it is wide— 260 miles from the northern upper Galilee border with Lebanon to the southern port city of Eilat on the Red Sea. Israel minus the territories is only 7,993 square miles overall, just slightly larger than one of America's smallest states, New Jersey.

If a Palestinian state were to be set up in the entire area that Israel captured in the Six Day War, excluding the Sinai Peninsula and the Golan Heights, it would only be 2,123 square miles in its "West Bank" part and 139 square miles in the Gaza Strip. The eastern portion would be on average just 83 miles long and 34 miles wide. The densely populated Gaza section would be even smaller; 24 miles long and less than 5 miles wide. A proposed Arab corridor between the two halves of the state would in effect cut Israel in two—a proposition not likely to be accepted by Israeli leaders. The West Bank portion of the proposed state is dominated by the Judean and Samarian hills, which afford a commanding view of Israeli coastal areas. The section of the coastal plane adjacent to Israel's pre-1967 border, from the southern Tel Aviv suburbs north to the town of Hadera, is only about 12 miles wide on the average. If the West Bank were no longer under Israeli control, the narrow coastal plane, home to well over a third of all Israelis, would be the only land bridge connecting northern Israel with the center and south, as it was before the Six Day War.

Israeli military analysts are naturally quite concerned over the potential for armed assaults from the proposed Palestinian state, especially from the hilly eastern section. Another worry is who would control such a state. There are six major factions and several splinter groups inside the PLO. Although Fatah is the largest, George Habash's Popular Front and Naif Hawatmeh's Democratic Front have many followers. Both groups are aligned with Syria which deeply mistrusts Fatah. The other three major PLO factions are also often at odds with Fatah. Yasser Arafat admitted in 1989 that he has little control over his constituent groups. How he would restrain their rivalries in an independent Palestinian state is anybody's guess.

Apart from internal PLO disputes, there is the huge problem of the two Palestinian Islamic fundamentalist movements who strongly oppose any peace moves toward Israel. Both have pledged to wage holy war until the "infidel state" is destroyed. Each has at times launched violent attacks against PLO supporters during the Palestinian uprising. Their demands, based on religious beliefs, are nonnegotiable. How will Fatah bring these growing movements into a peaceful settlement with Israel? And even if relatively moderate elements in the PLO succeed in overcoming their more radical opponents, how can Israel be certain that the PLO has abandoned its 1974 "phased program" to destroy Israel in stages? Will superpower sponsors of a peace treaty always be around to guarantee that the Jewish state is not swallowed up by a "secular democratic Palestinian state"?

If fully "free democratic elections" to determine the leadership of the proposed Palestinian state were held, as promised by Fatah, they would be the first in the entire Arab world. No other Arab nation has yet reached the stage of full democracy, although several are trying (municipal elections in Algeria in 1990 were won by Muslim fundamentalists, who call for a one-party theocratic state!). In light of the history of internal Palestinian violence and of the continuing deep divisions inside the PLO, it seems likely that such a state's "democracy" would most closely mirror Lebanon's, where ballots in the 1970s and '80s were replaced by bullets.

Arab leaders from Morocco in western Africa to Oman on the Persian Gulf must support any final resolution of the Arab/Israeli conflict, along with Muslim officials from non-Arab Iran, Pakistan, and elsewhere. Such a development seems remote, at best, as illustrated by

Iranian leader Ayatollah Khameini. Speaking on June 4, 1990—the first anniversary of his predecessor Ayatollah Khomeini's death—Khameini vowed that Iran will not rest until Israel is destroyed. Certainly Israel cannot fully rest until all of her declared enemies prove that they are ready to cease hostilities. It will not be true peace for Israel if, for example, Fatah moderates its positions, subdues its Palestinian rivals, signs a treaty, and then sets up a state in the territories, while Libya and Iran continue to support groups fighting for the destruction of "the Zionist entity." Both countries could carry on arming and training Lebanon-based militias. Lebanon would only cease to be a base of anti-Israeli activities if the many conflicts there were fully resolved—another remote possibility.

One of the Arab states which lies somewhere between Morocco and Oman is Syria, located just northeast of Israel. Nothing strikes me as more fanciful than the idea that Israel and the Palestinians can make peace while ignoring Syria, the other party along with Egypt and Jordan which lost land in 1967. Even if Syrian strongman Hafez Assad, an implacable foe of Israel, were replaced by a more moderate leader, Damascus could hardly give up its claim to the small piece of territory known in the West as the Golan Heights.

It is certainly true that Israel is much more likely to vacate the strategic Golan Heights than to pull out of east Jerusalem. Still, the ten thousand Israelis living in thirty-three settlements there would strongly—possibly violently—protest such a turnover, as would many thousands of Israelis who live on settlements like Hagoshrim in the Hula Valley just below the heights. Far too many Israelis remember the constant shelling and machine-gun attacks, which the Syrians launched from the area before the 1967 Israeli capture. In a peace settlement with Syria, Israel would probably at least insist that it hold onto the ridge and sloping hills just above the valley. Syria would demand the entire area back, but might agree to an international peacekeeping force being stationed on the heights just above the ridge. Although a settlement of the Golan dispute seems unlikely, it is at least possible.

Divided Arabs and Jews must also deal with a growing regional water crisis. The precious commodity is in short supply in all Mideast countries, with the few water sources under increasing pressure. Israel, Syria, and Jordan all vie for the waters which eventually flow into the Sea of Galilee and the Dead Sea. Growing populations are already taxing these and other water sources to the limit. Water would also be a major problem in the proposed minuscule Palestinian state. Analysts say the Mideast water shortage may well lead to future regional wars.

ARAB POWER AND ISRAEL

The vast wealth that poured into many Arab countries following the 1973 Yom Kippur War enabled the Arabs to purchase untold billions of dollars' worth of the latest Western and Soviet weapons systems and military equipment. Such arms are being acquired by countries whose land and population bases are vastly superior to Israel's. The apparent ending of the Cold War has led to stepped-up purchases of "bargain" weapons being dumped in Europe.

On the ground, Israel's armed forces are overwhelmingly outnumbered by her Arab enemies. As I complete this chapter, Syria and Iraq alone have standing regular armies of well over 1.5 million soldiers, compared to Israel's 150,000. Israel can muster another 500,000 men from its civilian population, but the Arabs can do much better than that. Syria is able to hit most Israeli targets with Soviet-supplied missiles equipped with chemical warheads. Iraq has missiles that can easily strike Israel; Iraq's western border is only 240 miles east of Jerusalem. Saudi Arabia has long-range Chinese missiles that are able to hit Israeli targets. Libya is thought to be building chemical weapons and acquiring advanced missiles. The number of tanks and combat jets that Iraq, Jordan, Syria, and the Gulf states possess are more than three times that of Israel's. To the west, Libya has about five hundred war planes. Algeria and Yemen also have substantial military resources, as does Morocco. Egypt has built up an impressive American-supplied military machine in the years since the peace treaty was signed with Israel.

It is undoubtedly true that some of these countries, especially Egypt and Morocco, are finished going to war with Israel. But others, especially Syria, Iraq, and Libya, seem intent on pursuing the jihad against the Jewish state. Non-Arab Iran says it wants to keep up the jihad struggle as well, with President Ali Rafsanjani calling in December 1990 for the setting up of a pan-Islamic army to annihilate Israel.

Many argue that Israel's nuclear weapons make all the above statistics irrelevant. While it is now undisputed that Israel does possess such weapons, this fact alone cannot compensate for Israel's extremely small population and land base in comparison to her enemies'. Iraq is about twenty times the size of Israel with a population four times as large. Saudi Arabia is more than one hundred times bigger. Tripoli, the capital of Libya—which is a mere eighty-five times the size of Israel—is well over a thousand miles west of Tel Aviv. Therefore, even if Israel responded to a devastating chemical, biological, or nuclear attack with all of her nuclear bombs, which is unlikely, portions of the Arab world would probably remain untouched. Tiny Israel, just slightly larger than Kuwait, could suffer serious damage and loss of life in a full-scale surprise missile attack. But the vast Arab world, more than four hundred times the size of Israel with close to 200 million people and massive underground oil deposits, could certainly recover in time from an Israeli nuclear blitz. If one adds to all this the likelihood that one or more Arab states will eventually possess nuclear weapons, Israel's position seems extremely precarious.

AMERICAN AID TO ISRAEL

Largely as a result of the Palestinian uprising, United States financial aid to Israel—about three billion dollars a year since 1985, to Egypt's two billion or so—has come under increasing attack. Critics note that aid to Israel and Egypt amounts to more than one-third of the United States' annual foreign aid budget. The statement is often heard that America supplies the equivalent of ten thousand dollars for every Israeli citizen, as if U.S. government checks are being handed out in the streets of Tel Aviv and Jerusalem! Israeli analysts note that most of the money immediately returns to the United States to pay off bank loans, helping somewhat to shore up America's troubled banking system. The rest, about 1.2 billion dollars, is military aid which for the most part must be spent in the U.S.—helping to keep people working at American defense establishments.

Israeli financial experts say that Israel would not need to receive so much U.S. aid, borrow so much from American banks, or invest so heavily in military procurement if the United States and other world powers were not selling vast quantities of advanced weaponry to Israel's Arab enemies. Trying to keep up militarily with her neighbors, Israel has the highest per capita defense budget in the world. They also note that Israel, unlike Egypt, has provided highly valued military information to the Americans, such as letting U.S. experts examine a Soviet-built Syrian Mig-29 whose pilot defected to Israel in February 1990. Information garnered has been worth tens of billions of dollars to the United States, say military analysts.

Israel also acts as a land-based "aircraft carrier" for American jets operating in the region, and as a friendly port for American ships in the eastern Mediterranean—important assets in this volatile and strategic part of the world.

ISRAEL MEETS THE PRESS

Many Israeli friends blame me and my media colleagues for what they believe are growing Western perceptions of them as hate-filled, intransigent people, gleefully oppressing Palestinians. Unfair press coverage has contributed heavily to a rise in worldwide anti-Semitic vandalism and other attacks in the past few years, they say. Israelis are portrayed as willfully depriving human rights to an oppressed minority, they complain, as if the Palestinians—part of the large Arab world—were imported black slaves whom the Israelis consider racially inferior, and therefore have a right to dominate. Although the comparison is often made, the situation is quite different from South Africa, they argue, where white minority leaders with no historical claim to the land deliberately set out to suppress the black majority based on racist beliefs. The Palestinians are not suffering because they are Palestinians, my Israeli friends argue. Israeli "oppression" is in reality mostly "suppression" of unwarranted Palestinian violence directed from the 1920s onward against Jews settling in their ancient homeland.

It seems to me that these arguments have merit. Israel, like any country, does have its racists and religious bigots, such as the late Rabbi Meir Kahane (murdered in late 1990 by an Arab Muslim in New York) and his followers. Yet, I have found most Israelis to be anything but racists. The Jewish people have suffered much bigotry and racial hatred down through the centuries, leaving most of them keen supporters of the concepts of tolerance and equality. Yet many Israeli Jews, especially those whose families came from Arab lands, or who lost loved ones in the various wars and terrorist attacks, do harbor hatred for their Arab cousins. However, I believe this is not primarily because of religious or racial reasons, but because of Muslim oppression over the centuries, and more so because the Arabs in general have repeatedly attacked the Jews both verbally and militarily in this century.

There is no denying that Arab citizens of Israel suffer discrimination in jobs, government funding, and so on. But again the main reason, I believe, is Israeli suspicions of the Arabs based on past wars and continuing terror attacks, and not because of ingrained racism. It is also true that Israeli businessmen usually pay Palestinian laborers less than Jewish workers. But again it seems to me that this is not the result of inherent racism, but simply because they can get away with it, thus cutting costs. In other words, it's a matter of greed—a sin undoubtedly shared by many business people around the world.

In racial terms, the Arabs and Jews are indeed cousins, as is obvious to anyone living in Israel. Israeli culture is heavily influenced by the larger Arabic Middle Eastern culture, which is natural enough since a majority of Israeli Jews are of Mideast origin. (However, this will change if Soviet Jews keep coming in large numbers.) Unlike blacks and whites, Jews and Arabs are of the same racial stock and have many shared cultural, religious, and social values which go back for millennia. This is why David

Ben Gurion thought in the 1930s that there was a chance that the emerging Jewish state could join a regional federation with neighboring Arab states.

The most popular Israeli foods and music reflect a strong Arab influence. The Hebrew and Arabic languages have many common words, since both originated in the same region. The Arab/Israeli dispute is a tribal religious conflict between relatives, not a racial struggle between two totally foreign and unrelated cultures.

Yet even if we journalists were scrupulously even-handed toward both the Palestinians and Israelis, there is no way that television pictures of armed soldiers shooting stone-throwing teenagers, or of young people being arrested and sent to crowded detention centers, could make Israel look like anything but a major human rights violator, no matter who is ultimately to blame for the situation. The Palestinians know this and have used such knowledge to their advantage.

Palestinian stringers working for Western news agencies during the early months of the uprising would sometimes call to recommend that a camera crew be sent to such and such a place in order to film a Palestinian demonstration. Such friendly advice helped assure that a constant stream of violent confrontations between Israeli soldiers and Palestinians made it onto television screens around the world. The ethics of acting on such tips bothered me, as they did some of my colleagues, yet everyone knew that action shots were what the editors back home wanted (in my case "action sounds," since I work in radio).

Naturally enough, the Israeli Army also tries at times to direct our efforts to gather the news, usually by limiting access to trouble spots. More than one reporter has been kicked, shoved, or arrested, and film has been confiscated. However, such restrictions and actions have been the exception rather than the rule. In comparison to the almost total news blackout which Britain imposed during the 1982 Falklands War, or the severe restrictions enforced during the American invasion of Grenada in 1983, Israel's record seems pretty good, considering that the uprising is in many ways a media war backed morally and financially by Arab states that threaten to destroy her. Neither the U.S. nor Britain faced even marginal threats from Grenada or Argentina.

Has press coverage of the uprising been biased against Israel, as my Israeli friends generally believe? Overall, I would say that the reporters I know have striven, as I have, to present a balanced and accurate picture. Yet we journalists are very fallible human beings. We have our own opinions. So do our editors overseas. Many of my colleagues tend to favor the Palestinian position over Israel's. A few are downright hostile toward the Jews. Other reporters display more subtle evidence of traditional Western anti-Semitic attitudes, usually without even realizing it.

I believe one of our faults is that we often judge Israel—located in the heart of the autocratic Middle East and on the western edge of Asia, a continent not exactly known for its great democracies—by the standards of a Western democracy at peace. Also some journalists seem to think that, since the Jews suffered the loss of a third of their people during the holocaust, they should now behave like angels toward people throwing stones, firebombs, and burning Israeli flags and performing other anti-Israeli acts.

I am frankly amazed that the perennially despised Jews, facing not only stones and firebombs, but real threats of widespread death and destruction from Arab neighbors have not reacted more harshly than they have.

Israeli and foreign human rights groups have been especially critical of Israeli army shootings that allegedly occurred in non-life-threatening situations. Other deaths which resulted from illegal use of firearms or beatings have been roundly condemned. Israeli Army leaders note that over a dozen soldiers were court-martialed for such abuses by mid-1989, followed by others in 1990.

However, human rights groups say their punishments were too light, thus failing to deter further violations. Israeli officials respond that such groups fail to take into account the warlike context in which the violence has been occurring, adding that many Israelis, some of them children, have also been killed or wounded. PLO and HAMAS uprising leaflets have called on Jewish soldiers and civilians to be killed, they note. They say human rights groups usually fail to condemn the inter-Palestinian killings which left over three hundred Arabs dead by 1991.

In terms of the real world, some seven hundred Palestinian deaths by Israeli soldiers in the first three years of the violent uprising were not that many, even if tragic. Nevertheless, world dismay that any unarmed civilians were dying was understandable, no matter who initiated the clashes.

Israeli leaders complain that the world media highlights each and every Palestinian death, while giving scant coverage to other violent world struggles. This criticism seems justified to me, although there are understandable political, historical, and religious reasons the press pays more attention to the Arab/Israeli dispute than to other conflicts. Israeli officials say that the international media hardly reported the deaths of over two hundred thousand Sudanese civilians—many of them children—during 1988. Pro-Israel media analysis groups echo this criticism, pointing out that American press reports featuring young Palestinian deaths were widespread during 1988.[6] Relatively few reports dealt with the Sudanese tragedy, they note, even though reams more were actually dying in the African nation. The groups did note, however, that the Palestinian casualties came mostly from army gunfire, and the Sudanese deaths mainly resulted from starvation caused by civil war.

It seems to me that in real-life Mideast, African, and Asian terms, Israel has acted with relative restraint in the face of an ongoing, violent civilian uprising. This does not excuse Israeli abuses, but it should be noted. On July 14, 1989, in the midst of a civil war, Somali soldiers fired indiscriminately into crowds of unarmed Muslims in Mogadishu, killing around 450 people. Saudi forces killed more than 400 unarmed Muslim rioters, mostly Iranians, in Mecca in late July 1987. The U.S. State Department said Iraq used chemical weapons to kill 600 to 3,000 Kurdish civilians in 1988. Around 500 civilians, some of them children, were killed in just a few days as Algerian forces put down fundamentalist-led food riots in 1988. Some 600 civil war refugees huddled in a church were massacred by Liberian government soldiers on July 29, 1990. Nobody knows how many hundreds or thousands of unarmed civilians were killed when Chinese forces crushed the Tiananmen Square student protests in early June 1989, or when Iraqi soldiers overran Kuwait in 1990. Such is the charm of the East. Of course, none of these countries claims to be a democracy, although others that do, such as Pakistan and India, have regularly used armed force against unarmed civilian rioters.

Israeli critics charge that media coverage of the Arab/ Israeli conflict often lacks historical context, especially in television and radio reports. Both Israelis and Palestinians complain that background context to individual clashes is also often nowhere to be found. Both charges are generally on target.

But in defense of my trade, I must point out that such omissions are mainly due to time constraints and not because most reporters are historically ignorant (although I do recall a newly arrived Associated Press reporter—one of hundreds of nonresident journalists who descended on Israel during the early days of the uprising—asking me to check her "facts," which I quickly saw were anything but that). More than once I complained to CBS radio editors in New York that my thirty-five- to forty-second spots sometimes seemed to obscure, rather than clarify, certain stories. But what can you do? There is simply very little room for background information on most commercial network newscasts.

Television reports tend to emphasize immediate, dramatic pictures over background context. The networks naturally want the viewer to stay tuned since more viewers means better ratings, which means more money. But overemphasis on "action shots" tends to give a false impression. Having used modern computer video editing equipment, I know how easy it is to rearrange shots to highlight the exciting. Most people don't stay home because three people were shot during a local bank robbery. Yet, if my friends in the States are any indication, when three are killed in a Gaza refugee camp, viewers far away from the action tend to think the whole of Israel is on fire. (Interestingly enough, many more people are killed each year in New York and Washington than in Israel, my Israeli friends point out, yet people still visit those cities.) Such false impressions have kept many potential tourists, whose visits are essential to Israel's economy, away from the Holy Land, say Israeli tourism officials. Frequent reports focusing on scattered violent confrontations, with very few or no reports on the overall peaceful situation elsewhere in Israel and the territories, is bound to give a distorted impression to TV viewers.

Another problem I see is the use of certain descriptive terms which convey more emotion than information. I cringe, for instance, when I use the words *occupied territories* in my reports, even though the phrase may be technically correct. I believe the arguments made by many Israelis, that the term is legally a misnomer, have validity. But more than this, I am aware that to many listeners, especially older ones, the words *occupied territories* conjure up pictures of Nazi Germany and Japan deliberately and ruthlessly occupying various sovereign nations before and during World War II. There is a vast difference between this and Israel's control—resulting from a war forced upon her—of two small strips of disputed land not far from her central cities. It would be far more accurate in historical terms to call the Soviet-dominated Baltic States "occupied territories," yet media reports have not done so. Certainly Tibet, forcibly taken over by China, is under resented military occupation. Many other portions of land are controlled by one nation and disputed by another. Yet with heavy media usage, everyone in the world knows that "*the* occupied territories" are the ones controlled by the tiny state of Israel.

Are the major news organizations determined to bash Israel? Probably not. But they are certainly not immune to the forces which exist in the real world, especially financial ones. Although it would be hard to prove, it at least seems plausible to suggest that some of the media's major commercial sponsors—the large oil companies who operate in the Arab countries; automobile manufacturers whose customers won't purchase cars if there's no gasoline to run them; and major banks full of petrodollar deposits—have an interest in pleasing the Arabs more than the Jews. It doesn't seem far-fetched to assume that such business giants might have some influence in corporate media headquarters, as well as at the White House.

The American President has certainly seen government projections that the United States will need to import increasing amounts of oil from the Mideast as the 1990s progress. The region had 70 percent of known world oil reserves in 1990. Imports from Saudi Arabia doubled between 1986 and 1989, and increased over six-fold from Iraq. By the time of the Iraqi invasion of Kuwait a quarter of America's oil imports came from the Persian Gulf. With Europe increasingly reliant on Mideast oil supplies, as Japan always has been, it is not hard to imagine that Western governments and businesses will be increasingly receptive to Arab interests in the coming years. Would the quick Western military buildup in the Persian Gulf region have occurred if Iraq were a medium-sized African state that overran a small, poor neighbor? The rapid multinational response to Saddam Hussein's occupation of Kuwait was certainly undertaken with strategic Western oil interests in mind. There's a lot of black gold under those Arab desert sands, and everybody knows it.

CONCLUSION

The Arab/Israeli struggle is unique among world conflicts. At its center is a city sacred to almost half the people on earth. After centuries of domination by Christians, then by Muslims, then by Christians during the Crusades, then once again by Muslims, Jerusalem is now under Jewish control, although Jews comprise only a tiny proportion of the world's population.

The two religions that dominated the Holy Land for many centuries are, for the most part, unhappy that Jews once again control the land. But both realize that the ancient prophets they revere, plus most other great men and women of the Bible, including Jesus, were Jews. While Christians debate whether or not the Jews have a right to sovereignty in the ancient Jewish homeland, Muslims overwhelmingly agree that it is not the will of Allah, as revealed in the Koran.

Immigrating Jews over the past hundred years encountered deep-seated resistance and growing hostility from many Palestinian Arabs—Muslim and Christian. The Arabs' opposition was partly due to understandable fears of what a sovereign Jewish state might mean for their future. But it was even more so the result of preconceived prejudices based on religious beliefs.

The Jewish people suffered frequent persecution during their centuries of exile from the Promised Land, mostly from Christians, but also from Muslims. Such persecution did not wane, but actually increased, as the "enlightened" industrial revolution spread in Europe and Russia. The overwhelming majority of Jewish immigrants who came to the Holy Land from the 1880s until 1948 were trying to escape powerful attempts to destroy them, first during the pogroms in Russia and eastern Europe, and later during the Nazi reign over most of Europe and parts of northern Africa. Most Jewish immigrants since 1948 have fled oppression in Muslim-Arab countries and under communist regimes in eastern Europe and the Soviet Union. The need for a Jewish homeland is quite evident to such immigrants and their offspring. Israel is indeed a refuge for the Jewish people, especially those suffering persecution or threats of annihilation.

Many Palestinian Arabs became refugees as the Jewish state came into existence. Others fled their homes during the 1967 Arab/Israeli war. With natural growth, some 1.4 million Palestinians living in Jordan, Syria, and Lebanon are today registered as refugees. Another 800,000 live in Judea, Samaria, and the Gaza Strip. Although wealthy Arab states and others could have supplied money to resettle them, the Palestinians "would remain refugees, to be utilized during the following years by the Arab states as a powerful political and propaganda pawn against Israel," as Benny Morris puts it.[1] The refugees are housed, fed, and receive medical attention through United Nations relief agencies (which received more than one-third of their operating funds in 1990 from the United States), along with private charitable organizations.

It was not inevitable that the Arabs of Palestine became refugees. Western-oriented Jewish Zionist leaders did not intend to displace them, believing the land was big enough to house both peoples, which it was. However the Arabs, of whom most are Muslims, were basically duty-bound to reject the idea of Jewish sovereignty in the Holy Land. Many also feared that immigrating Jews would take revenge for the centuries of oppression, and sometimes persecution, suffered by their Jewish co-religionists under Islam. Muslim religious leaders, especially the Jerusalem Grand Mufti, played upon those fears. Violent attacks were launched upon the Jews in the 1920s and '30s, leading naturally enough to a hardening of Jewish attitudes toward Palestinian Arabs. In the midst of a war launched by calls from the entire Arab world for the Jews to be thrown into the sea, and on the heels of the holocaust, most Jews were not sad to see the Arabs flee when the main refugee flight occurred in 1948.

Finding a peaceful solution to the Arab/Israeli conflict is next to impossible, as many world diplomats have discovered over the past four decades. Hatred of the Jews is still strong in much of the Arab world, as any casual reading of the Arab press will show. The idea of a sovereign Jewish state in the heart of the Muslim world is, and will always be, grating to many Muslims. Jewish Israelis, while deeply desiring peace, are overwhelmingly skeptical of Arab, and especially Palestinian, intentions. The various Arab/Israeli wars and years of PLO terrorism have left deep scars. Undoubtedly most Palestinian refugees, stateless and living in substandard conditions, harbor deep hatred of Israeli Jews.

Although our secular century obscures the fact, the Arab/Israeli dispute is overwhelmingly a struggle over an ancient city sacred to both peoples. The Jewish people have yearned for Jerusalem ever since their exile from the Holy Land. Most Muslims, whose ancestors fought hard to prevent Christian domination of Islam's third holiest city, are not about to abandon willingly the demand for complete sovereignty over east Jerusalem, where the mosques of Omar and al-Aksa sit on the ancient Temple Mount. Anwar Sadat made this point even as he received back the Sinai Peninsula in 1978. Palestinian and other Mideast Christians are generally more sympathetic toward the Jews, having also suffered under Islam. Yet most are still opposed to Jewish control over Jerusalem.

Jewish sovereignty in the Middle East seems to contradict the teachings of the Koran, and thus calls into question the validity of Islam itself. Jewish attachment to Jerusalem's Old City has existed for thousands of years and continues to play an important role in the religious life of the nation.

Israel annexed east Jerusalem in 1967, a move supported by the vast majority of Israeli Jews. Polls show very few Israelis would willingly surrender sovereignty even if they came to believe that the Arabs as a whole were truly ready to make peace.

To say the least, I have painted a fairly dark picture. What can I do? I wish I could honestly say, as some of my colleagues and many world governments do, that peace will come if only "Likud Party intransigence" is modified. But I believe that the conflict runs much deeper than *any* political party, statesman, or government can successfully deal with. Having extensively covered the conflict at its center, I believe my analysis is an accurate portrayal of the situation.

I know of many good and sincere people—Arabs, Jews, and others—who are working to bring about reconciliation and an end to violence. I am also acquainted with many hurting people on both sides of the conflict, and I wish I could write that peace is just around the corner. But strong forces, based on ancient religious beliefs, are at work in the struggle. They are not about to disappear. Of course, it is always possible that a more powerful force will one day succeed in ending the Arab/Israeli dispute. I do not believe that the world powers alone have such strength, despite the tremendous economic influence they exert over the antagonists, especially Israel. Still, they will probably keep trying, and may surprise me and many others by somehow forcing the two sides to lay aside their deep division, especially over

Jerusalem. A devastating war could also lead to a de-facto resolution of the Arab/Israeli conflict.

Many Christians, basing their beliefs on Daniel 11 and Paul's second letter to the Thessalonians, expect that a worldwide leader with supernatural powers—the "antichrist" strongman of the books of Revelation and Daniel—will impose a peace settlement in the strife-torn region. This leader will allow the Jews to rebuild the Temple in Jerusalem, or come onto the scene after it is rebuilt, and eventually seat himself in it and declare that he is God. In the end, he will prove to be no friend of the Jews, nor of true Christians, who will refuse to worship him or participate in his worldwide economic system.

Although a journalist and not a prophet, I am personally convinced that there are strong supernatural forces at work behind the Arab/Israeli dispute. I cannot help mentioning that I often perceive a certain glowing, otherworldly light behind the conflict—a light that shows up some very dark shadows. Why does the United Nations spend such a disproportionate amount of time on this struggle? Is it simply because the world body helped to create the Jewish state? Why does one of the smallest countries on earth have one of the largest permanent foreign press corps? Is it just that "Jews are news," or because wealthy oil states and three major religions play a role in the Arab/Israeli conflict? There is a fascination, an intensity to this struggle that seems to go beyond normal explanations.

If it is true, as the Bible says, that the God of Israel has forever wedded his name to this tiny strip of disputed land, then *that* is what makes this conflict so unlike any other. If he indeed intends to establish his earthly reign in Jerusalem, and this design is opposed by his heavenly and earthly adversaries, then no other reason must be given for the fact that Jerusalem is "a very heavy stone"

(Zech. 12:3) in the way of a man-made peace process. If these things are true, then Arabs and Israelis are participants in a story whose ultimate implications are far greater than any human being can comprehend.

Israel is increasingly at the center of international criticism, protest, and condemnation. With serious threats all around and growing trials at home, it seems that Jacob's troubles can only increase as the world heads toward the twenty-first century. I think it is fair to speculate that the many biblical prophecies that speak of extremely dark days for the world just before the kingdom of God is fully established on earth may be nearing the time of their fulfillment. Is an "antichrist" dictator about to appear who will enforce a "final solution" of the Mideast conflict? Will a full-scale military attack leave Israel greatly weakened and open to foreign domination during the short time span known to many Christians as the Great Tribulation, as Revelation 11:2 and Zechariah 14:2 seem to indicate? What of the long-anticipated and dreaded final battle of Armageddon, which the book of Revelation says will involve armies numbering two hundred million soldiers (Rev. 9:16)? Only God and time will fully reveal the answers to these questions.

Whatever lies in the future, it is quite clear that the complex Arab/Israeli conflict already reeks of hatred, death, and destruction. Yet I believe there is hope even today for the troubled Middle East. Every one of Abraham's children—Arab and Jew—has the same opportunity as I of receiving God's gift of eternal life, offered in his chosen Messiah. Quite understandably, this does not seem like a valid road to peace to most Muslims and Jews, who have witnessed much hypocrisy and violence over the years from Gentile followers of Jesus— further stoking the holy war fires blazing in the world. But Israel's Messiah does have the power to bring reconciliation and peace to individuals and societies, ending all wars both internally and between nations. His is the only peace process that will ultimately succeed in turning Arab and Israeli swords into ploughshares . . . finally resulting in everlasting *shalom* for the Promised Land.

EPILOGUE

Air raid sirens were wailing throughout Israel once again. But this time, it was not Holocaust Martyrs and Heroes Remembrance Day. Or was it? I and several friends were just completing an unusual Sabbath evening supper at Lance Lambert's Jerusalem home. All of us were eating rapidly—we even skipped several prepared courses—fearing that air raid sirens would sound at any moment. It was day number two of Operation Desert Storm, and Iraqi missiles had already struck Israel the night before as Saddam Hussein desperately tried to turn the U.N. authorized attack against him into another full-scale Arab/Israeli war.

The telephone, which is normally shut off during the Sabbath, rang. A friend in the know was calling to warn us that another Iraqi missile attack was expected sometime during the evening. We picked up the pace of our eating and attempted to maintain a pleasant dinner conversation despite the nervousness we all felt.

Suddenly, the sirens sounded. The Lambert household flew into action. They knew just what to do. Their survival plan had become routine over the previous two nights. The American-led air assault against Iraq had begun early Thursday morning. From that moment on, everyone wondered when and how Saddam would respond. He didn't leave anyone in suspense for long. During the pre-dawn hours on Friday, the first Iraqi missiles struck Tel Aviv and Haifa. Now everyone was on edge, expecting another Iraqi strike.

Lance's two dogs were ordered down the stairs, and three large cages housing exotic birds were rushed down right behind them. A quick search was made to locate any of Lance's four Siamese cats not already down in the anti-chemical shelter, sealed off with plastic sheeting and masking tape.

On call for CBS radio, I grabbed a nearby portable telephone and rapidly descended down the stairs, dialing network headquarters in New York City along the way. Within minutes I was on the air, telling listeners throughout America that another missile alert was underway in Israel. With a gas mask perched on top of my head, I reported that Israeli state radio was ordering everyone to proceed immediately to anti-chemical home shelters and to put on their protective masks. Soon the radio announced that a missile attack was in progress.

As dinner guests donned their masks, I slipped into a back bedroom to escape the rising noise level in the improvised shelter. When I returned to the room five minutes later, I was taken aback by the strange, science fiction-like scene before me. My friends, recognizable now only by their clothes and hair, were quietly listening to the radio. Closest to the door was Lance, who looked up at me from his favorite chair. His gas mask could not conceal the extremely sad look in his eyes.

Were these really the same people who were eating an elaborate Sabbath meal with me only minutes earlier? How could it be that Lance, whose father was gassed to death at Auschwitz and who suffered through the Nazi blitz of London as a boy, had to wear a gas mask in his own home on the Jewish Sabbath—ready for a threatened deadly chemical attack from an Arab dictator waging a unilateral war against Israel? I immediately returned to the back bedroom, feeling like I needed to spend a couple of quiet minutes by myself.

We were soon allowed to leave our protected shelter. The suspected missile attack, we were told, had been a false alarm. But several hours later, three Iraqi missiles did come crashing down on metropolitan Tel Aviv, leaving around a dozen Israelis injured and many families homeless. Fortunately, their bodily wounds were not serious. But if one of the missiles had landed just thirty feet or so from where it had, a shelter housing nine families would have been destroyed, undoubtedly leaving its occupants dead or badly wounded.

In truth, many residents of Tel Aviv, Haifa, and elsewhere were deeply wounded by the Iraqi missile strikes, despite the fact that chemical warheads were, at least in the initial attacks, not deployed. They were emotionally shaken that a brutal regional dictator—calling himself the new Nebuchadnezzar, the one who revived the ancient Babylonian Empire and conquered Jerusalem—had repeatedly threatened to "liberate Jerusalem" by launching indiscriminate terror attacks from the sky on Israeli civilians. They were traumatized as they hastily donned gas masks and placed their children in protective plastic tents whenever sirens sounded. Psychologists said among the worst victims were elderly holocaust survivors who were trying to cope with the prospect of sudden death by gas, and this while huddled in their homes in the heart of Jewish Israel. Of course young children, unable to fully understand why they were quickly snatched from their beds in the middle of the night as sirens sounded and who later sometimes heard loud explosions, were receiving memories that will probably haunt them the rest of their lives.

Despite the missile threat, however, most Israelis were relieved as the American-led assault on Saddam's Iraq got underway. They hoped the powerful onslaught would eliminate the threat that the Iraqi dictator would drag the entire Middle East into another full-scale Arab/ Israeli war.

As the January 15 United Nations deadline for Iraq to leave Kuwait approached, Israeli leaders had feared the worst—that Saddam would suddenly fire off his substantial missile arsenal aimed at Israel. Had he done so, many lives would have undoubtedly been lost. Israel's airport, and its nuclear reactor in the Negev desert, might have been hit. Government leaders in Jerusalem would have been forced to respond in a major way, no matter what effect this might have had on the international coalition arrayed against Iraq. Autocratic rulers of Jordan, Syria, and other Arab states such as Algeria and Yemen would have found it hard to resist widespread popular support for Saddam's holy war to "liberate Palestine." But Saddam did not open fire, despite reported advice by several of his top generals that he do so.

The threat posed by Iraqi missile attacks eased with the arrival in Israel of the most advanced version of the American Patriot anti-missile system, manned for the time being by U.S. forces. However, several Israelis were killed and more than one hundred wounded, when a number of missiles reached their targets in the first few days after the Patriot's deployment. President George Bush had promised that America would help defend the Israelis from Iraqi missiles if Israel refrained from taking them out in a preemptive operation, and he was apparently keeping his word. The demonstrative U.S. commitment to Israel's security helped defuse fears that the Arab countries would rally around Saddam in his holy war against the Jewish state. Still, Israelis were warned that the complex Patriot system—originally designed to take out aircraft, not missiles—would not totally eliminate the serious threat posed by Syrian, Iraqi, or Libyan chemical-tipped warheads.

The anticipated destruction of Iraq's war-making potential should diminish the short-term nuclear threat against Israel, and dash hopes among many Palestinians, various Arab states, and Iran that Israel can be greatly weakened, or even destroyed, in a new Mideast war. Nevertheless, this does not mean the stalled Arab/Israeli peace process will spring back to life soon after the war is over. The Israelis will say—quite understandably—that there is simply no one to talk to. Memories of PLO and other Palestinian leaders warmly embracing a man who takes great pleasure in sending deadly missiles on civilians in Tel Aviv will not be soon forgotten in Israel, even if they are in the rest of the world. The fact that Palestinians in the territories almost unanimously view Saddam as a great Arab leader and potential savior bodes ill for the proposed Palestinian state just next to Israel's major cities. Apart from the PLO's stand, Israelis will long remember that Palestinians in Nablus, and elsewhere, along with Arabs in Damascus, Amman, Algiers and other Arab capitals, gathered in the streets to cheer when reports of missile strikes on Tel Aviv were aired on radio and television.

Yasser Arafat's call for Palestinians everywhere to support Saddam's holy war for the Promised Land demonstrated once again the main reason why the Arab/Israeli conflict continues after so many decades: Most Palestinians still rally when a serious cry of war is made against the Jewish state. Arafat and a few other PLO leaders have spoken in recent years about compromise solutions to the Israeli/Palestinian conflict. But show him, and most of his followers, an Arab leader who appears to be strong and ruthless enough to possibly destroy or greatly harm the "Zionist entity" and they wholeheartedly embrace him. This tendency, first demonstrated by fervent Palestinian backing for Nasser, does not increase the prospects that Israel will anytime soon hand over east Jerusalem to PLO control, no matter which Israeli political party is in power. In supporting Saddam, the PLO—Israel's supposed negotiating partner—has once again demonstrated its uncanny ability to repeatedly convince most Israeli Jews that its intentions are altogether evil.

Israel has been widely portrayed in recent years as a powerful Goliath oppressing helpless Palestinian Davids. But the fact is Israel still feels quite threatened by mainly Soviet-armed neighbors who take great joy in the thought of her destruction. Israel's fears do not reflect an unwarranted "ghetto mentality," as is often charged, but stem from real and continuing threats from heavily armed neighbors like Iraq and Syria. Israel's inability, without American help, to prevent Iraqi missiles from hitting coastal cities demonstrates anew that the Jewish state is not some invincible military giant, but a small country that has good reason to feel threatened when confronted by much larger nations like Iraq and Syria. What if a nuclear warhead had been on one of the Iraqi missiles which hit Tel Aviv—a real possibility if the Israeli Air Force had not destroyed Iraq's nuclear reactor in 1981? Israel's main population center would have been devastated.

Even if Israeli leaders had ignored western concerns and launched a preemptive strike on Saddam's Scud missile launchers, it would have been difficult to successfully destroy all of them, as it was for much larger allied forces in the opening stages of the war. Israel could have done the job in time, but not before many missiles—probably including chemical ones—had rained down upon her.

The Palestinians may not have missiles or an air force, but they do have many powerful Arab and Muslim friends who possess vast arsenals of deadly weapons. Israel also has powerful friends, but in recent years they have been increasingly reluctant to lend her their support. Maybe by the time the war against Iraq is over,

Israel's western friends will have a better understanding of the serious challenges and anxieties the Jewish state faces regularly in her struggle to survive in the volatile Muslim Middle East.

APPENDIX
KEY MAPS

The British Mandate, 1920

MEDITERRANEAN SEA

Sidon

Damascus

SYRIA

IRAQ

FRENCH
MANDATE

Haifa

Tel Aviv

Amman

Gaza

Jerusalem

PALESTINE

B R I T I S H   M A N D A T E

TRANSJORDAN

ARABIA

EGYPT

The British Mandate, 1922

GOLAN HEIGHTS Ceded to the French Mandate of
Syria in 1923 and captured by Israel in 1967.

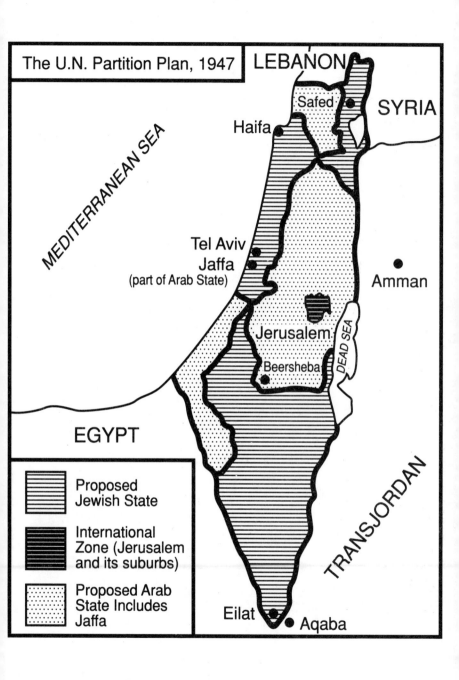

The U.N. Partition Plan, 1947

LEBANON
SYRIA
MEDITERRANEAN SEA
Safed
Haifa
Tel Aviv
Jaffa
(part of Arab State)
Amman
Jerusalem
DEAD SEA
Beersheba
EGYPT
TRANSJORDAN
Eilat
Aqaba

Proposed Jewish State

International Zone (Jerusalem and its suburbs)

Proposed Arab State Includes Jaffa

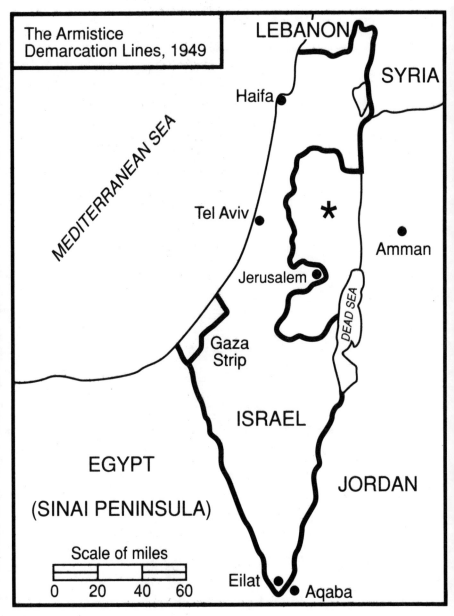

The Armistice
Demarcation Lines, 1949

LEBANON

SYRIA

MEDITERRANEAN SEA

Haifa

Tel Aviv

*

Amman

Jerusalem

DEAD SEA

Gaza
Strip

ISRAEL

JORDAN

EGYPT

(SINAI PENINSULA)

Scale of miles

0   20   40   60

Eilat

Aqaba

★ Area annexed by Jordan in 1950 and renamed "West Bank"

NOTES

CHAPTER 1 MY ROAD TO ISRAEL

1. This is a summary of events based on testimony and interviews of Arabs, Jews, and foreigners at the site. I believe this is as accurate an account as can be given, although both Palestinians and Israelis might dispute some of the points. All agree that it was a chaotic and fast-moving event, and so a complete reconstruction is not easy to make.

   Many Palestinians insist that no calls to jihad were made over the mosque loudspeakers, but many witnesses testified under oath that they heard such calls at the beginning of the riot. I believe their testimony is accurate, although I think calls to "slaughter the Jews" may have come from the rioters themselves and not over mosque loudspeakers as some testified.

CHAPTER 2 RACHEL WEEPS

1. Edward H. Flannery, *The Anguish of the Jews* (New York: Paulist Press, 1985), 1.
2. Ibid., 40.
3. Ibid., 41.
4. Ibid., 50.
5. Ibid., 51.
6. H. L. Ellis, *The Lion Concise History of Christianity* (London: Lion Publishers, 1983).
7. In fact, proportionally fewer Jews than Gentiles died from the plague, undoubtedly because of strict Jewish dietary and hygienic laws garnered from the Bible such as ritual hand-washing before each meal.

CHAPTER 3 BUSTING OUT OF ARABIA

1. *The Koran* (London: Penguin Books Ltd., 1978), translated from Arabic into English by N. J. Dawood, 317. All subsequent quotations from the Koran are from this translation. Also note that most Islamic versions of the Koran are in chronological, not numerical, order.
2. Ibid.
3. Ibid.

4. G. H. Jansen, *Militant Islam* (New York: Harper & Row, 1979), 21.

CHAPTER 4   SUFFER THE LITTLE HOLY LAND

1. Samuel Katz, *The Jewish Presence in Palestine* (Jerusalem: Israel Academic Committee on the Middle East, 1976).
2. *The Koran* (London: Penguin Books Ltd., 1978), translated from Arabic into English by N. J. Dawood.
3. James Parkes, *A History of Palestine from* A.D. *135 to Modern Times* (London: Victor Gollancz Ltd., 1949), 214.
4. Mark Twain, *The Innocents Abroad* (London: 1881), quoted by Parkes, ibid., 441–442.
5. Ibid., 349.

CHAPTER 5   RETURN TO ZION

1. Arieh Avneri, *The Claim of Dispossession: Jewish Land Settlement and the Arabs* (Tel Aviv: Yad Tabenkin, Hebrew ed. 1980, English ed. 1982).
2. Walter Laqueur, *A History of Zionism* (New York: Holt, Rinehart & Winston, 1972), 239.
3. Ibid., 240.
4. Ibid., 239.
5. Ibid., 242.
6. The population of Palestine at the beginning of the first immigration wave is disputed. Most Arab sources say estimates of 400,000 are too small. Avneri, quoting Professor Roberto Bacci who authored a book on the topic, says 523,000 people lived in the land in 1890—431,800 Muslims; 57,400 Christians; and 42,900 Jews.

   He thus calculates that 425,000 to 440,000 Arabs lived in Palestine in 1880. The numbers at the beginning are important since disputes also rage over how many Arabs immigrated into Palestine before 1948. British records show that the Arab population increased by 120 percent between 1922 and 1947, writes Avneri.

   He and others believe this unusually large population increase must have been at least partially due to wide-scale Arab immigration—legal and illegal—into Palestine during the period (Desert and mountain borders were largely open, notes Avneri). Therefore, at least a portion of the "Palestinians" who fled in 1948 were relatively recent immigrants from Egypt, Syria, Trans-Jordan, etc.

CHAPTER 6   JACOB COMES OUT ON TOP

1. Laqueur, *A History of Zionism,* 529.
2. Ibid., 573.
3. Reports at the time spoke of more than two hundred killed; but a survivor from the village, Muhammad Sammour, told correspondent Eric Silver of the British *Guardian* newspaper in April 1983, that 116 residents had died. Sammour said he was one of the representatives of the five clans that lived in the village and who met in Jerusalem just after the slaughter to count the dead.
4. Laqueur, *A History of Zionism,* 585.

CHAPTER 7   ARABS AND JEWS AT WAR

1. Benny Morris, *The Birth of the Palestinian Refugee Problem, 1947– 1949* (Cambridge, Great Britain: Cambridge University Press, 1987, paperback ed. 1989).
2. Ibid. This latter conclusion is one of the things which has made Morris' book so controversial. Israeli critics say he has deliberately ignored evidence that local and regional Arab leaders did indeed order out prominent Palestinians, knowing this would lead by example to wide-scale flight. Such commands, mainly issued verbally, they say, were picked up by Israeli and British intelligence. They say Morris, who was born the same year as the Jewish state, tends to exaggerate Israeli confidence and military strength, viewing the 1948 struggle through the eyes of one who has only known Israel as a military giant.

   Morris notes that he lacked Arab documents on the period, but says he pieced together a fairly accurate picture of Arab activities from Israeli and British documents. Some question the validity of this approach. The fact that he relied on Hebrew and English translations of Arabic radio broadcasts and other Arabic material in Israeli and British archives has also been criticized. Despite uneasiness with the way Morris interprets some of the material he presents, and agreement with some of the criticism mentioned above, I believe his book is overall the best to date in detailing the refugee flight.
3. Ibid., 298.
4. Ibid., 294.
5. Quoted by historian Martin Gilbert in *The Arab/Israeli Conflict: Its History in Maps* (London: Weidenfeld and Nicolson, 2nd ed., 1976), 67.

CHAPTER 8   FROM OPTIMISM TO DESPAIR

1. Gilbert, *The Arab-Israeli Conflict,* 103.
2. Thomas Friedman, *From Beirut to Jerusalem* (New York: Farrar Straus Giroux, 1989), 69.
3. Ibid., 70.
4. Ibid., 70.
5. Ibid., 73.
6. Ibid., 58–59.
7. Eugene Rostow, U.S. Undersecretary of State for political affairs in the late 1960s, presented the legal arguments behind this position in the April 16, 1990, issue of *New Republic* magazine: "The Jewish right of settlement in the West Bank is conferred by the same provisions of the Mandate under which Jews settled in Haifa, Tel Aviv, and Jerusalem before the State of Israel was created." He notes that Article 25 of the Mandate gave Great Britain and the League of Nations "discretion to 'postpone' or 'withhold' the Jewish people's right of settlement in the Trans-Jordanian province of Palestine," adding that the British did just that in 1922. "The Mandate does not, however, permit even a temporary suspension of the Jewish right of settlement in the parts of the Mandate *west* of the Jordan River." He adds that the 1949 armistice line—which in effect became Israel's pre-1967 borders—did not legally constitute Israel's permanent borders.

   The Mandate provisions for settlement in *all* of Palestine west of the river did not end in 1948, writes Rostow, but continue to have legal force to this day. Therefore, Israel has a legal right to build settlements in those portions of Mandatory Palestine captured in 1967. Other legal arguments concerning the application of the Fourth Geneva Convention are also given in the article.

CHAPTER 10   THAT ELUSIVE PEACE

1. It has become popular among Mideast Arabs in recent years, along with neo-Nazis and others, to maintain that East European and Russian Jews are not descendants of ancient Jews at all. Therefore, they have no right to live in the Holy Land. This case was made in a Saudi Arabian-sponsored ad printed in October 1988 in major American newspapers: "In A.D. 740 a large kingdom of Europeans, located in modern-day Russia, converted to Judaism. This group had no biological connection with any of the original Jews." Therefore, "most" of the Jews in Israel are not biological Jews, but descendants of European converts, also known as "Askenazi" or

"White Jews" who can "make no Biblical claim to the Arab lands in Palestine, including Jerusalem."

This argument is based on the conversion to Judaism in the eighth century of leaders of the Khazaria Kingdom located in south central Asia. Subsequently many Khazars converted to Judaism and were dispersed when the Russians destroyed the kingdom in the eleventh century.

But it is also known that at least some Jews from the West moved to Khazaria to escape persecution. More importantly, it is well documented that many west European Jews moved east to Poland, Lithuania, etc., during the Middle Ages after they were forced out of France, Germany, Austria, etc. (This is why Yiddish, a German-Hebrew mixture, was the main language of such East European Jews.)

Certainly Khazar's Jewish converts, as converts elsewhere, mixed over the years with known physical descendants of Abraham, but it is historically absurd to maintain that "European White Jews" have no ancient Jewish ancestry. Such widely believed myths, propounded by a leading "moderate" Arab state, illustrate the deeply held Arab prejudices against Israel.

2. For instance, Israel's 700,000 Arab citizens, unlike Arabs in some other Mideast nations, have full voting rights and read a non-government-controlled Arabic press, subject to Israeli censorship, but still freer than in all regional states except Egypt and Lebanon. Unlike in Syria, Iraq, and elsewhere, they cannot be held in prison without being formally charged with a crime. They have full religious freedom, unlike Muslims in Saudi Arabia, who are still officially subject to the death penalty if they convert.

Of course, Palestinians in the territories do not enjoy all of these rights, and many have been imprisoned without trial and others apparently tortured. Yet overall, they have been treated relatively well, in comparison to the way Syria, Iraq, Algeria, Saudi Arabia, and others have handled internal riots and rebellions in the past decade. (Read Thomas Friedman's excellent report on Syria's crushing of the fundamentalist rebellion in the city of Hama, *From Beirut to Jerusalem.*)

Israel's comparatively good human rights record may not be apparent to many people because media reports tend to highlight criticism of Israel by such groups as Amnesty International, while only lightly reporting stronger, but routine allegations of torture and other abuses in Syria, Sudan, and other regional countries. Media outlets rightly maintain that Israel's record is and should be of more concern to Americans and other Westerners because of strong Western political and economic support for Israel. Still, media focus on Israeli human rights abuses, paying less attention to the misdeeds of other regional states, probably leaves many Westerners with the false impression that Israel's overall record is the poorest in the region.

3. This is undoubtedly why the Vatican, which opposes Israeli sovereignty over Jerusalem, has yet to officially recognize Israel. Every pontiff since 1948 has turned down invitations to visit the Jewish state (although Pope Paul VI came through Jordan to east Jerusalem before the Six Day War). Pope John Paul II has met Israeli leaders several times in Rome, as he has Yasser Arafat.

4. Twenty-one states were members of the Arab League following the 1990 merger of North and South Yemen. Several African member states are mostly non-Arab, but largely Muslim.

5. Israel and the U.S. are jointly working on an "anti-missile missile" to intercept and destroy incoming missiles. Part of the SDI program, the so-called "Arrow" missile is expected to be more effective in intercepting incoming missiles than the current U.S. "Patriot" system.

6. Among groups that monitor media coverage of Israel are: CAMERA (Committee for Accuracy in Middle East Reporting in America), P.O. Box 17322, Washington, DC 20041; and Americans for a Safe Israel, 114 E. 28th Street, New York, NY 10016; Zionist Organization of America, 4 East 34th Street, New York, NY 10016.

CONCLUSION

1. Morris, *The Birth of the Palestinian Refugee Problem 1947–1949*, 296.